Higher Education in the Making

SUNY series in Constructive Postmodern Thought
David Ray Griffin, editor

Higher Education in the Making

Pragmatism, Whitehead, and the Canon

George Allan

STATE UNIVERSITY OF NEW YORK PRESS

Published by
State University of New York Press, Albany

© 2004 State University of New York

All rights reserved

Printed in the United States of America

No part of this book may be used or reproduced in any manner whatsoever without written permission. No part of this book may be stored in a retrieval system or transmitted in any form or by any means including electronic, electrostatic, magnetic tape, mechanical, photocopying, recording, or otherwise without the prior permission in writing of the publisher.

For information, address State University of New York Press, 90 State Street, Suite 700, Albany, NY 12207

Production, Laurie Searl
Marketing, Jennifer Giovani

Library of Congress Cataloging-in-Publication Data

Allan, George, 1935–

  Higher education in the making : pragmatism, Whitehead, and the canon / George Allan.
    p. cm. – (SUNY series in constructive postmodern thought)
  Includes bibliographical references and index.
  ISBN 978-0-7914-5990-4 (pbk. : alk. paper)
    1. Education, Higher—Curricula—United States. 2. Postmodernism and education—United States. 3. Pragmatism. 4. Canon (Literature) I. Title. II. Series.

LB2361.5.A36 2004
379.1'99—dc22   2003064726

for Malcolm Evans
a gracious friend and persistent critic

Contents

	Acknowledgments	ix
	Series Introduction	xi
ONE	Crumbling Cathedrals	1
TWO	Content Canonists	17
THREE	Procedural Canonists	35
FOUR	Anti-Canonists	53
FIVE	Relative Canonists	71
SIX	Canonical Dynamics	89
SEVEN	Canonical Dialectics	107
EIGHT	Pragmatic Canonists	127
NINE	Education for a Democracy	145
TEN	Religious Education	165
ELEVEN	Education for Our Common Good	183
TWELVE	Cathedral Ruins	199
THIRTEEN	Constructive Pragmatics	215
	Works Cited	233
	Note on Supporting Center	239
	Index	241
	SUNY Series in Constructive Postmodern Thought	245

Acknowledgments

Chapters 1–8 are genealogically connected to three essays published long ago. However, those earlier ideas have been greatly transformed—rethought, extended, extruded, modified, melded, cantilevered, tempered, deepened, and distributed in and amongst newer ideas—and so their presence is not always detectable. Nonetheless, these essays deserve mention since they set me on the journey that led to writing this book. They are "The Canon in Crisis," *Liberal Education* 72 (1986): 89–100; "The Process and Reality of an Educational Canon," *Contemporary Philosophy* 12 (1989): 3–8; and "Process Philosophy and the Educational Canon," *Process Studies* 20 (1991): 93–105. The original version of this last essay was presented at a "Conference on Process Philosophy of Education: Confluence and Construction," sponsored by the Association for Process Philosophy of Education, Cornell University, 1991, and published in a slightly altered version after long delay as "Modernism, Post-Modernism, and the Pragmatic Recovery of an Educational Canon," in Robert Neville and Tom Kasulis, eds., *The Recovery of Philosophy in America: Essays in Honor of John Edwin Smith* (Albany: State University of New York Press, 1997), 93–114. Excerpts from it, plus some comments about academic deans, appeared as "Political Correctness and the Middling Dean," *American Conference of Academic Deans, Proceedings,* January 1992: 18–25.

Chapter 9 is a slightly modified version of "Playing with Worlds: John Dewey, the Habit of Experiment, and the Goods of Democracy," published in *Soundings* 79 (1996): 447–68. A version of chapter 10, with a significantly different second section, was published as "Whitehead and Dewey: Religion in the Making of Education," in Janus A. Polanowski and Donald Shelburne, eds., *Whitehead's Philosophy: Points of Connection* (Albany: State University of New York Press, 2004). A briefer version of chapter 11, "Weaving Our Common Good," was a Plenary Lecture at the Third International Whitehead Conference, on Process Thought and the Common Good, sponsored by the Center for Process Studies, Claremont, California, 1998.

An earlier book of mine, *Rethinking College Education* (Lawrence: University Press of Kansas, 1997), used a typology of three kinds of educational purposes institutionalized in American colleges and universities: the Faithful Community, the Guild of Inquirers, and the Resource Center. This typology reappears in this book, altered by the shift in focus from educational purposes to educational norms, as Content Canonists, Procedural Canonists, and Anti-Canonists. As I argue, it is also similar to the three kinds of University Bill Readings discusses: the University of Culture, the University of Reason, and the University of Excellence. The alternative to all three approaches, which in this book is termed a Pragmatic Canon, has affinities to the approach in *Rethinking College Education* that I describe as an academic institution "without any essential purpose." The basic similarity between the notions in this book and the other one is that in both cases what is essential, I argue, is the learning process itself, not whatever theoretical or practical outcomes it might happen to produce.

My arguments have been influenced by the opportunity to participate in a series of Liberty Fund colloquies organized by Timothy Fuller and Eugene Miller under the rubric "Education in a Free Society," in particular two colloquies in 1997, on "Ideas of the University" and "The Rise of the Medieval University," and another in 1999 on "Challenges to Liberal Education in the twenty-first Century."

Introduction to SUNY Series in Constructive Postmodern Thought

The rapid spread of the term *postmodern* in recent years witnesses to a growing dissatisfaction with modernity and to an increasing sense that the modern age not only had a beginning but can have an end as well. Whereas the word *modern* was almost always used until quite recently as a word of praise and as a synonym for *contemporary,* a growing sense is now evidenced that we can and should leave modernity behind—in fact, that we *must* if we are to avoid destroying ourselves and most of the life on our planet.

Modernity, rather than being regarded as the norm for human society toward which all history has been aiming and into which all societies should be ushered—forcibly if necessary—is instead increasingly seen as an aberration. A new respect for the wisdom of traditional societies is growing as we realize that they have endured for thousands of years and that, by contrast, the existence of modern civilization for even another century seems doubtful. Likewise, *modernism* as a worldview is less and less seen as The Final Truth, in comparison with which all divergent worldviews are automatically regarded as "superstitious." The modern worldview is increasingly relativized to the status of one among many, useful for some purposes, inadequate for others.

Although there have been antimodern movements before, beginning perhaps near the outset of the nineteenth century with the Romanticists and the Luddites, the rapidity with which the term *postmodern* has become widespread in our time suggests that the antimodern sentiment is more extensive and intense than before, and also that it includes the sense that modernity can be successfully overcome only by going beyond it, not by attempting to return to a premodern form of existence. Insofar as a common element is found in the various ways in which the term is used, *postmodernism* refers to a diffuse sentiment rather than to any common set of doctrines—the sentiment that humanity can and must go beyond the modern.

Beyond connoting this sentiment, the term *postmodern* is used in a confusing variety of ways, some of them contradictory to others. In artistic and literary circles, for example, postmodernism shares in this general sentiment but also involves a specific reaction against "modernism" in the narrow sense of a movement in artistic-literary circles in the late nineteenth and early twentieth centuries. Postmodern architecture is very different from postmodern

---

* The present version of this introduction is slightly different from the first version, which was contained in the volumes that appeared prior to 1999.

literary criticism. In some circles, the term *postmodern* is used in reference to that potpourri of ideas and systems sometimes called *new age metaphysics,* although many of these ideas and systems are more premodern than postmodern. Even in philosophical and theological circles, the term *postmodern* refers to two quite different positions, one of which is reflected in this series. Each position seeks to transcend both *modernism,* in the sense of the worldview that has developed out of the seventeenth-century Galilean-Cartesian-Baconian-Newtonian science, and *modernity,* in the sense of the world order that both conditioned and was conditioned by this worldview. But the two positions seek to transcend the modern in different ways.

Closely related to literary-artistic postmodernism is a philosophical postmodernism inspired variously by physicalism, Ludwig Wittgenstein, Martin Heidegger, a cluster of French thinkers—including Jacques Derrida, Michel Foucault, Gilles Deleuze, and Julia Kristeva—and certain features of American pragmatism.[1] By the use of terms that arise out of particular segments of this movement, it can be called *deconstructive, relativistic,* or *eliminative* postmodernism. It overcomes the modern worldview through an antiworldview, deconstructing or even entirely eliminating various concepts that have generally been thought necessary for a worldview, such as self, purpose, meaning, a real world, givenness, reason, truth as correspondence, universally valid norms, and divinity. While motivated by ethical and emancipatory concerns, this type of postmodern thought tends to issue in relativism. Indeed, it seems to many thinkers to imply nihilism.[2] It could,

---

1. The fact that the thinkers and movements named here are said to have inspired the deconstructive type of postmodernism should not be taken, of course, to imply that they have nothing in common with constructive postmodernists. For example, Wittgenstein, Heidegger, Derrida, and Deleuze share many points and concerns with Alfred North Whitehead, the chief inspiration behind the present series. Furthermore, the actual positions of the founders of pragmatism, especially William James and Charles Peirce, are much closer to Whitehead's philosophical position—see the volume in this series entitled *The Founders of Constructive Postmodern Philosophy: Peirce, James, Bergson, Whitehead, and Hartshorne*—than they are to Richard Rotry's so-called neopragmatism, which reflects many ideas from Rorty's explicitly physicalistic period.

2. As Peter Dews points out, although Derrida's early work was "driven by profound ethical impulses," its insistence that no concepts were immune to deconstruction "drove its own ethical presuppositions into a penumbra of inarticulacy" (*The Limits of Disenchantment: Essays on Contemporary European Culture* [London: New York: Verso, 1995], 5). In his more recent thought, Derrida has declared an "emancipatory promise" and an "idea of justice" to be "irreducible to any deconstruction." Although this "ethical turn" in deconstruction implies its pulling back from a completely disenchanted universe, it also, Dews points out (6–7), implies the need to renounce "the unconditionality of its own earlier dismantling of the unconditional".

paradoxically, also be called *ultramodernism,* in that its eliminations result from carrying certain modern premises—such as the sensationist doctrine of perception, the mechanistic doctrine of nature, and the resulting denial of divine presence in the world—to their logical conclusions. Some critics see its deconstructions or eliminations as leading to self-referential inconsistencies, such as "performative self-contradictions" between what is said and what is presupposed in the saying.

The postmodernism of this series can, by contrast, be called *revisionary, constructive,* or—perhaps best—*reconstructive.* It seeks to overcome the modern worldview not by eliminating the possibility of worldviews (or "metanarratives") as such, but by constructing a postmodern worldview through a revision of modern premises and traditional concepts in the light of inescapable presuppositions of our various modes of practice. That is, it agrees with deconstructive postmodernists that a massive deconstruction of many received concepts is needed. But its deconstructive moment, carried out for the sake of the presuppositions of practice, does not result in self-referential inconsistency. It also is not so totalizing as to prevent reconstruction. The reconstruction carried out by this type of postmodernism involves a new unity of scientific, ethical, aesthetic, and religious intuitions (whereas poststructuralists tend to reject all such unitive projects as "totalizing modern metanarratives"). While critical of many ideas often associated with modern science, it rejects not science as such but only that *scientism* in which only the data of the modern natural sciences are allowed to contribute to the construction of our public worldview.

The reconstructive activity of this type of postmodern thought is not limited to a revised worldview. It is equally concerned with a postmodern world that will both support and be supported by the new worldview. A postmodern world will involve postmodern persons, with a postmodern spirituality, on the one hand, and a postmodern society, ultimately a postmodern global order, on the other. Going beyond the modern world will involve transcending its individualism, anthropocentrism, patriarchy, economism, consumerism, nationalism, and militarism. Reconstructive postmodern thought provides support for the ethnic, ecological, feminist, peace, and other emancipatory movements of our time, while stressing that the inclusive emancipation must be from the destructive features of modernity itself. However, the term *postmodern,* by contrast with *premodern,* is here meant to emphasize that the modern world has produced unparalleled advances, as Critical Theorists have emphasized, which must not be devalued in a general revulsion against modernity's negative features.

From the point of view of deconstructive postmodernists, this reconstructive postmodernism will seem hopelessly wedded to outdated concepts, because it wishes to salvage a positive meaning not only for the notions of selfhood, historical meaning, reason, and truth as correspondence, which were central to modernity, but also for notions of divinity, cosmic meaning, and an enchanted nature, which were central to premodern modes of thought. From the point of view of its advocates, however, this revisionary postmodernism is not only more adequate to our experience but also more genuinely postmodern. It does not simply carry the premises of modernity through to their logical conclusions, but criticizes and revises those premises. By virtue of its return to organicism and its acceptance of nonsensory perception, it opens itself to the recovery of truths and values from various forms of premodern thought and practice that had been dogmatically rejected, or at least restricted to "practice", by modern thought. This reconstructive postmodernism involves a creative synthesis of modern and premodern truths and values.

This series does not seek to create a movement so much as to help shape and support an already existing movement convinced that modernity can and must be transcended. But in light of the fact that those antimodern movements that arose in the past failed to deflect or even retard the onslaught of modernity, what reasons are there for expecting the current movement to be more successful? First, the previous antimodern movements were primarily calls to return to a premodern form of life and thought rather than calls to advance, and the human spirit does not rally to calls to turn back. Second, the previous antimodern movements either rejected modern science, reduced it to a description of mere appearances, or assumed its adequacy in principle. They could, therefore, base their calls only on the negative social and spiritual effects of modernity. The current movement draws on natural science itself as a witness against the adequacy of the modern worldview. In the third place, the present movement has even more evidence than did previous movements of the ways in which modernity and its worldview *are* socially and spiritually destructive. The fourth and probably most decisive difference is that the present movement is based on the awareness that *the continuation of modernity threatens the very survival of life on our planet*. This awareness, combined with the growing knowledge of the interdependence of the modern worldview with the militarism, nuclearism, patriarchy, global apartheid, and ecological devastation of the modern world, is providing an unprecedented impetus for people to see the evidence for a postmodern worldview and to envisage postmodern ways of relating to each other, the rest of nature, and the cosmos as a whole. For these reasons, the failure of the previous antimodern movements says little about the possible success of the current movement.

Advocates of this movement do not hold the naively utopian belief that the success of this movement would bring about a global society of universal and lasting peace, harmony, and happiness, in which all spiritual problems, social conflicts, ecological destruction, and hard choices would vanish. There is, after all, surely a deep truth in the testimony of the world's religions to the presence of a transcultural proclivity to evil deep within the human heart, which no new paradigm, combined with a new economic order, new child-rearing practices, or any other social arrangements, will suddenly eliminate. Furthermore, it has correctly been said that "life is robbery": A strong element of competition is inherent within finite existence, which no social-political-economic-ecological order can overcome. These two truths, especially when contemplated together, should caution us against unrealistic hopes.

No such appeal to "universal constants," however, should reconcile us to the present order, as if it were thereby uniquely legitimated. The human proclivity to evil in general, and to conflictual competition and ecological destruction in particular, can be greatly exacerbated or greatly mitigated by a world order and its worldview. Modernity exacerbates it about as much as imaginable. We can therefore envision, without being naively utopian, a far better world order, with a far less dangerous trajectory, than the one we now have.

This series, making no pretense of neutrality, is dedicated to the success of this movement toward a postmodern world.

David Ray Griffin
Series Editor

Chapter 1

Crumbling Cathedrals

A Towering Problem

The majestic towers of English cathedrals, because of their height and thus their unusual weight, have become a serious problem. As they sink steadily, persistently, into the marshy soil of the sceptered isle at a faster rate than the buildings they adorn, important structural cracks and stresses have begun to appear. In some cases, such as at York, significant emergency repair to the foundations has been necessary to prevent the tower's complete collapse.

I want to draw an analogy between these cathedral tribulations and those of another but equally magnificent structure, the American system of higher education—in particular, the traditional liberal arts college, including its more recent surrogate, the university undergraduate arts and sciences curriculum. It too is a lofty accomplishment, and it too is collapsing under the weight of its own successes, not only to its own detriment but also to that of the culture it adorns. I doubt that any commission or task force admonishing that the cracks in academe be replastered, the trim replaced, and the walls repainted will be able to stop its slow but steady disintegration. The problem is with the undergirding, with the cultural pilings and intellectual footings upon which everything else depends. For that kind of problem, far more serious repairs are required.

In approaching issues about education and the social good, my tendency is to use adaptive change as the primary criterion for assessing the value of an idea or the worth of a practice. This proclivity means that my way of thinking is intertwined with two related modes of thought: pragmatism and process philosophy. It might be expected, therefore, that I would look favorably upon the crumbling of old things, such as long-entrenched educational theories and programs of study, because of the promise of the newly emerging possibilities thereby permitted. And of course I certainly do. The issue is not change, however, but the character of that change. For the perishing of old achievement does not guarantee the fashioning of better achievement, even when the old is without question very bad and almost anything novel would seem an improvement. I am walking in the footsteps of Whitehead, James, and Dewey when I claim that we cannot live without cathedrals, even though we are always having to repair them and so are always transforming them.

The pragmatic approach to education I will develop is not opportunistic, at least not in the sense presumed by those who dismiss pragmatism as a willingness to do whatever is needed in order to get what you're after—a wily, unprincipled Machiavellian "it's true if it works." Nor is my approach one that embraces change uncritically, that follows the logic of the Whig interpretation of history: whatever is newer is better. Educational pragmatists are adaptive, however. They prize imagination and the innovation it makes possible as crucial resources in a world where changes are rife and failure to adjust to them is a recipe for disaster. There are no treasures secure from rust or moth, no cathedrals that can get by solely on what their original builders wrought.

The pragmatic approach to problem solving is rooted in a theory of knowledge, in a claim that the best way to understand things is in terms of their use. A bit of knowledge is not a description of something but a means of interacting with it in order to achieve some purpose. What it describes is a course of action for us to follow, in order to find something we are seeking, or having found it to use it properly. That's an apple tree if when I walk up to it I can pluck its fruit and, eating it, enjoy certain predicted tastes, textures, and nutritional benefits. It's an apple if it keeps the doctor away.

Knowing changes as our purposes change and as our situations are altered. This dynamic approach to knowledge is suited to a world where there are no fixed essences, no timeless first principles or fundamental elements, no absolute origins or ultimate destinations. Permanence is crucial—form, structure, rule—to give sense, orientation, and significance to things. But whether these structures are discovered or invented, they too change, although more slowly than the things they order. The laws of nature, the axioms of logic and mathematics, the necessary conditions for organic life or personal happiness or social stability: none of them are unchanging or eternal. So my pragmatic claim about the best method for learning about a thing is tied to a claim about the nature of things. The truth-claim that works does so because of how the world works. Pragmatism as a theory of inquiry dovetails with a process ontology, a metaphysics that, while denying neither, makes change more fundamental than permanence.

Our answers to the questions of how we know and what we know shape our answer to the further question of how best we might comport ourselves under such conditions. Our ethic, our view about what is worthwhile and what conducive to our personal fulfillment, the pragmatist says, needs to take account of the community we share with other persons and the environment of other things and organisms in which we live out our lives. We are a part of nature, interdependently changing as it changes. We are changed by what envelops us, gladly or not, voluntarily or not, and we in turn change this encompassing world because of how we know it, what we think it is and we are, and what we think it and we might best become.

Pragmatism in this sense is an example of what David Ray Griffin calls "constructive postmodernism." It calls into question the eternal verities that are the hallmark of modernism, the timeless and universal standards by which the fleeting and parochial achievements of the world are measured and judged excellent or deficient. But it also rejects the nihilistic attempt to demolish verities of any and every sort, to deconstruct all the traditional hierarchies based on truth, goodness, and beauty, on faith, hope, and love. The pragmatism I use and defend in this book is neither modern nor antimodern, but rather their reconciliation. It advocates hierarchies of excellence but also their critique, recognizing that no values are forever, that the best of our creations are limited and so always in need of improvement. Griffin says that constructive postmodernism "seeks to overcome the modern worldview not by eliminating the possibility of worldviews as such, but by constructing a postmodern worldview through a revision of modern premises and traditional concepts" (xiii). It is therefore appropriate that this book be a part of the SUNY Series in Constructive Postmodern Thought, because it seeks to overcome the traditional modern view of an educational canon not by eliminating the possibility of canons, but by constructing an understanding of an educational canon based on a revision of its philosophical premises and traditional concepts.

Education is about how we know, about ourselves as learners and teachers of the how and what of knowing. It is about the historical and contemporaneous human communities that support and impede our learning and hence our development. And it is about the natural systems that make all of these conditions for education possible. In examining the non-pragmatic theories of education that ground many of the current interpretations of what constitutes good teaching and effective learning, I will argue that they have contributed and are contributing to the collapse of American higher education because they rest on inadequate philosophical views about knowledge, human nature, and moral value. I will sketch a pragmatic alternative to these philosophical commitments while I am developing the pragmatic theory of education I think offers a more adequate, more viable approach than those currently in vogue.

All of this philosophizing in good time, however. What follows in this first chapter is an attempt to trench around the problem of our crumbling cathedrals of higher learning in order to identify where their foundations have been weakened and for what reasons. I hope in subsequent chapters to explain why they are in need of our urgent attention and how they might best be repaired.

The Growing Weight of Knowledge

The walls of academe are out of plumb. There is more for students to learn these days than our colleges and universities have the capacity to teach. The traditional frameworks for organizing what needs to be learned are too narrow or too rigid or are wrongly segmented. They are twisted, extruded, mixed, melded, delaminated, relayered in an attempt to retain some reasonable shape and sequence to an undergraduate course of study. These patchwork attempts are sometimes clever, sometimes bizarre, but seemingly always ineffective. This incapacity is particularly evident in liberal arts curricula, which have traditionally been assigned the task of providing students with a generalized educational foundation for their subsequent career involvements or for their advanced professional and technical studies.

In the last century, however, the relevant content for such a general education has burgeoned uncontrollably. There are at least four reasons for this loss of control: the expansion of knowledge, its democratization, its globalization, and a decline in how much a student can be presupposed already to know. They are each a familiar feature of classrooms and curricula these days.

First, the expansion of knowledge. Within the traditional academic disciplines there has been an information explosion, often combined with the elaboration of whole new areas of theory or application. In the natural sciences new kinds of instruments for detecting, measuring, analyzing, and interpreting data have revolutionized both subject-matter content and method. Once upon a time, biologists studied the world's flora and fauna, observing their behaviors, analyzing their structures, ordering them into species and genera, tracing their genealogies. Now they also study atoms and molecules in order to understand and to alter the cells of which those organisms are composed. Geologists are no longer content to be earth scientists, but now they also investigate extraterrestrial landscapes. Chemists, working with nuclear resonators and magnetic spectrometers in addition to test tubes and Bunsen burners, synthesize not only new molecules but also new elements. Astronomers scan the heavens with their ears as well as their eyes, and spend most of their time peering at computer printouts. Physicists require new kinds of mathematics to permit their speaking coherently about the extremely small and the extremely large, then require new kinds of logic and a touch of mysticism in order to make quantum mechanics consistent with gravitational theory or to justify how their account of the Big Bang could possibly be compatible with their account of time's reversibility.

Seemingly without end, this inexorable expansion in the content of the natural science disciplines creates a difficult pedagogical conundrum. Instructors brood over how to reconcile the difference between, on the one hand, what most students must know in order to possess a basic understanding of the everyday natural world around them and, on the other hand, what students need to know as the first step toward becoming a professional scientist. Take biology, for example. Learning how to identify the backyard birds and roadside flowers in a region, or studying how the sexual practices of various kinds of mammals have evolved in order to provide an insight into human sexuality: these would be wonderful ways to kindle the interest of casual students in biology. Potential majors, however, need to learn the basics of taxonomic theory, the Latin names of key kinds of flora and fauna, and both the molecular and ecological mechanisms explained by the neo-Darwinian synthesis. How can any introductory biology course accommodate both these agendas?

Combine these incompatible student needs and interests with the problem of learning how to use increasingly complex instruments in order to gain access even to the basics, and the very notion of a general science course becomes an oxymoron. The choice seems to be either a superficial science appreciation course or a prematurely narrowing introduction to a scientific subdiscipline—either a nonlab "Science for Dummies," a course that is about science but does no science, or an introductory survey course limited to a restricted subject area such as botany or inorganic chemistry or discrete mathematics.

Not only is there so much more content to teach these days, but it seems less and less to be composed of elements that are related in a systematically hierarchical fashion. The problem is not simply that chemistry presupposes physics, biology both, and geology all three. It's that aspects of each intertwine and then branch off in surprisingly independent ways, so physicists investigating subatomic phenomena need to know topology rather than calculus and find they have more in common with molecular biologists than physical chemists. What a biology major needs to study in order to be prepared for a career as a molecular biologist has little to do with what another biology major should take in preparation for becoming an ornithologist. The forks in the road leading to scientific competence come sooner than they once did, and the roads diverge more sharply. We can only wonder how long it will be before a student's first science course options are limited to an array of very narrow access points to very narrow non-overlapping fields of study.

Social studies has fared no better, having become over the last century a collection of social sciences. In economics and psychology, statistical analysis and mathematical modeling now serve as tools making the prediction of human behavior a reality—or at least a plausible expectation. Anthropologists now do their fieldwork in Chicago as well as in New Guinea and, while the physical anthropologists are now hard to distinguish from biologists, the cultural anthropologists are easily mistaken for social psychologists or semiologists. Popular culture replaces the circulation of elites as the focus of social analysis; historians become sociologists and sociologists historians. Political scientists these days learn their theory by reading Foucault as well as Plato and Machiavelli, they study American government not only by reading the *New York Times* and the *Congressional Record* but by manipulating data bases of precinct-by-precinct voting patterns, and they use systems theory to guide them through a comparative study of the various extant and historical forms of governance.

For the humanities, philosophy is no longer limited to its traditional concerns about the nature of Being, the conditions for happiness or justice, and the proper method for discerning universal and necessary truths and maybe even Truth Itself. It has also taken a linguistic and a phenomenological turn, attempting to clarify the meaning of scientific, moral, artistic, and commonsensical truth claims—and more recently attempting as well to deconstruct any and all such claims. Religious studies now finds its subject matter as much in the social sciences as in theology and ecclesiastical history, as much in the mass media as in scripture. Foreign language courses have expanded into the equivalent of area studies programs, and literary criticism has interpreted the notion of a text to include a motley range of cultural artifacts. The fine arts, outdoing themselves in shattering conventional standards of taste, topic, and style, have turned art and music historians into psychologists, biographers, and gossip mongers concerned more with connoisseurship and patronage practices than with matters of iconography, provenance, and formal analysis.

This expansion in knowledge has not meant that the old learning is repudiated; it goes on as before. But to it is added all this newness, and there is no end of it in sight. At the same time, however, these mainstreams of knowledge have lost their monopoly on determining the intellectual currents of the day. There has been a democratization of what counts as knowledge, and it constitutes a second reason why educators have been losing control over the content that a general education should provide.

The academic tradition has come under attack by voices representing concerns and perspectives it had typically neglected. Women have called into question the male dominance of what the disciplines find worth studying—and the culture worth doing. Racial, ethnic, and cultural minorities—Native Americans, African Americans, Hispanic Americans, Asian Americans—insist upon their own agendas with respect to what issues need to be analyzed, what experiences celebrated, what assumptions affirmed or jettisoned. Gays and lesbians come out of the closet and demand that their stories also be taken seriously. Even Americans of European origin follow a similar pathway, insisting upon a curricular way to study, and hence to celebrate, their often newly rediscovered immigrant heritages.

The proliferation of studies programs in all these areas has followed roughly an identical pattern. Initially there are ad hoc discussion groups and courses, supported by ad hoc collections of interested faculty and students advocating the significance of their interests by quiet persuasion or shrill proclamation, by negotiation and compromise or by confrontational agitation. From these experiences, interdisciplinary courses and programs emerge, which eventually develop into disciplines in their own right, complete with majors and a scholarly tradition of central texts, key concepts, landmark events, and a proper methodology. American Studies was the pioneer and paradigm in the second half of the last century for this extension of the franchise of academic respectability. It was soon followed by Jewish Studies, Islamic Studies, Women's Studies, Black Studies, Hispanic Studies, more recently by Africana or Diaspora Studies, Gay or Lesbian Studies, Celtic Studies, Aboriginal American Studies, Gender Studies.

Advocates of positions or methods not in general favor—advocates of Thomistic ontology, Marxist economics, Personalist ethics, enactment language instruction, holistic therapy, extrasensory perception, animal rights, detective fiction, creationism—have taken heart from these developments and set about forming their own academic interest groups. Caucuses of these rebels against the taken-for-granted began to appear at professional meetings half a century ago and by now have matured into subdisciplines and even whole new disciplines, complete with their distinctive methodological claims and a growing body of books, articles, journals, and conferences.

So add this democratization of relevant knowledge to its expansion, a growth that complements the thickening of traditional knowledge by increasing the scope of what is considered legitimate and important. But now also add deparochialization as a third reason for why we no longer can agree on what the content of a basic education should be, much less on how to design an introductory course that would have any warrant for being called a survey of its salient features or even of the key points of access to those features.

Our academic disciplines are at last taking effective cognizance of subject matters other than Western civilization and of bodies of learning other than those created by Western scholars. This has resulted in the spread of comparativist approaches. A political science course on the city is now likely to involve Tokyo and Mexico City, Peshawar and Chichén Itzà, as well as London and Paris, New York and Chicago, Athens and Jerusalem. A religion course on the nature of belief will not take Christian or Judeo-Christian approaches as normative, but will attempt to develop suitable categories out of a survey of the world's religions, including the practices of precivilizational cultures.

And through the history of science we have become increasingly aware that modem science is dependent on nonscientific attitudes and habits, on culturally constrained interpretive frameworks and conceptual paradigms, that need to be understood in order to understand the limits and the potential of science as currently practiced. Knowledge has become a global phenomenon.

To these three widenings of the perimeter of the things needing to be learned, we must also add the increased educational burden placed on the undergraduate liberal arts curriculum by a significant decline in the taken-for-granted knowledge traditionally provided by home, religion, and school. Our students arrive on campus at the beginning of their freshman year knowing shockingly little of the facts, ideas, and practices that constitute the repertoire of information and skills that is the necessary presupposition for the metaphors, allusions, examples, and routines—the habits of head, hand, and heart—that make teaching possible.

Governing concepts and guidelines, information as structured by some principle or purpose, are things we typically convey by their analogy to everyday experience, commonsense belief, and childhood memory. The texts and artistic creations studied in the humanities were created by people steeped in the history and culture of Greece and Rome, Judaism and Christianity, infused with the exacting rhythms of farm work and craft guild, permeated with the tricks and sensitivities needed to survive the relentless onslaught of violent storms, cruel barbarians, and hard-hearted tax collectors. Science as a method, a body of truth, and a technology was fashioned by these same people and is a creature, thus, of these same steepings. But things have changed. The Good Shepherd has little meaning as a religious symbol for a person raised in an urban environment. The resonance Huxley intended by titling his futopian novel *Brave New World* is unheard by ears unaccustomed to Shakespeare. The point of calling the outermost planet of our solar system Pluto is lost to those who think it was named after a Disney cartoon character.

Our intellectual heritage in its most fundamental aspects is deeply imbedded in the habits of thought and practice that define our world. But if this stock of cultural know-how has not been inculcated in the young before they arrive on campus, then the higher in higher education is undermined. In order to teach college-level materials, the undergraduate faculty increasingly must first teach the taken-for-granted materials those presuppose. Faculty, however, are usually not prepared to do so. Consequently students are taught theories and interpretations of facts that they lack the proper cultural background to grasp. Faculty complain about lazy students, then adapt to what they take to be a realistic assessment of how things are by lowering their expectations, and eventually assign students grades that imply they know more than clearly they do. When the wellsprings of our creativity dry up, when we let down our guard, when we reap what we have sown, when the yoke of our oppression becomes unbearable—or rather, when these metaphors die but nonetheless remain in our speech as mere cliches—it is no wonder that our imagination fogs over, our ideas are put in irons, and we are in danger of wrecking on conceptual shoals of our own making.

In sum, knowledge has become for us more complex, broader in kind and in scope, thicker in theme and content, its presuppositions no longer presupposed. The sheer mass of what we need to learn is too much for the connective mortar that has traditionally held it together. Because the pointing has cracked and is falling away, the bricks and stones are loosening, shifting, breaking apart. Its walls no longer running true, the cathedral of learning is in danger of collapse.

The Disintegrating Foundations of Knowledge

If there are problems with the walls and the mortaring, the cause might have to do with the foundations. Perhaps we are putting an inappropriate amount of weight on them. Or, given that the superstructure has grown, perhaps the foundations need to be strengthened. In either case we would be well advised to ask about the fundamentals that undergird what we know. We need to pay attention to whatever basic ideas or first principles or primary facts there are that support the remainder of our ideas, methods, and information.

The aim of education, if we take this approach, is threefold. First, we need to do the best we can to bring our intellectual disciplines into harmony with these fundamental features of knowledge. Second, we need to transmit this precious heritage of what we know to the members of each new generation so that tomorrow's leaders will be able to see to the heart of things in order thereby to grasp firmly their enduring meaning and significance. For, third, it is only in this way that nature can be predicted and controlled, our communities made secure and just, and ourselves fulfilled. Only by knowing—and knowing how to utilize—basic truths and the methods for obtaining them, will our lives be constructed on a firm foundation, secured against the shifting sands of change and chance.

Notice the Aristotelian perfection of our argument. Students are the material cause of education: the unformed, unlearned raw material. The formal causes of education are the basic governing principles of the various academic disciplines. The final cause or goal is that those fundamental truths be actualized in the students, making them at least informed and at best learned young men and women. The efficient cause is the desire of students to fulfill their potential, to be responsible citizens, effective workers, and good persons.

The process of educating the nation's youth, when thus construed, will work as it should just so long as everything about it is so organized that these four conditions for education are in harmony: basic knowledge taught in the proper way to rightly motivated students who are expected upon graduation to become a new generation of leaders. Wherever this harmony breaks down, we think the fault must lie in some unfortunate intruding distortion. For only when the education process has somehow gone awry does the acorn grow into a stunted oak, the child become an irresponsible adult, the society suffer the taint of injustice. Only when the foundations of the cathedral of learning are undermined does truth come into conflict with hope, moral rectitude find itself at odds with societal authority, the welfare of others seem incompatible with our own happiness.

And yet, as we have seen, this Aristotelian view of things is in disarray. The problem has not been a distortion of knowledge but just the opposite: its increasing weight has been more than its ancient foundations can bear. The distortion has not come from some external intrusion, some invasion of barbarians intent on razing the cathedral of learning. It has come from the faithful themselves, building their tower too high, overburdening the carrying capacity of its foundations.

The opponents of those who advocate focusing education on the inculcation of basic truths argue that such a monochrome approach may have been thought sensible when the students in our colleges and universities were all middle- and upper-class white protestant boys preparing for the professions. Students then all seemed the same, and seemed to need the same truths and ideals in order to flourish, because the cultural influences shaping them were pretty much the same. It was easy enough to turn the familiar and recurrent into the universal and necessary, and to ascribe ultimacy to the harmony between what we taught and what our students and our nation needed.

But now add WASP girls, add blacks, add Lithuanians and Vietnamese, add Spanish-speaking Catholics and saffron-robed Buddhists, add the poor. Add young people who see themselves as alienated from the cultural mainstream, those who want to be caught up in its currents as soon as possible and those who want to divert it or dry it up. Add the worlds of style and mood, of metaphor and imagination, found on MTV, in the shopping malls, and on the street corners where drugs are bought and sold. From this welter arises no single shade of potency, no primary colors in which to paint one's life, no palette of goals and callings normatively suited to the fully functioning adult. Whatever our students make of themselves by their own arbitrary, context-bound choices, is what they will fundamentally be. These acorns won't all become oaks, and some may not wish even to be trees. That's their own choice, we say, and their own choice is as good as any other choice.

So we imagine a new sort of educational cathedral. We talk confidently, with the casual air bred of familiarity, about the cultural relativism of art and morality, the ideological basis of social belief and practice, and even the revolutions in scientific paradigms. We revel in the relativism, in a polymorphous embrace of all the various knowledge structures. Each of us is our own god creating our own worlds, all of them valid, none of them able to withstand the argument that their claims to special status reduce merely to special pleading. In our cathedral there are many rooms, each with their own foundations or built as temporary modular units that need no foundations at all. What we had once thought were objective truths, we now see as only historical conveniences. Our politics, our science, and our morality are all strategies of social control, matters of asserting hegemony rather than truth.

We go even farther, for we are invited to invent new realities with our fertile imaginations and then, assisted by our Macintosh graphics programs and our Microsoft spreadsheets, to explore their possibilities, to delight in our new-found liberation. But we no longer think that what we create are models of anything more basic than themselves. We think that what we know rests on nothing more fundamental than someone's inventiveness. Our intellectual and moral disputes, the clash of our interests and our armies, are conflicts among our various world-creations. We should respect each other's differences, argue our own case, seek to persuade others to our point of view, invent new and reconciling perspectives. But beyond or behind this interchange there is nothing, no hierarchy of importances, no objective order of things, no self-evident truths, no commonly accepted commonsense guiding principles. No authorized referee exists who can settle our disputes and crown the rightful victor with the laurel wreath of objectivity, certitude, completeness, or legitimacy.

These days, when we are all our own truth makers, there may no longer be a need for cathedrals in which we might come together in order to acknowledge a common authority for what counts as true and so for what justifiably commands our allegiance. We should be pleased to have come to a realization that a conversation among the pluralism of voices clamoring to be heard in the intellectual marketplace is all that viably remains.

Now apply these relativist developments to the academic curriculum. Surely there is more to studying than learning the ways by which the sons of the governing white elite can best prepare themselves to carry on the tasks set them by their fathers. Even were this race-class-gender elitism still our aim, the explosion in that knowledge has made the old listing of the needed courses woefully inadequate. But there are now all those other new kinds of courses evoked by new definitions of the elite and by anti-elitist alternatives. There are all those courses that have nothing to do with preparing students to govern but are focused instead on how to secure a job or retrain for a new one, that offer senior citizens a substitute for shuffleboard. It should be no surprise that the listing of courses in a college catalogue nowadays often looks something like the *Weekly Shoppers' Guide,* and the members of the curriculum committee seem like politicians trying their best to cope with the multiple pressures of conflicting special interest groups.

We can see this dissolution of the traditional justification for foundational knowledge in the trajectory over the last two centuries of the requirements for graduation at most American undergraduate arts and sciences colleges. At first, everything was required because it was generally agreed that to be educated meant to study certain specific subjects and to acquire certain specific skills. Not only were Latin, geometry, and moral philosophy high on that list, but these fields had an unambiguous content. Studying Virgil, Euclid, and Aristotle was the necessary condition for attaining civilized adulthood.

Eventually "all" became "some" as electives were introduced. One needed geometry but not necessarily Euclid, science but not necessarily geometry. Laboratory work need not be replicating standard experiments in physics or chemistry but might instead involve specimen collecting in botany. Philosophy could mean not just the Greeks but modern philosophers: Descartes, Kant, the Scottish commonsense realists. It was even possible to substitute a modern language for Latin, with English literature therefore added as an alternative to the classical literatures. If an elective curriculum meant that it might henceforth be possible to graduate from college without having read Virgil, one could at least take comfort in knowing that the student was reading Shakespeare instead.

The "some" became over the decades increasingly attenuated, however, and was defined eventually in terms of very broad ranges of academic endeavor. Some natural science was required, some social science, some humanities—the choice was the student's, properly advised by a faculty mentor. Now we no longer can agree that there is any one text or author that a person must have studied to be worthy of an undergraduate diploma: neither Plato's nor Whitehead's philosophy, neither the Preacher's nor the Buddha's wisdom, neither Galileo's nor Einstein's physics, neither Shakespeare's nor Woolf's fiction, neither Machiavelli's nor Strauss's advice, neither Yung-lo's nor Norton's anthology.

Nor can faculty agree on any short list of concepts that are musts for an arts and sciences undergraduate student to know: not the second law of thermodynamics, not the dialectic of class struggle, not the evolution of species, not formalist criticism, not multiple regression analysis, not the Whig interpretation of history, not the hermeneutical circle. Where once our predecessors had agreed that some very specific ideas and methods are absolutely essential to know and be adept at utilizing, we can say now only that some vaguely defined general kinds of such things are important.

There are those in higher education who have given up even this pale confidence in the difference between the important and the trivial, the worthwhile and the fashionable. In many institutions, a content requirement has been completely eschewed and graduation expectations defined in terms of skills, of competencies learned and demonstrated in whatever subject context the student might prefer. Other undergraduate programs have abandoned even this. Graduation for them has become the accumulation of a certain total of academic credits involving classes, internships, life-experiences, self-instructional packets, distance learning contracts—a course of study the mix and pattern of which results from personal choice, perhaps influenced by faculty advice but not requiring faculty consent. These free choice schools still insist upon a major, however, inverting in interesting fashion their eighteenth- and early-nineteenth-century predecessors who insisted upon the breadth of one's study but had no notion of a major. Before too long, however, even the major will likely disappear as a graduation requirement.

We are left with curricula that express the likes and dislikes of faculty whose personal preferences have shaped the scope of what they are competent to teach. This palette of offerings is then modified by the likes and dislikes of students whose preferences multiply the sections of some courses and sound the death knell of others, causing business courses to burgeon and sending Milton scholars into early retirement. And our curricula often express as well the likes and dislikes of benefactors and legislators who exact a price for their financial largesse.

Ruined Choirs

The trajectory is manifest: from objective truth to cultural worldviews, from universal norms to personal preferences. Our deconstruction of learning in the name of intellectual liberation from the arbitrary tyrannies of traditional, mainstream, and regional objectivities entails the arbitrary elimination of any and every imposed definition of what subject matters we must study, what skills we must acquire, to what virtues we must aspire. When anarchy is loosed upon the educational world, hierarchies of knowledge and developmental sequences from basic to specialized learning fall apart. Is this collapse good or bad? Do the foundations need to be restored, remodeled, or eliminated? Is the cathedral to be shored up, or should it be torn down and a new one built in its place? Or is the cathedral simply best left in ruins?

As Bill Readings points out in *The University in Ruins,* the trope of a culture in ruins has a long history, one that has relevance for the meaning of higher education. The ruins of Nineveh and Tyre, of the Athenian Acropolis and the Roman Forum, engage our emotions. They are sermons about the fleeting character of human accomplishment, the vanity of believing that one can defy the ravages of time. But they are also celebrations of a former glory, of a time of grandeur, of noble achievement. They show us a social good that our ancestors once possessed but that has since been lost: a golden age commanding our admiration. Ancient ruins evoke in us a romantic nostalgia for lost causes, for ideals no longer realized or never realized. But they also stir us to dream of revival. Perhaps we can reconstitute what has been lost in a way and form appropriate to our own times. We can restore the glory that was Greece; we can create a New Rome as the worthy successor of the Republic or the Empire.

In this phoenix-like trope of a culture rebuilding itself out of its ruins, the educational institutions are taken as the builders, as the instruments of the reconstruction. They will take up the shards of the past and make them whole again. The culture that remains, the cultural remains of a former glory, will be wrought by education into that glory redivivus. According to this understanding of what a ruin means, the mission of the liberal arts in the contemporary world should be to effect "the mediating resynthesis of knowledges, returning us to the primordial unity and immediacy of a lost origin" (Readings: 169). First, the arts and sciences faculty should teach their students how the traditional academic disciplines, now so deeply fragmented, can be integrated. Second, under the aegis of the ideal of a culture's integrity—what Hegel called the spirit of an age, a *Weltanschauung,* a cultural framework of beliefs, values, and practices—an actual intellectual unity should then be hammered out and inculcated in the rising generation. Third, these students should carry this ideal and its abstract theoretical expressions into their homes and workplaces, and there begin to build the institutions that will give it concrete historical embodiment.

Thus, educators are attracted to ruins because they imply an aspiration. The task of education is to transform a dead or dying past into a vital living present. Our problem, however, is that it is this instrument of renewal itself that is dead or dying. Not only is the metropolis of Western civilization, and with it the American city on a hill, becoming a ruin, but so also is the cathedral of learning that offers us a possibility for rebuilding it.

Over the course of the next three chapters, I will explore what I take to be the primary ways in which it is proposed that American undergraduate education in the liberal arts be revitalized. Each of those ways centers around the notion of an educational canon—the first based on content, the second on method, and the third a repudiation of canons of any sort. My strategy will be, first, to look at the philosophical presuppositions of each proposed approach, its presumptions concerning what knowledge is, how humans can acquire it, and for what purpose. In the light of these presuppositions, I will then explore the claims each approach makes about what is most important for students to learn and what irrelevant, what crucial and what discretionary—the normative guidelines for becoming properly educated. I will conclude by sketching some of the curricular and pedagogical implications of these considerations. In chapter 5, I will consider a fourth approach, that of relativism, but will argue that its various versions turn out to be temporalized restatements of the first two approaches.

The three approaches to a revitalized educational mission, featuring three differing notions of the canonical conditions for a proper education, can be ordered historically—first the classical/medieval and next the modern, both of them hierarchical approaches, then on to the deconstructive postmodern egalitarian alternative. These approaches are better taken, however, as competing voices in a current debate. They should not be understood as stadia on a downward or upward trajectory, neither desirable phases of a progressive emancipation of learning from the straitjacket of tradition nor dolorous moments in the progressive loss of a nurturing tradition. They are plausible, but seemingly incommensurable, positions: each vying for our attention and commitment.

Indeed, I will argue, the most important features of the various approaches to education have to do with a dispute about the nature of hierarchies, and so the first two approaches can be taken as more similar than different. The debate, therefore, is basically a dialogue, a disputation between canonists of all kinds and anti-canonists, between those who believe in natural hierarchies and those who find hierarchies artificial and harmful. After examining these views and their underlying polarity, I will be ready, beginning with chapter 6, to elaborate a middle way, a nonpolarizing approach to education and its canons—a pragmatic theory about how best to conceive of the higher learning with regard to its philosophical grounds, its normative character, and its practical dynamics.

Chapter 2

Content Canonists

Foundationalism

These arguments about what should be taught, about what it is important for every student to learn, are not merely cat fights between those enamored by the new and those who prefer the tried and true. The dispute is over two claims about reality, one contending that it is ordered hierarchically into essential and accidental elements, one insisting that it is not. If some aspects of the world are essential, then the study of any particular thing needs to give primary attention to those aspects, since in one way or another it is dependent on them. If there are no essences, however, if the aspects of the world are all happenstantially related, then the study of any particular thing needs to take equal account of all the various aspects that at a given time might have some bearing on it.

Foundationalism is the assertion that ideas, methods, and the purported facts on which they are based and which they generate—concepts, hypotheses, interpretations; protocols, models, experimental designs; sense data, images, digital readouts—must be judged in terms of their adequacy to an objective correlate upon which they depend. True ideas "mirror" an external reality that serves as their foundation (Rorty 1979). When the form and content of our mental image is an undistorted reflection of the form and content of an external reality, when our sentence asserting that this is so has the same structure as the structure of that about which we are making an assertion, then our mental picture is accurate and our assertion true. "The cat is on the mat" is true if and only if there actually is a cat related to a mat by being located on it.

There can be as many models of reality, as many interpretive frameworks and intellectual perspectives, as there are people to invent them, but no more than one of them is "privileged." Only one representation of reality can mirror it accurately. Is it Aristotle's representation, or Galileo's, or Einstein's? At least two of these are in some manner wrong: inadequate, overstated, parochial. Maybe all three. It may well be that no human being has yet come up with a fully accurate picture of things, nor ever will. But the existence of an objective foundation for knowledge remains as the ideal, the norm, by means of which what is flawed can be recognized as flawed, without which the very notion of a flaw could not even be thought.

The reality our theories attempt to mirror is not a hodgepodge of particular facts. It has generic characteristics and relational structures. The particular facts are elements of systems, and these systems are elements of wider or more complex systems governed by general laws, perhaps even by universal ones. The natural order is not the bewildering flux of novel realities it often seems to be. There are underlying uniformities that these supposed novelties illustrate. The apples are ripening in the orchard, the leaves are turning a brilliant red; the fog rolls in at dusk, obscuring the bright sparkle of the evening star. When the apple falls it will plummet to the ground whereas the leaf will drift down slowly, but they are both constrained by the same gravitational force, described by Newton's three general laws of motion—which laws also govern the behavior of the water molecules in the fog and the orbital and rotational motions of Earth and Venus.

The objective world so understood is organized hierarchically. Every individual thing is an instance of a kind of thing: this thing here in front of me is a cat, that object under it is a mat, you and I are both human beings. If each individual is an instance of a kind, then those kinds must be instances of a kind of kinds, and this ordering of kinds must continue until some one highest kind is identified. Moreover, if its kind is what gives a thing its reason for existing and is therefore a standard by which the quality of its existence can be judged, then the whole system of kinds can have no discernible reason, nor in consequence any inherent value, unless it too has a reason for existing and hence a criterion for determining its worth.

The system of natural kinds, stretching from conditions that only minimally enform the fluid flux of matter to the ultimate condition that gives sense and value to the universe, constitutes what Arthur Lovejoy, paraphrasing Alexander Pope, calls a "Great Chain of Being." All things are linked together and each had its proper place, the "number of links ranging in hierarchical order from the meagerest kind of existents, which barely escape non-existence, through 'every possible' grade up to the *ens perfectissimum*..., everyone of them differing from that immediately above and that immediately below it by the 'least possible' degree of difference" (59). Natural things compose a rational system rather than an arbitrary collection because the form of each thing, its essence, provides the universal and necessary conditions for its existence.

To be is to be enformed, and the being of the creatures is the result of God's timeless determination of them in their kinds, an ordering of things both rational and right because divinely ordained.

Modern science has secularized this hierarchy, replacing an interventionist Christian God with an uninvolved deistic Creator and eventually with a nondivine although still mysterious Big Bang. The natural kinds have ceased to be timeless, fixed essences, having been replaced by evolving structural conditions. What remains constant amid these changing beliefs is the principle of hierarchy, the conviction that the universe is intelligible, that it can be understood because its components comprise a single rational system. The ideal of an ultimate Theory of All Things is thought to be a realistic realizable goal for scientific inquiry.

Foundationalists likewise understand actual human societies as organized hierarchically, based on inherent differences among the persons involved. At the bottom of the hierarchy is a large class of workers, of slaves or serfs or industrial proletarians, at the top a small controlling elite of landowners or nobles or managers. Location on the hierarchy is a matter of property rights, birthright, or the proper recognition of natural talent, all of these understood as intrinsic qualities. Deference is due those with a higher status than our own in recognition of their superior worth. We would be doing violence to the natural order of things were we to disdain our betters or aspire to their status. Yet every station in life confers an honor appropriate to it, which others are obliged to acknowledge. The servant deserves respect as a servant, the master as a master. Our excellence is a function of our effectiveness in fulfilling our appropriate social role, just as an acorn's excellence is constituted by its effectiveness in becoming a sturdy oak.

The particulars of any given society's hierarchy will be unique, of course, a matter of its history, of special circumstances and responses. They all share certain structural similarities, however, general features by which they can be compared and classified with respect to their success in realizing the normative ideal of a well-ordered human community. For instance, their governments can be classified as monarchies, oligarchies, or democracies, their kinship systems as matriarchies or patriarchies, their economies as capitalist, socialist, or communist. These differences can then be ordered with respect to their intrinsic value: from worst to best. Foundationalists may argue over the classifications and the rankings. They may dispute Plato's claim that there are only six basic kinds of government, or they may accept the six but reject his preference for a monarchy headed by a philosopher. But all foundationalists will agree that there really is a best form of government and a best set of societal rules, an ideal that we must strive to understand and, having understood it, strive to realize.

This belief about the objective correlate to true beliefs dominated Western thought throughout its classical and medieval periods; it is still the common sense of most Westerners today. The paradigm of this tradition, Socrates, constantly questions his Athenian compatriots about their claims to know the truth of things, to know what it means for a person to be good or a society just. He says that he lacks their know-it-all confidence, that he "does not have knowledge but is guessing." There is one thing, however, that he does know: "I certainly do not think I am guessing that right opinion is a different thing from knowledge" (*Meno* 98b). Objective knowledge may be hard to come by, but such a thing exists and it is not the same as anyone's—or even everyone's—opinions, interests, or preferences. Error, evil, and incoherence can in principle be distinguished from truth, goodness, and beauty.

When applied to education, foundationalism is the presumption that our perceptions, practices, and interpretive reflections can justifiably be grouped in terms of subject matters that are organized internally and with respect to each other in a manner that mirrors the way in which the world is organized. The organization of learning into a *trivium* and *quadrivium* of arts is explicitly hierarchical. The trivial arts come first because they have to do with the necessary conditions for learning, with what Eva Brann calls "significant speech"—initially grammar which transforms sounds into speech, then rhetoric which uses grammared speech to communicate with others, and finally logic which organizes such communication into forms of valid reasoning. On this foundation, a student is then able to undertake a study of the quadrivial arts, "the arts of intelligible things," arts "traditionally ordered according to increasing corporeality, from dimensionless arithmetic through plane and solid geometry, to astronomy (the application of mathematics to moving bodies) and music (the study of bodies executing harmonious motions, that is, physics)" (Brann 1979: 119).

Nowadays our organization of learning is expressed first of all as a hierarchy among the natural sciences. Because the complex things of physical nature are constructed out of simpler basic components, physics and chemistry are said to be the most basic of the natural sciences. They explicate the nature and behaviors of the ultimate building blocks of the universe, the atoms or subatomic elements that combine to form the molecules of which the stars, stones, plants, and animals of everyday experience are composed. Physics is finally more basic than chemistry because chemical reactions are special instances of its more general laws. Biology is physics and chemistry applied to organisms; geology applies all three disciplines to an understanding of the Earth or any other planetary body.

This hierarchy in the kinds of knowing is then extended into the social sciences as attempts to use the general principles of the natural sciences to explain and predict the behaviors of human beings individually and in groups. Economists, psychologists, and physical anthropologists have had the most success in becoming scientists in this sense. Most departments of government have at least gestured in that direction by renaming themselves political science departments. Many historians see their discipline as a science: an application of the other social sciences to the past, to a study of the beliefs and behaviors of persons no longer living and of the institutions they once wrought. Even humanists often attempt to transform their disciplines into sciences, or handmaidens of the sciences. For instance, the currently dominant understanding of philosophy in the English-speaking world and Scandinavia is that since it is not a science it can discover no new facts nor develop any theories for predicting them. Philosophy can play a useful role, however, in clarifying the character of the assertions scientists make about the world, and in exposing the pretensions of non-scientists when they attempt to make truth assertions of their own.

This hierarchy of the disciplines is justified by the foundationalist presumption that every thing is an instance of some kind of physical thing and so must be located somewhere within the hierarchy of the kinds of natural entities. E. O. Wilson names this presumption "consilience," which he describes as the idea "that all tangible phenomena, from the birth of stars to the workings of social institutions, are based on material processes that are ultimately reducible, however long and tortuous the sequences, to the laws of physics" (266). We might try to reject Wilson's and Lovejoy's vision by arguing for a dualism between physical and mental kinds of things or by claiming that there are natures superior to the natures of natural things, organisms, and persons. But dualisms of any sort are incoherent, and so supernaturalists have been losing their battle with scientists ever since Galileo. The Great Chain of Being, interpreted naturalistically as a chain of ever more complex systems of physical phenomena, is the objective world that our knowledge mirrors.

Foundationalism so construed defines unmistakably the task of pedagogy. There is at minimum a best approximation to a fully adequate picture of reality. The consensus of scientists and humanists, their theories and interpretations having withstood the test of time, of endless confirmation and attempts at refutation, circumscribes that best approximation. Accordingly, the purpose of a general arts and sciences education—of an undergraduate liberal arts education—is to teach a rising generation the skills required to make such distinctions, to introduce young people to the treasures of an intellectual heritage that, tempered by the fires of sustained constructive criticism, can confidently be offered as composing the sum of what is genuinely known to be the case.

The Great Books Canon

A "canon" is a normative measure. The term derives from the Greek for a straight rod, a measuring stick: hence a standard, a set of instructions. A canon is what people in authority use to indicate what those under their jurisdiction are supposed to do. Musical compositions are called canons when their initial subject is then taken up sequentially by the various other parts in strict imitation. What canons do to people is what cannons do to projectiles and canyons to rivers: they canalize them into a definite well-ordered trajectory. Ecclesiastical obedience is a matter of canon law; the sacred scriptures of the faith comprise a canon; the resident clergy at a cathedral, their lives ordered by the juridical canons of the Church, are themselves called canons. With respect to the cathedral of learning, therefore, the foundations of knowledge can be thought of as canonical truths and the faculty who teach such truths can be called its canons. Appropriately, the chief academic officer of an undergraduate college, the head of its faculty, is given the same title as that given the superior canon for a cathedral: the dean.

The *Oxford English Dictionary*'s second definition of "canon" captures explicitly its educational function: a canon is "a general rule, fundamental principle, aphorism or axiom governing the systematic or scientific treatment of a subject." It determines the essential or core features of a subject, the basic structure of relationships that characterize it, those upon which the other features of the subject, the accidental or peripheral ones, depend. Thus, an intellectual canon with respect to some subject matter is the set of rules for determining what materials—ideas, methods, heuristics, texts, data—are crucial for someone to know if he or she is to grasp that subject adequately. The intellectual canon is a sorting device, a way to separate important from unimportant knowledge. It is a way not only to distinguish truth from falsehood but also to distinguish core truths from peripheral ones, a way by which to find a path that leads us out of the confusions of our own experience and the conflicting claims of self-proclaimed experts, that leads us to the foundations upon which they all rest and by which they can be judged.

By an obvious process of metonymy, the intellectual canon is usually taken as designating those central materials themselves rather than the rules for their determination. The intellectual canon becomes an "educational canon" when the relevant subject matter is taken to be human knowledge in general and the emphasis is not upon its creation but upon its transmission. In disputes about the character of American undergraduate education, the canon is usually at issue: What are the texts that contain those ideas essential for American young people to know in order for them to become responsible citizens? As William Bennett puts it, paraphrasing Matthew Arnold, the educational canon is "the best that has been said, thought, written, and otherwise expressed about the human experience" (3)—what Allan Bloom calls "the rare, the refined and the superior."

Advocates of canonical education view with dismay the decline over the last century in the "authority of tradition." They see an old consensus about what it is important for anyone to know eroded by the acid rains of academic professionalization and cultural fragmentation. The expansion in the complexity and scope of information has meant a need both for increasingly specialized skills and for greater breadth of experience and sensitivity in order to acquire or understand that information. According to the supporters of a canon-based education, the result of this expansion has been, on the one hand, the emergence of a professionalized faculty more interested in their narrow research programs than the general education of students and, on the other hand, a politicized faculty more interested in persuading students to accept their blinkered ideologies and support their polarizing political agendas than in teaching them to think critically and independently. These two factional, fracturing tendencies have led, the content canonists argue, to a dangerous "dispersal of authority," to a "loss of integrity in the bachelor's degree" (Rudolph 1985; Cheney 1989).

A curriculum without "integrity" (Rudolph) is one without "coherence" (Cheney), one in which "intellectual authority" is replaced by "intellectual relativism" (Bennett). The dreary roster of evidence showing the failure of the American educational system to teach its young people what they need to know is said by these canonists to be the result of this fragmentation, this collapse of any commonly agreed upon distinction between important and unimportant materials. The solution they advocate, therefore, is that we recover the old and proper integrity of the undergraduate curriculum by reaffirming the centrality, and hence the authority, of those fundamental structures of understanding that have been defined by the traditional educational canon. In *The Higher Learning in America,* Robert Maynard Hutchins famously summed up this view by means of a logical sorites: "Education implies teaching. Teaching implies knowledge. Knowledge is truth. The truth is everywhere the same. Human education should be everywhere the same" (66).

"Some books are more important than others," says Bennett (10), and these should be studied with care. They bring students into "the company of great souls" (11), confront them with "the questions that are central to human existence" (29), and so by the universality of that encounter provide them with a common heritage that serves as "the glue that binds together our pluralistic nation" (30). Gertrude Himmelfarb makes the same appeal to centrality and universality: "The canon—any canon—assumes that there is such a thing as great books containing great and enduring ideas and truths worthy of being studied and valued. Moreover, it assumes that these ideas and truths transcend time and place, race and ethnicity, class and gender, country and nationality" (4).

Italo Calvino characterizes a great book—a "classic"—as one "that has never finished saying what it has to say" (128), that we therefore read and reread, finding it always fresh, unexpected. Its significance is therefore all-encompassing: it "takes the form of an equivalent to the universe" (130), persisting "as a background noise even when the most incompatible momentary concerns are in control of the situation" (132). Eva Brann echoes Calvino's encomium by identifying books worthy of inclusion in the St. John's College curriculum as ones that have "indefinitely rich interpretability without loss of definite meaning," that are "original" in the double sense of standing at "the origins or foundations of human knowledge" and of being able to "bring forth something new" in the minds of those who read them (1999: 164). Great books also have "independent interpretability": the richness of their content is sufficiently self-interpreting "so that students and tutors need no background preparation" to learn from them (165).

Brann adds, and all traditional canonists would agree, that what is great is also difficult. What students learn in studying great books is "the array of conditions associated with excellence: that what is finest often denies itself to easy access; that to live admiringly with things above oneself is a source of dignity; that genuine hierarchies confer respect on all their members; that even what is greatest, or especially what is greatest, offers itself to critical judgment" (161). Learning properly undertaken in dialogue with great souls involves "concentrated, particular, and laborious immersion," which is the only way by which one can "stack the mind with exemplars of the highest quality" (161).

James Garfield, when the President of Hiram College, supposedly made Brann's point more succinctly in his retort to a parent who was complaining about his son being forced to study the classics rather than subjects relevant to a career in business or the professions: "Well, it all depends upon what you want. When God wants to make an oak, He takes a hundred years, but He takes only two months to make a squash" (quoted, Carnochan: 135). And, of course, Spinoza put it even more succinctly in that wonderful last sentence of his *Ethics:* "All excellent things are as difficult as they are rare" (223).

In *To Claim a Legacy,* Bennett identifies the great souls whose books he thinks should compose our educational canon. He explicitly limits himself to Western civilization, and his examples are all from the humanities—as defined by the National Endowment for the Humanities, which includes history and any subdiscipline of a social science that in its concepts, methods, and conclusions is not scientific, such as, for instance, political theory. Bennett's great souls "include, but are not limited to" the following (11):

- *Classical antiquity:* Homer, Sophocles, Thucylides, Plato, Aristotle, Virgil.
- *Medieval-seventeenth century:* Dante, Chaucer, Machiavelli, Montaigne, Shakespeare, Hobbes, Milton, Locke.
- *Eighteenth to twentieth century:* Swift, Rousseau, Austen, Wordsworth, Tocqueville, Dickens, Marx, George Eliot, Dostoevsky, Tolstoy, Nietzsche, Mann, T. S. Eliot.

- *American:* the Declaration of Independence, the Federalist Papers, the U.S. Constitution, Hawthorne, Melville, Lincoln, Twain, Faulkner, M. L. King Jr.

To which Bennett adds, almost as an afterthought, the Bible and these works of art: the Parthenon, Chartres Cathedral, Michelangelo's Sistine Chapel ceiling, the music of Bach and Mozart.

Lynne Cheney, Bennett's successor at NEH, offers in *50 Hours* her own paradigm of a "cultures and civilizations" core curriculum that is similarly focused. It devotes three of the six courses in the core to Western civilization (19–20). Her list, reorganized by Bennett's categories, adds and subtracts from his:

- *Classical antiquity:* added, Livy; omitted: Aristotle; Homer is included in the initial globally inclusive core course on "The Origins of Civilization."
- *Medieval-seventeenth century:* added: Augustine, Cervantes, Luther, Descartes; omitted: Montaigne.
- *Eighteenth to twentieth century:* added: Voltaire, Goethe, Mill, Flaubert, Woolf; omitted: Swift, Tocqueville, George Eliot, Tolstoy, Mann.
- *American:* added: Douglass, Edwards, Emerson, Thoreau, Webster, Chief Joseph, Whitman, Dickinson, Frost, Wright; omitted: Hawthorne.

Cheney's courses include the Bible and all of Bennett's artists and works of art, but add Monet, Picasso, Copley, Cassatt, and O'Keeffe. Her list of musicians substitutes Beethoven for Bach.

We have to go to the St. John's College curriculum (provided, e.g., in Casement, Appendix B) before the natural sciences and mathematics find their proper place in the canon. They are a part of Cheney's model core curriculum, but as teaching a method of inquiry rather than as a source of great books. Students at St. John's study, among other scientists, Euclid and Ptolemy, Galileo and Newton, Harvey and Lavoisier, Dedekind and Lubachevsky, Mendel and Einstein. Moreover, since the St. John's list is a four-year course of study not a fifty-hour core, it can be far more inclusive in its humanities great books. For instance, it complements Sophocles with Aeschylus, Euripides, and Aristophanes. Students read Berkeley and Hume after Locke, and they study Francis Bacon, Adam Smith, Kant, Hegel, Darwin, and Freud. St. John's readings in literature expand on the NEH lists to include Rabelais, Racine, Joyce, Kafka, Conrad, and Flannery O'Connor. Despite its far greater length, the St. John's list has few American authors, however. It includes William James, but only through his *Psychology: the Briefer Course,* and it offers no Hawthorne, Dickinson, Thoreau, Whitman, or Faulkner.

My own eyebrows rise at the omission of the American pragmatists from all three of these rosters of Western civilization's great souls. Cheney lists William James, and quotes him at the end of *Tyrannical Machines* in support of the claim that an education in the canon teaches critical judgment: "We learn what types of activity have stood the test of time; we acquire standards of the excellent and durable" (52). But there is no indication of James's pragmatism here, as there is none in the St. John's use of him. Incredibly, none of our three canons include John Dewey. Nor is Charles Sanders Peirce on any list, even though he, Wittgenstein, and Heidegger—all three omitted—are, along with Einstein and Freud, the most original—in Brann's sense—and influential thinkers of the twentieth century.

Criticisms of this sort are cheap shots, however, superficial ditherings around the edges of the canonists' argument. Bennett was quick to note that his list is by no means exhaustive. He also acknowledges that it would benefit from more attention to great souls who are not Western nor culturally mainstream nor male. His point and Cheney's is not that education should be confined to reading what they recommend, but that for Americans what is essential to their education can and must be learned from a traditional collection of works by their own and West European authors, along with certain Hebrew, Greek, and Roman predecessors. On this foundation one can then construct a fuller cultural edifice of other authors who are worth reading, a house of intellect that is wide, diverse, and generously pluralistic. But it will be a house built upon the sand, say Bennett and his colleagues, unless first it reaches to bedrock by means of a canon such as the one they propose. Cheney exemplifies this sequencing by following her one pre-Western and three Western core courses with two non-Western requirements, although in the form of a choice of any two among five "other civilizations" (one of which, incoherently, is a "Latin American Civilization" course that begins with the European conquest (21)).

Back to the Basics

Those who spearhead a back-to-basics movement as the proper way to respond to the current explosion in things to be learned escape being merely curmudgeons insofar as they are guided by a foundationalist understanding of things. If the hierarchical organization of an academic discipline can legitimately aspire to reflect the hierarchical nature of how the world is organized, then they are right to object that educators are pandering to political pressure, to special interest groups and emotional arguments, when they accept new claims about what needs to be learned as on a par with the old, familiar list of essentials.

Certainly the educational canon changes over time: new great souls need occasionally to be added to the pantheon. New books, ideas, and authors will from time to time be thought worthy candidates for inclusion, and some provisionally included can later be judged unworthy. Any canon changes, but the proper way to add or subtract from its roster of the great is by a process of historical winnowing: the test of time, the verdict of history. Attempts to short-circuit this process are dangerous because they substitute the passions and biases of the present moment for the considered and reflective judgment temporal distance makes possible. Making hasty alternations in an established tradition of what is considered fundamental is gratuitously destabilizing.

Thus, foundationalist supporters of an educational canon can legitimately argue that computer science or American studies are not proper undergraduate majors on the grounds that they have arisen as applications or conglomerations of supposedly more basic disciplines. A liberal arts curriculum, or at least a general education core, should be limited to the subjects students need to know no matter what their subsequent specializations might be. Students, says Eva Brann, should be prevented from entering prematurely into the sustained study of a specific field of knowledge. They "should be granted a period of enforced inchoateness before they go on to advanced study in the field they choose" (1979: 118). Just as the public schooling movement fostered by Horace Greeley was based on the claim that all children in a democracy should be taught by eighth grade the knowledge essential for citizenship, so in these more complex times those basic requirements should be enlarged to involve completion of a secondary school diploma or, for those wishing to prepare for one of the professions, a baccalaureate degree.

The only way to save the content of a student's basic education from becoming an arbitrarily growing pile of this and that is to insist that it be limited to what is essential. The importance of standards is to validate not so much the quantity or quality of what a student has learned as its character—not whether it is difficult or profound but whether it is essential. American studies, interesting and relevant though it might be, is a peripheral subject, resting on the twin foundation of American history and American literature. Computer science is a burgeoning specialty of discrete mathematics, a subdiscipline of a subdiscipline. First master the basic discipline, then later on explore its extensions and applications.

Advocates of a traditional canon might be skeptical concerning the legitimacy of black studies or women's studies, for instance, insisting that these movements to democratize the academic disciplines are rooted in a confusion between the obvious value of consciousness-raising and the requirements of a genuine field of knowledge. Rooting out prejudice is a necessary task for educators, not only the prejudice of their students and themselves but also that of the great souls they study. But to do so responsibly, we must first understand what we are claiming has been distorted by prejudice. We should never throw truth out with the error that the bathwater of our critiques is washing away.

We should reject Aristotle's disparaging view of the rational capacity, and hence the access to political decision making, of those who compose the complement class of free Greek men—women, children, slaves, and foreigners. But to abandon a study of Aristotle altogether, on the grounds that his whole philosophy is incurably infected by this or any other of his prejudices, is to blur the distinction between what is essential and what accidental to his philosophy—a distinction, indeed, key to that philosophy itself. Aristotle's ideas and his methods have so deeply shaped our beliefs that we cannot understand ourselves except by understanding him. The limitations of his position need to be pointed out, some of his ideas and methods condemned or ridiculed for their pernicious or silly claims, others of them praised for their insight and prescience. But all of his ideas should be explored as pathways toward an understanding of the intellectual and moral horizon of the Greek world, and their lineage should be traced from then to now. It will tell a story of how those strengths and limitations in some ways stubbornly persisted and in some ways were transformed by events and by the inner dialectic of their own possibility for self-transcendence. We must in the end move beyond Aristotle, but only by moving through him not around him. First Aristotelian studies, then women's studies.

Foundationalist canonists pursue a similar line of reasoning in regard to the globalization of knowledge. Cultures other than Western culture have their own great souls, key ideas, and enduring artistic and literary expressions. The arrogance that once bred indifference to other cultures and their achievements, that justified dismissing them as primitive, heathen, or wrongheaded, has long since been exposed for what it is. We have much to learn from our cousins who live in other lands or other times. But our Western heritage, which is the basis of who we are, of our habits of mind and heart, must first be well-learned before another civilizational tradition can be usefully investigated. We have to know ourselves before we can understand how we are like and unlike others. To see beyond our cultural horizons we must first see to them.

The strategy in all these cases is the same: lay a firm foundation, then build on it. The foundationalist complaint is that by rushing too quickly to what is new, to the immediately exciting and relevant, students pay a severe penalty. They learn a lot of particulars but not the principles by which the particulars are related, and so they never get a good grip on the contextualizing framework that gives a subject its significance, that discloses its presuppositions and hence both its limits and its possibilities. Entranced by the trees, they miss the forest. Taking the time to get the basics right is how students can equip themselves to build their own viewpoints, to develop the wherewithal to come up with their own novelties and relevance, suited to changing times and conditions, rather than being limited to whatever ideas and ideals others have happened to dangle before them.

Basic intellectual, vocational, and life skills, as well as values and value judgments, can only be acquired when the environment for their acquisition is texts written by authors who help us distinguish the core from the periphery, the enduring from the ephemeral. We learn to think well by studying a great thinker, not by reading comic books. We learn to write well only if we are at the same time reading those who write well about important things. Perhaps it is not as quaint as it might at first have seemed to advocate recapturing in contemporary modes the ideals of a classical British education: teaching students the elitist and parochial truths of their cultural heritage in the guise of the lives and writings of its greatest heroes, so as by their example to prepare those students for the duties of citizenship in a complex world. Excellence breeds excellence, and for the difficult discipline of study that this truth entails there is no shortcut.

These high standards with respect to intellectual content suggest a parallel concern with high standards in evaluating students. If all texts are equally valuable, all topics of similar worth, then it follows that they are all roughly on a par. This leveling effect also applies to student achievement. If the value of something is a subjective attribution, then the quality of a student's work should similarly be focused on his or her subjective qualities: the effort expended, the hours spent, the commitment evidenced. If, however, there is indeed an essential core of materials of unquestionable value that must be learned by any liberal arts undergraduate, and if such learning is difficult to achieve, but not unreasonably so, it can be expected that a bell curve of achievement levels will result. A typical student, working diligently, would be expected to earn more C grades over four years than B and A grades combined. That this is not so at most colleges and universities is evidence not of faculty slovenliness but of something more endemic: the collapse of any strong sense of an unquestioned standard of excellence regarding what must be learned for a student justifiably to be called educated.

The Agonized Academic

The ideal way to institutionalize the sort of education the content canonist advocates is to create what Bill Readings calls the "University of Culture" (ch. 5; for a similar notion see Allan 1997: ch. 2: "The College as Faithful Community"). Its mission is to provide the young people of a nation with the beliefs and values of their ancestors, thus preparing them for the responsibility they will have as adults to assure their nation's future by embodying those same beliefs and values in their current practices and by inculcating them in the successor generation. The University of Culture is "the model for an institution in which the present could fuse past tradition and future ambition into a unified field of culture" (68).

As students at such an educational institution, the focus of our education would be on personal development: becoming civilized in order to become good citizens. Learning would be a *Bildung,* a journey in self-discovery, in the increased actualization of our inherent potential. It would be accomplished by internalizing the best in our tradition, turning what was merely a history into our heritage. This heritage could be ethnic and geographic, a matter of familial ties and emotional loyalties, of blood and soil. The German Idealists, however, whom Readings identifies with the University of Culture, tended to understand a national tradition as more than this. They thought our journey of cultural internalization needed to involve our rational faculty as well as our feelings. They believed that the task of educators is to get behind the accidents of the nation's mythic expressions and historical contingencies to the deeper truth that grounds them—not to repudiate those particularized features of the nation's ethnic character but instead, in Schleiermacher's words, to rationalize them so that "the nation will come to embody an ethnicity that is raised to rational self-consciousness" (quoted, Readings: 64). Schiller inverts the argument, but to the same effect: "Reason is given organic life through historical study. Humanity does not achieve the moral state by rejecting nature but by reinterpreting nature as an historical process" (quoted, Readings: 63). Cardinal Newman's "Christian gentleman" is the Anglo-American version of this approach: adults who have learned, in family and church as well as in school, "certain habits, moral or intellectual," that are culturally rooted, are prepared "to fill their respective posts in life better, ... [to be] more intelligent, capable, active members of society" (Newman: 7).

An educational institution subscribing to the University of Culture vision will be inherently conservative, for it holds to a cultural version of a key biological feature of organic development: that the ontogeny of a cultivated citizen should recapitulate the phylogeny of the culture's history. Revolution, however, because it repudiates that history, cuts young people off from the necessary conditions for their proper development into productive adults. Therefore, America and France, as revolutionary nations, need a substitute for ethnic heritage if they are to retain a traditional understanding of the role of education. According to Readings, they find their substitute by making a double move.

First, these newly formed nations broaden what counts as the tradition the University is to inculcate. It is no longer the tradition of a particular nation but rather that of the whole of Western civilization. What was repudiated in

1776 and 1789 were contingent historical articulations of some of the basic features of Western beliefs and values. The *Declaration of Independence* and the *Rights of Man and the Citizen* appeal to the deeper truths of this pan-European political tradition against attempts by the Hanover and Bourbon monarchies to distort it for their personal benefit. Hence, both new governments found their exemplars in earlier Western cultural expressions—indeed, in the earliest: those of Periclean Athens and the Roman Republic.

Second, the revolutionary nations make this tradition a result of their own decisions, not a consequence of their history. As befits a free people, they make their "tradition appear to be the object of a democratic choice rather than the sheer burden of heredity" (Readings: 84). So they fashion an intellectual canon as their substitute for the inherited tradition of which their revolution deprived them. They take the associated educational canon to be part of this social contract, an agreement among the nation's founders, protected and perpetuated by its cultural elite, concerning what the people should be taught about the bedrock of their fresh-minted beliefs and values. Although the great books identified by this educational canon are supposedly judged worthy of inclusion on rational grounds, their authority derives in no small part from the aura of that for which they are the substitute: "This canon is, in fact, the surreptitious smuggling of *historical* continuity into the study of supposedly discrete and autonomous artworks" (84). The canon is a democratic artifact, something chosen by the people. But it is also sacred, for it expresses the ideas and describes the practices that made our cherished freedoms possible.

George Santayana, in his brilliant 1911 essay on "The Genteel Tradition in American Philosophy," argues that this investiture of recent choice with the trappings of hoary tradition is precisely what we should expect would happen in a time when the cathedral of learning is on the edge of ruin. A concern for finding and defending one's canonical foundations is the likely response for a small elite to make that sees itself, and the beliefs and values that give it significance, gravely threatened. Surrounded by an alien and hostile world of alternative values, the members of a threatened elite will respond by intensifying their commitment to their own values. They are embattled saints in the midst of a sinful land, protecting their bastion of civilization against the barbarian at its gates. Santayana's name for this siege mentality is "the agonized conscience." It is the temperament of those who inhabit "a small nation with an intense vitality, but on the verge of ruin, ecstatic and distressful, having a strict and minute code of laws, that paints life in sharp and violent chiaroscuro, all pure righteousness and black abominations, and exaggerating the consequences of both perhaps to infinity" (190).

I think we can see the agonized conscience expressing itself educationally in the strong sense of ought that traditional canonists typically exude. They have a clear notion of what they think it means to be civilized, to be a learned or cultured person, and they insist that this notion function as a normative ideal governing all decisions regarding the content of courses and the shape of programs of study. They are then scandalized should there be any divergence from that ideal, especially if the problem lies not in the failure to live up to it but in an indifference or disdain for its authority or in a sloven carefree attitude toward its importance. Teaching properly what is essential to the survival of civilization is a serious matter. It calls for a vigilant enforcing of canonical guidelines, a constant attention to standards, lest the academy be damaged beyond repair by those who willfully or in ignorance—sinners or barbarians—would undermine its foundations.

The problem, of course, is that the ideal of the content canonist is atavistic, nostalgic, a form of pedagogical romanticism. The back-to-basics solution is, after all, a demand that we go back. Aristotle, Lovejoy, and Alan Bloom may be right in their insistence that the world is ordered hierarchically and that without permanent norms of judgment and categories of understanding, grounded in the essential features of that order, experience is rendered meaningless. But the categories they offer us are, in fact, inadequate to experience, more culture-bound than they would acknowledge. And this bit of awkwardness simply cannot be ignored.

For instance, Aristotle's prejudices run deep. His views regarding who has the capacity to reason can easily be corrected by ascribing to all human beings the rational capacity he ascribes only to Greek males. But his claim that the highest end this reason serves is the contemplation of timeless immaterialities is rife with the implicit denigration of temporal change that justifies Dewey's drumbeat of criticism against both him and Plato for turning people away from the concrete fixable "problems of men" and toward ethereal chimeras. Or to take another example, the notion of natural hierarchies when applied to human communities slips all too readily into cultural chauvinism, into the conviction that our own culture is at the pinnacle of the hierarchy. Even such a sophisticated educator as Cardinal Newman could say, thinking he was uttering nothing controversial, that "in the language of savages you can hardly express any idea or act of the intellect at all: is the tongue of the Hottentot or Esquimaux to be made the measure of the genius of Plato, Pindar, Tacitus, St. Jerome, Dante, or Cervantes?" (quoted, Readings: 287). Such blinkered beliefs, Aristotle's as much as Newman's, are simply inadequate to the world as we now know it. A people, says Santayana, who are "full of solemn memories" but who live in a place and an era for which those memories are unsuited, are engaged in a futile activity, attempting to put "an old wine in new bottles" (186).

Despite its accuracy in regard to the need for objective, enduring norms in the determination of what students should learn, the back-to-basics advocates do not deal effectively with the contemporary explosion in knowledge merely by commanding it to go away. Significant contributions to knowledge did not end with the Great War—the white male bourgeois Western bias in the canon is no fairy tale—the deconstruction of normative absolutes is no passing fad—Bunker Hill, the Bastille, and Appomattox really happened. The call for a return to the good old days when Western civilization was the only civilization, when men were men and truth was self-evident, when one could tell the players by the color of their hats, or more likely by the color of their skins, is an idol of the tribe. Neither should we, nor can we, ever go home again.

Chapter 3

Procedural Canonists

Methodism

The medieval synthesis of the thirteenth century brought closure to a longstanding conflict among authorities in the Western world with regard to scientific, societal, and moral truths. The remarkable coherence of the notion of a Great Chain of Being is based on a series of reconciliations. Reason and revelation, it was finally agreed, were not incommensurable faculties for attaining truth. The sacred and the secular were not hostile realms, a City of God opposed to and repudiating the City of Man, but complementary, the authority of each absolute in its realm but buttressed by the other. Faith and works were not mutually exclusive foundations for morality, because faith needed to be expressed in acts of benevolence and it was in turn strengthened by those activities.

Within a century, however, this coherence was beginning to break down, buffeted by new expressions of theological skepticism, new forms of political consolidation, and inventions such as the navigational compass, the telescope, and double entry bookkeeping that gave access to new worlds for people to explore and exploit. The religious wars of the sixteenth century were at the confluence of all these unsettling changes, adding death, starvation, and homelessness to the mental and spiritual battles being waged. Some way out of this confusion had to be found, and the route finally taken was to shift the focus of concern from assertions about what is or is not the case to a consideration of the procedure by which one arrives at those assertions. The modern world is based on the claim that methods are more fundamental than results, that ends are guided, achieved, and justified by the means that make them possible.

It is no accident, therefore, that Descartes was in the midst of a military campaign in Germany during the winter of 1619, serving under the Duke of Bavaria, when the ideas came to him that would eventuate in his *Discourse on Method.* It is no accident that in 1637 he published this monograph on "rightly directing one's Reason and of seeking Truth in the Sciences" while self-exiled in Holland in order to avoid being incarcerated by the French government at the behest of Church authorities for his supposedly heretical views. "When I regard with a philosophic eye the various activities and pursuits of men at large," he says, "there is hardly one but seems to me vain and useless" (8). The problem, he thinks, is that people base their activities on false information and that too many of their judgments are ill-considered. It is not that people are incapable of good sense, but rather that "it is not enough to have a sound mind; the main thing is to apply it well" (7). Applying one's good sense well requires a proper method, however, a way by which accurately to distinguish truth from falsehood, good judgment from bad.

Descartes rejects as inadequate the whole traditional Western intellectual canon of great souls and their great books. Great literature "stimulates the mind" and the "memorable deeds related in historical works elevate it"—"the reading of good books is like a conversation with the best men of past centuries"—but they are not trustworthy sources of truth because so weighed down by "superstition and error" (10). Even philosophy is not a helpful guide because "there is no point but is disputed and consequently doubtful," and the "other sciences," because built on philosophy's first principles, are no better. All these resources are like "proud and magnificent palaces built only on sand and mud" (11).

Descartes is left with only his own capacity for good sense as a resource: his reasoning powers. He resolves to carve out for himself, to create out of his own rational reflection on error and its avoidance, "the true method" by which to achieve "knowledge of everything" that his "mind could grasp" (19). Since others have this same rational capacity, he hopes that his results will be of help to them as well as to himself. As he remarks at the conclusion of the *Discourse:* "I am writing in French, my native language, rather than in Latin, the language of my teachers, because I hope for a better judgment of my opinions from those who use only their natural reason in its purity than from those who only trust old books" (56).

Descartes' method is a simple four-step procedure. First, to accept as true "only what presented itself to my mind so clearly and distinctly that I had no occasion to doubt it." Second, "to divide each problem I examined into as many parts as was feasible." Third, to then move in "an orderly way" from "the simplest objects" to "knowledge of the most complex." And fourthly, "to make throughout such complete enumerations and such general surveys that might be sure of leaving nothing out" (20–21). Analyze what is to be known into its simplest units, accept only those that are clearly and distinctly known, that cannot be doubted, then from these simple units synthesize what is complex, all the time carefully checking your work.

In the last part of the *Discourse*, Descartes puts his method to work. He sets about calling into question everything he had previously taken as true, and he finds that the one simple fact he knows clearly and distinctly, the one truth that cannot be doubted, is "that I, who was thinking this, was something" (31). From this foundation, Descartes then famously proves the existence of God. Thereafter, with the assurance God's goodness gives that the natural light of his reason can be trusted, he goes on to discern the universal and necessary first principles of science, the mind-body dualistic nature of persons, and the moral conditions for the good life.

However, Descartes's *je pense donc je suis* proved not to be as firm a foundation as he had claimed, much less the proof of God deduced therefrom, and the basic laws of his science were soon superseded by Newton's. What remained was the method. Not the conclusions of which he was so confident, but the rules that were the source of that confidence. Not the objective features of reality nor the reflections of that reality in the mind of the knower, but the mirror, the instrument by which what is known can be said to be a true picture of what is.

The Cartesian method generates an axiomatic deductive system of truths. Its paradigms are the methods of the logician and the geometer: first, determine a small number of self-evident and absolutely general axioms or first principles, then—by means of a rigorous method for explicating what is implicate in those axioms—derive theorems and intermediate principles of decreasing generality that are no longer self-evident, that provide knowledge never before understood or appreciated. Such a system is as hierarchical as any medieval hierarchy of natural kinds, every bit as pyramidal as the Great Chain of Being. But the hierarchy is not ontological: it is not an order of beings. It is a rational procedure for guiding empirical inquiry.

Accordingly, a person's status in the hierarchies of a social order is not a matter of heredity and tradition but of merit. Those who are able both to determine and to pursue their ends rationally should be more successful than those whose beliefs are burdened by superstition and whose practices are antiquated. Achievement based on a clear and distinct understanding of available resources and options deserves our praise and respect. Success warrants and should confer honor, and the greater the success the greater the honor. The "man of reason"—the gentleman scientist and the mercantilist entrepreneur—becomes the societal paradigm. A new aristocracy of wealth and knowledge replaces the old aristocracy of family lineage.

According to this Cartesian way of thinking, an academic discipline attains the honorific status of an objective science by avoiding the biases of cultural tradition and individual self-interest. It does this by accepting as a fact appropriate to its subject matter only what has been derived from an application of rational method. As Eva Brann points out, because reason is "essentially a tool, it needs a matter that supplies it with *evidence* on which to work. *Experience* is the term for the way of obtaining such evidence," and what is experienced comes "packaged as 'phenomena,' 'facts,' 'data,' or 'information.' That is to say, experience is a way of receiving the world as *prepared* material for reasoning. It delivers wood not trees" (1979: 134).

An academic discipline organizes these prepared facts into a system by treating them as instances of governing principles, principles that are themselves instances of more general principles, and so on until all the known facts and principles of the discipline are subsumed under a single unifying set of first principles. For a discipline to be a science, its truths must constitute an axiomatized system of truths, and mathematics is the means by which such systems are most effectively developed and their truths most unambiguously expressed. Physics is thus the queen of the sciences since its theories are rigorously mathematical, its facts fully quantified, and its system strictly hierarchical. The social sciences are trying to rise to this norm of systematic quantified knowledge, with mixed success. The arts and humanities trail far behind, so entrapped by their proclivity to prefer beauty rather than truth that they seem unlikely ever to arrive at anything even approximating mathematically expressible axioms.

This notion of a hierarchy of disciplines based on method rather than subject matter need not entail that the method be applied in a single invariant manner, however. It is reasonable for us to adjust the method to suit the character of the subject it rationalizes. We can tailor our mathematics to the context of its application. We can use statistical approximations when it is not possible to specify a precise result—for instance, in dealing with complex interactive systems that behave in causally determinate but unpredictable ways. We can make room in our analyses for emergent properties of complicated things such as organisms, properties of the whole that cannot be reduced without loss of information to the properties of their components. Steven Pinker, for example, distinguishes "greedy reductionism" which attempts to "explain a phenomenon in terms of its smallest or simplest constituents" from "good reductionism" which "consists not of *replacing* one field of knowledge by another but of *connecting* or *unifying* them." He talks about "levels of analysis"—physical, biological, cultural, and others: "None of these levels can be replaced by any of the others, but none can be fully understood in isolation from the others" (70, 71).

The mind-body dualism to which Descartes was led by his method even permits the development of two differing and incommensurable kinds of science, and hence two kinds of scientific method: an experimental method for analyzing physical entities and a hermeneutical method for understanding mental entities. Historians can go so far as to defend a kind of scientific method in which a story serves to connect facts meaningfully, providing an account of a development from origin to ending that explains what happened without utilizing generalizations of any sort—a story that is well ordered with regard to psychological and chronological sequencing. The key to a disciplinary method having scientific status is not that it uses covering law generalizations but that its explanations are consistent and coherent, that they make rational sense.

The point of methodism is as an antidote to the fragmentation of knowledge, and its educational value is its applicability across the burgeoning variety of new disciplines. It offers a way to fashion a common ground for knowledge that is based on an epistemology rather than an ontology, on how to go about acquiring knowledge rather than on the character of what is acquired. The original ideal may have been modulated, a single rational method becoming a variety of rational methods, as many ways to doing science as there are bodies of knowledge, as many modes of inquiry as there are kinds of truth. Nonetheless, the underlying motivation remains: to resolve the endless squabbling about foundations and essences by turning our attention away from the what toward the how of knowledge.

The Great Ways Canon

The modernist shift from a foundationalist to a proceduralist approach gives rise to a different notion of canon: the intellectual canon is the scientific method and the educational canon is composed of the techniques and attitudes that students need to acquire in order to think as a scientist thinks. This sort of canon is at least as old as the practices of the librarians at Alexandria who, in the centuries before their great collection of manuscripts was destroyed, first by Roman and then by Moslem invaders, prepared lists of manuscripts that they judged to be the best examples of the various genres of works in their possession. Their criteria of selection had to do with form and style, with matters of literary method rather than content. "The morality of the contents were of little interest to them, but consistency of characterization was, as well as subtlety of diction and versification, elegance of ornamentation, and imaginative power" (Kennedy: 225). Quintillian, a couple of centuries later in his *Institutio Oratoria,* echoes this emphasis on method: he intends "to provide a reading list for students that will enrich their facility for style, supply models to imitate, and provide a knowledge of sources to which they can allude" (quoted, Kennedy: 225).

In the Middle Ages, this interest in the formal aspects of a text becomes the *trivium*—a grammar of thought and its expression, a method for the study of anything whatsoever. As John of Salisbury argued, for instance, grammar is "the science of verbal expression and reasoning" (Book 1, ch. 23). It involves not only considerations of syntax, but also learning how to read any text accurately—"to understand everything that can be taught in words" and interpret it properly—and learning how to communicate what one has learned to others, "speaking and writing correctly," that is, truthfully (Book 1, ch. 21). The *trivium* method was not taught as an abstract procedure but always through imitation of the classical authors. It therefore required a canon of great works, great not with regard to their content but to the grammar they exemplified. Thus, John of Salisbury describes the teaching method of his mentor, Bernard of Chartres, as involving great texts of

> poets and orators who were to serve as models for the boys in their introductory exercises in imitating prose and poetry. Pointing out how the diction of the authors was so skillfully corrected, and what they had to say was so elegantly concluded, he would admonish them to follow their example. (Book 1, ch. 24)

By nineteenth century America, this extended sense of grammar as a nurturing of our rational faculties by the study and imitation of great pieces of writing had become a cliche. Studying Greek and Latin, studying the languages themselves as well as what was written in them, was thought to be the best way to train a student's mind. The difficulty of the texts required mental discipline, and that discipline was thought to serve students well in their practical postbaccalaureate pursuits. The classics were valued "less as literature than as language—repositories of grammatical and syntactical structures which, the Yale Report insisted, employed 'every faculty of the mind ... the memory, judgment, and reasoning powers.' " Thus, for instance, Princeton in 1846 forced one of its professors to resign "because he was teaching Greek literature as well as Greek language" (Levine: 76–77).

In *Prescribing the Life of the Mind,* Charles Anderson articulates a contemporary version of this methodist tradition. The "public purpose" of the university, he argues, its "real work," is "to produce useful ways of thinking, ... to create systems of reason, practices of inquiry" (57). The mission of higher education is to teach "thought ways"—"habits of mind"—that "work well in comprehending the world and deciding what to do in it," that prepare students "to think clearly and carefully about all the affairs of everyday life"(59). A thought way is a normative method: a guide for how best to think through a problem, first by determining what it is—comprehending the problem—and then by working out a solution that will resolve it. That the methods to be taught are normative is a point Anderson underscores in the title of his book. The university should be not merely a neutral repository of culture wisdom, nor merely an agora for the exchange of views, a high-priced debating society. Its task is to "*prescribe* a program for the life of the mind," which means "educating people to adopt certain habits of thought and to renounce others" (19). Education is a matter of learning a discipline, a discipline in the sense not of a body of knowledge but of a procedure for acquiring it.

The core of an arts and sciences curriculum, the courses designed to teach the educational canon, is thus for Anderson composed of the basic thought ways. He proposes five courses (121–141):

1. *Civilization:* a general orientation to one's education, concerned with "how we came to think as we do." Its aim is "to show the genesis, the development, and the rationale of the systems of analysis, the disciplines of mind, that the university deems worthy of teaching" (124). Notice the prescriptive character of the purpose: it is not really how we came to think as we do but how we came to believe that certain ways of thinking are normative for us.
2. *Science:* a "mastery of the fundamentals of scientific inquiry" which, since scientific thinking is the dominate mode of thinking these days, means bringing students into "the life of the mind of their time and place" (128).
3. *Human Situation:* exposing students to diverse perspectives through the study of other cultures, exposing them to "that relativizing experience which is so essential to critical and practical reason" (134). The point is not to appreciate cultural diversity as such but to sharpen one's reasoning powers through such experiences.
4. *Humanities:* "to teach us how to go beyond the thin theory of knowledge, to teach us how to extract a fuller measure of meaning from the world, and to provide us with deeper, more explicit, guidelines on how to make our way in it" (136–37). Again, the purpose is not edification but utility: deepening our analytic and interpretive skills, honing them into more sophisticated tools of inquiry.
5. *Practical Studies:* a "study of a few versions of systematic practice in some detail" (141). Firsthand awareness of the concepts and appropriate techniques relevant to a few representative professions or trades, and of the reasons for their development, provides another context for developing methodological skills.

Anderson really has one method in mind, the scientific method as taught in the second core course. The other core offerings are ways by which students can enhance their sophistication in the use of that method: learning about its history and its specific professional applications, widening and deepening their sense of the world for which that method is a guide.

Most other proposals for a procedural canon are pluralistic, however, expanding the canon to embrace a variety of equally important basic methods. The Association of American Colleges and Universities monograph *Integrity in the College Curriculum*, for instance, identifies nine "methods and processes, modes of access to understanding and judgment" that it thinks are essential for every undergraduate student to know—not only to know about but to know how to utilize (Rudolph 1985: 15). It takes these intellectual skills as the conditions for nurturing "qualities of mind and character" (25) that have in the past enabled and should once again now serve to enable "generations of men and women to grasp a vision of the good life, a life of responsible citizenship and human decency" (6).

The AAC&U's nine basic methods for knowing are:

1. Inquiry, abstract logical thinking, critical analysis.
2. Literacy: writing, reading, speaking, listening.
3. Understanding numerical data.
4. Historical consciousness.
5. Scientific method.
6. Informed and responsible moral choice.
7. Art appreciation and experience.
8. International and multicultural experiences.
9. Study of one academic field in depth.

The first seven of these intellectual skills reflect the key content subjects of a traditional education: logic, literature, mathematics, history, natural science, ethics, the arts. The eighth is a contemporary rendition of the European Grand Tour that young scholars were advised to take between completing their formal education and settling into their life's work. The ninth skill is an acknowledgment that this life's work nowadays is highly professionalized and that it is better for students to know one of the particular available methods well than to seek after the one foundational method originally thought to underlie the rest.

Harvard, under the leadership of its Provost, Henry Rosovsky, designed a new kind of general education requirement in the late 1970s. The Harvard College Core Curriculum Program, still in effect, replaces a traditional content-oriented core or set of distribution requirements with one based on method. It identifies a number of "ways of thinking" to which students need to be exposed. The Core

> does not define intellectual breadth as the mastery of a set of Great Books, or the digestion of a specific quantum of information, or the surveying of current knowledge in certain fields. Rather, the Core seeks to introduce students to the major approaches to knowledge in areas that the faculty considers indispensable to undergraduate education. It aims to show what kinds of knowledge and what forms of inquiry exist

in these areas, how different means of analysis are acquired, how they are used, and what their value is. The courses within each area or subdivision of the program are equivalent in the sense that, while their subject matter may vary, their emphasis on a particular way of thinking is the same. (visit <http://www.registrar.fas.harvard.edu/Courses/Core/index.html>, for a list of the web pages containing this statement and those cited below; as of June 2003)

The content of what students study in any given course that is appropriate to one of the ways of thinking varies widely, but all such courses introduce students to the same basic method.

Harvard's Core (since Fall 1999) requires eleven courses, organized into seven categories:

1. *Foreign cultures* (one course). A course about a major culture distinct from that of the United States. Its aim is "to expand one's understanding of the importance of cultural factors in shaping people's lives," including one's own, as well as to "introduce methods of studying a culture, and the issues involved in approaching a culture not one's own."
2. *Historical Study* (two courses). A course on the background and development of major contemporary issues and a course on the documented details of some transforming event or events. Their aim is "to develop students' comprehension of history as a form of inquiry and understanding."
3. *Literature and Arts* (three courses). A course focusing on literary texts and methods of literary analysis, a course on a nonliterary form of expression, visual or musical, and a course on a creative cultural epoch in history. Their aim is "to foster a critical understanding of artistic expression, and to exemplify the ways in which the humanities are an arena for scholarly examination and discussion."
4. *Moral Reasoning* (one course). A course on "significant and recurrent questions of choice and value that arise in human experience." Its purpose is "to acquaint students with the important traditions of thought that have informed such choices in the past," to "enlarge" their "awareness of how people have understood the nature of the virtuous life," and "to show that it is possible to reflect reasonably about such matters as justice, obligation, citizenship, loyalty, courage, and personal responsibility."
5. *Quantitative Reasoning* (one course). A course the purpose of which is "to introduce students to mathematical and quantitative modes of thought." Some courses "emphasize theoretical aspects of mathematics or statistical reasoning," others "explore the application of quantitative methods to questions in the natural sciences, social sciences, or humanities."
6. *Science* (two courses). Courses concerned with the physical sciences and courses emphasizing biological, evolutionary, or environmental science. Their common aim is "to explore the phenomena, ways of observing and

understanding them, theories that synthesize them, and the undergirding methodology that, taken together, result in the scientific perception of our world."

7. *Social Analysis* (one course). A course that aims "to acquaint students with some of the central concepts and methods of the social sciences and to show how these approaches can enhance our understanding of contemporary human behavior."

These kinds of courses parallel fairly well categories 3–8 of the AAC&U report, if we combine the natural and social science methods. We can then take AAC&U's first two categories, the methods of Inquiry and of Literacy, as general features of any method. Its ninth category, the study of one field in depth, is accounted for at Harvard and most other colleges and universities, of course, by the academic major. Only two of Harvard's core course justifications, those for the Foreign Cultures and Moral Reasoning requirements, mention content as important, an interesting flash of traditionalist recalcitrance amid the otherwise explicitly methodist commitments.

The Great Ways approach is about technique: a style of analysis and synthesis, of exegesis and interpretation, that we are to bring to a subject matter. It is sensitive to the peculiarities of what it studies, and so often does not propose a universal method, a single route to knowledge that is independent of what it is about. Nonetheless, the best method for analyzing and interpreting a subject matter is always understood as independent of whatever methods may have been utilized originally in its creation. We would use symbolic logic not Aristotelian logic in order to analyze the validity of Aristotle's reasoning. We could rerun Priestley's experiments in order to determine the chemical composition of air, but our reason for doing so would be antiquarian, our results unacceptably imprecise for any scientific purposes. Nor is Shakespeare's method of composition the method of literary criticism by which we seek to interpret his plays and to understand how he created them.

The Great Books approach is humanistic because of its interest in the persons who created the books or art objects it celebrates, and even when its subject is about institutions and actions its interest is in the actors. We study about Julius Caesar by reading his *Gallic Wars;* we learn about the American Civil War by reading Lincoln. The Great Ways approach, in contrast, is scientific because it is interested in the findings and the theories, not the explorers and the theoreticians. But both approaches agree that knowledge is hierarchical, that certain achievements and methods of achievement are more significant than others, that some are foundational to appreciating and utilizing the rest, that these should be identified as composing an intellectual canon, and that teaching this canon to students should be the first priority of educational institutions.

On to the Specialties

If the amount of information to be learned is growing exponentially, and if there is no permanent core of content by reference to which most of this growth can be pruned away, then our obvious response is to learn a method for learning whatever content we might care to know. As we have seen, however, that method is readily pluralized: the scientific method becomes the methods of the several sciences. The only sensible way to deal with this excess is to limit our efforts to some portion of the whole. The best a single individual can hope for is to encompass adequately some specific way of organizing knowledge, some specific method and the specific discipline it has generated. But even this limitation often proves insufficient, and so we settle for subdisciplines and specializations within subdisciplines. The rest we ignore, or study only insofar as it is relevant to our specialty.

Hence, the basics to which we need to return, the essentials of our education, are no longer defined absolutely but relatively. What is basic to an understanding of the Italian Baroque in painting is different from what is basic for an expert in high-energy plasma gas instabilities. Nothing is basic pure and simple. A tradition of agreed-upon truth is retained, but relative to a specialized region of knowledge. We know what is the case for the subdiscipline that defines our expertise. We know its canonical methods of inquiry—its protocols for hypothesis formation, experimental testing, and warranted validation or verification—and we know its established reservoir of information and theory. Outside this framework, we are no longer expert and so are without authority, lacking the competence to discern truth, able only to express an opinion.

This relativization of what is essential has gone hand in hand with the professionalization of the faculty, with the segmentation of knowledge into disciplines. Competence in a field is now determined by certification after completion of a prescribed course of study at an appropriately accredited postbaccalaureate institution. Graduate study in geology or sociology or religion is just as preprofessional as study in a law school or medical college. Graduates are licensed to ply their trade: in the case of professors, to teach their discipline to neophytes and to undertake scholarship contributing to the body of knowledge they teach. This Germanic model of education stands in sharp contrast to the English model that was in vogue when most of our nation's liberal arts colleges were founded. The learned amateur once celebrated as being able to teach all or most all suitable college courses has been replaced by the professional able to teach only what he or she is licensed as being competent to teach.

The process of disciplinization is a more recent phenomenon than one might expect. For instance, most of the current social sciences had no separate standing in undergraduate curricula until after World War I. The very notion of a major at my own institution is an innovation of the 1920s. The relative stability of the traditional disciplinary majors over the most recent half-century masks somewhat the continued use of mitosis as the technique for dealing with an area that has become glutted with content. Biology has become an administrative convenience for grouping together specialists in botany, zoology, ecology, neurophysiology, and molecular analysis. In psychology, newly minted professors usually hold their doctorates in a discipline that combines the term "psychology" with some qualifier such as "social," "developmental," "biological," "clinical," or "cognitive." No one is simply a biologist or psychologist anymore, and hence no one is really prepared to teach a single course that would survey the whole of his or her field as traditionally defined. Consequently, students no longer earn a degree in biology or psychology but in botany or ecology, experimental or cognitive psychology. Those students satisfying a distribution requirement are exposed not to the traditional discipline as a whole but only to one of its offspring modalities.

The problem with the pluralism produced by expertise is that it separates us into intellectual enclaves. Specialized knowledge, distinctive methodologies, technical vocabulary, separate journals, and professional meetings all conspire to make it difficult for us to comprehend one another. Each of us knows something well, but we lack any practiced sense of its wider significance, of how it fits properly within the general scheme of things. College and university campuses are supposed to be alive with intellectual challenge and cooperation, but too often they have degenerated into a mere juxtaposition of isolated departments. Indeed, the isolation is often intradepartmental. Many academic departments have become nothing more than an undiscipline of convivial colleagues who have lost even the awareness of having lost their common concern for a shared intellectual enterprise. Is it only in our nightmares that we imagine a time in which there are as many distinct disciplines on a campus as there are professors, each with its own major requirements and probably each with its own half-time secretary—teaching a curriculum where even majors are dispersed into arbitrary collections of courses, of which an arbitrarily defined number are needed to graduate? Or can we go farther still, the courses modularized into topic units defined by the hour exam in which they culminate, the course grade merely the arithmetic sum of the hourlies?

This fragmentation of curricular and intellectual matters, with the resultant collapse in general education, is the inevitable consequence of abandoning a belief in overarching integrative concepts. We have excised the connecting girders that provide a meaningful framework of intelligibility for the manifold of experience. We no longer have a way to construct from the welter of hourlies some intelligible referent for the word *baccalaureate* printed on our diplomas. There are, to be sure, countless instances where groups of faculty and, indeed, whole campuses manage to cooperate in the invention of programs that enhance symbiotically the integrity of the various disciplines by blending and blurring the accustomed boundaries of disciplinarity. But the societal press of things is toward further and further subdividings.

This trend may be one of the prime causes of the student ignorance we love to deplore. Often the problem is not ignorance as such but spotty knowledge. Never having had a survey course in world history or even Western civilization, students may be reasonably informed about the Progressive Movement in the United States but have no clue as to what the Cluniac Reform was or why Socrates was executed. We expect our students to have a general education, but we ourselves contribute daily to the undermining of the conditions that give that expectation any sense.

The professionalization solution is far more in the mainstream of American higher education than is the back-to-basics movement, although the latter has been growing in importance as a reaction to the former. But specialization is as much a form of wishful thinking as is its opposite. It defines the core of importance differently than the basics advocates do, and it is more relativistic, admitting the legitimacy of other cores of importance for other experts with other concerns. But it ignores the reality of the contemporary world. It tries to duck away from the fact that information is not ultimately capable of segmentation, that its justification lies in its usefulness to the liberation of the human spirit and the resolution of actual world problems, neither of which are segmentable realities. Specialization creates hierarchical expertise, but all the pundits of the information society say that leadership and citizenship in the twenty-first century require, above all else, thinking and judgment that are systemic and integrative. Splintering human knowledge into an endless array of subdisciplines is as irrelevant to our needs as attempting to recover its essential core.

The Agonized Academic (continued)

The shift from the content of an education to the procedures for acquiring it makes no difference to the agonized conscience. The advocates of methodism see themselves every bit as embattled as their foundationalist counterparts. It seems ludicrous that university and college scientists, a privileged elite by any of the usual measures of success, should describe themselves as a struggling minority threatened on every side by intellectual barbarism. But the threat confronting those who are practitioners of a scientific method is real, nor is it merely some historical happenstance, a current but probably ephemeral danger. It is in the very nature of their method that it should be under attack.

Santayana explains the logic of the agonized conscience as a linking of three beliefs: "that sin exists, that sin is punished, and that it is beautiful that sin should exist to be punished" (189). There is an ideal that ought to be realized, a failure to live up to this ideal that results in an appropriate punishment, and an admiration of the exquisite rightness of this arrangement. We feel "a fierce pleasure in the existence of misery, especially of one's own," in the "scandal" of our failure to do what we know we ought to have done and the misery of having to suffer the consequences. The fierce pleasure is due to our recognition that our failure and misery are "requisite, since otherwise the serious importance of being as we ought to be would not have been vindicated" (189).

The agonized stance to the procedural canonists replaces a properly God-fearing way of life with a proper method of inquiry as the ideal to be realized. Knowing the right method is the litmus test for showing that we have been properly educated, that we can think like scientists. Misery is endemic to science: the failed experiment, the misguided hypothesis, the incompletely specified procedure, the tainted equipment, the ambiguous or non-replicable results. The misery becomes a scandal when the failures are thought to have been avoidable, when they are caused by shoddy preparation, ignorance of other relevant work, unimaginative hypothesis formation, bias in the interpretation of results, or tampering with the data in order to make them confirm a hypothesis. Granted that humans are fallible, that anyone can make a mistake, the point of a method is to push error toward the vanishing point. As the last of Descartes's methods made clear: we must be sure to check our work—and to check the purity of our commitment to the method. "Vigilance over conduct and an absolute demand for personal integrity" (Santayana: 190) are the sine qua non of good science.

Good science is the keystone to the arch of knowledge that links our desires to their fulfillment, and education is the key to the keystone. Unless young people are trained to be good scientists, the archway will begin to crack. A commitment to mastering the techniques of experimental inquiry, an aspiration to methodist excellence, is the sign that a student has promise. Those who are afraid of math, who are unwilling or unable to think quantitatively, are without promise: undisciplined, essentially lazy, precisely the barbarians who threaten science and hence the well-being of society. The scandal of higher education is the declining numbers of students who want to major in the sciences, the growing number who find it too hard, who take as little science as possible and where some is required seek out courses that involve as little math as possible. Unless the sciences attract students early, indeed in their pre-college years, they will be lost. Hardly anyone switches into the sciences from the humanities, although many budding scientists fall by the wayside and end up majoring in literature or history.

Thinking like a scientist is an unnatural skill, requiring self-discipline and extensive training. Our natural propensity is to react to a problem emotionally and from blind habit, to do what seems expedient without knowing what the facts actually are and without systematically exploring the reasonable alternatives for arriving at an effective solution. As John Dewey ceaselessly lamented, if only the methods of the natural sciences would be applied to our societal and personal concerns, the prejudice and ignorance that plagues our lives could be dissipated. That our educational institutions seem to be doing less not more to support this ideal is indeed a scandal.

The scandal runs far deeper, however, seeping out around the edges of a basic dilemma. Because the methods of science are skills that need to be both taught and practiced, scientists require well-equipped laboratories in which to carry out their experiments and properly designed classrooms in which to train up their successors. Scientists are dependent upon social institutions to provide these resources. Colleges in the United States were founded to inculcate the essential content of the nation's cultural heritage. But methodism declares its independence from any content, demanding the unfettered freedom to follow wherever that method might lead. The procedural canonists can bear allegiance to no particular content because they adulate a method that presumes no substantive preconditions and is restrained by no predetermined limits on what it might conclude. Yet this method must be learned and applied under the aegis of a college or university. It must function under the guardianship of an institution that is beholden for its continued existence to its funding sources, whether they be religious denominations, governmental agencies, or wealthy individual benefactors.

Immanuel Kant addresses this awkwardness in a little monograph published toward the end of his life: *The Conflict of the Faculties*. He distinguishes the "higher" university faculties of theology, law, and medicine, all of them content oriented, from the "lower" arts and sciences faculty of philosophy, which is based not on a content but solely on its commitment to rational method. The educational mission of the higher faculties is to play a "heteronomous" role: to support the commands of government, to serve the end at which it aims, which is the creation of a stable and thriving social order. The higher faculties do this by teaching the nation's citizens right from wrong and indicating the conditions of their salvation, by designing and explicating the laws by which they are governed, and by providing for their health. The educational mission of the lower faculty, in contrast, is to "use its own judgment about what it teaches" (26): to be "autonomous." "Now the power to judge autonomously—that is, freely (according to principles of thought in general)—is called reason" (43). The lower faculty, Kant argues, is "independent of the government's command with regard to its teachings"; "having no commands to give, [it] is free to evaluate everything" (26).

What makes the higher faculties higher, of course, is their direct proximity to the government and other cultural benefactors whose interests they serve. The purposes of the higher faculties are thus practical: they have to do with values, obligations, and pains and pleasures, with the conditions for living a satisfying life. Insofar as they are successful in what they do, the citizenry regard them, says Kant, as "soothsayers and magicians," as "miracle-workers" (49), because they provide what the citizens desire: rules for keeping their health, for staying on the right side of the law, and for attaining personal salvation. The citizens are not interested in truth but in comfort, in the satisfaction of their wants and interests as these are structured by a realm of power and command.

A conflict between the higher and lower faculties is therefore inevitable. The one serves power; the other is the unfettered servant of truth. If the higher faculty were to claim a rational basis for its teachings, it either "offends against the authority of the government that issues order through it" or it opens itself to the rational criticism of the lower faculty, which—since the higher faculty is poorly prepared to defend itself rationally—may result in serious damage to "the dignity of its status" (35). The inverse consequences would follow were the lower faculty to attempt to function as a higher faculty: it would either offend against reason or fall victim to charges that it had not properly interpreted its governmental mandate.

Hence, the two kinds of faculty are on a collision course where peace is possible only if neither trespasses on the other's turf. It is the nature of those who command, however, to wish to extend their command. "Consequently the philosophy faculty can never lay aside its arms in the face of the danger that threatens the truth entrusted to its protection, because the higher faculties will never give up their desire to rule" (55). The "vigilance" required of the agonized conscience is due to the scandalous fact that its autonomy is heteronomous, that it is unfettered only with the permission of the benefactors of the institutions upon which it depends.

Bill Readings characterizes what he calls the "University of Reason" (ch. 5; see also Allan 1997: ch. 3: "The College as Guild of Inquirers") in terms of this Kantian dilemma: a situation in which professors and students are trapped in an "aporia between reason and institution," a contradiction between the demands of rational inquiry and the demands of national interest. The University—understood as referring to Kant's lower faculty, to all the academic disciplines that adhere to the scientific method, including the arts and sciences at both the undergraduate and graduate level—is "a fictional institution" because, although it is a heteronomous creation, it acts "as if" it were autonomous (60).

Unfettered teaching means helping students become autonomous individuals, people who are independent thinkers, who will be critical of their country's beliefs and practices insofar as these are based on unthinking habit, superstition, or injustice. The established authorities are likely to deem such people agitators, to see them as both ungrateful and unpatriotic. Unfettered research means pursuing an ideal of truth or beauty without regard for its societal implications. The establishment will see such pursuits either as trivial, if they are in the sciences, or offensive, if in the arts. The public, Readings argues, takes "the blind acceptance of tradition" (57) as its criterion of value, thus as the test of whether what goes on at an educational institution is worth supporting. The informed citizen, the well-paid employee, the successful entrepreneur, the civic leader: these mainstream images of how education pays off adorn college and university catalogues as evidence of why the tuition they charge is justified, an investment that promises a better return on capital than an average basket of S&P stocks.

Kant thinks that this conflict will be resolved by the triumph of autonomy. The enlightened despot in an unenlightened age may need to impose by fiat an effective form of government and an appropriate mode of education. He will then invite the university thereby established to teach his nation's citizens the skills of autonomy. As the lower faculty succeeds in this undertaking, it will "prepare the way for the government to remove all restrictions that its choice has put on freedom of public judgment" (Kant: 59; see also Readings: 59). The ruler will accomplish by arbitrary command what an enlightened citizenry, a public composed of rational individuals, would have freely chosen to do. As the public becomes more rational, thanks to the education in autonomy provided by the university's arts and sciences faculty, top-down command will be replaced by free democratic choice. And so it would come to pass that "the last would some day be first": the lower faculty would become the higher, the one closest to the government. For in that day, "the government may find the freedom of the philosophy faculty, and the increased insight gained from this freedom, a better means for achieving its ends than its own absolute authority" (Kant: 59).

The scandal of American education, of course, is that the resolution of the conflict between education and government has moved in exactly the opposite direction. The tension has been lessened by the colleges and universities becoming less autonomous in what they say, in what they teach, in what they do. The expense of supporting the scientific method has escalated dramatically—the cost of the salaries needed to attract and retain fully credentialed science faculty, the cost of the paraphernalia required to carry out the sophisticated experiments that are the cutting edge of contemporary science and technology, the cost of classrooms and laboratories where students can learn to use such equipment and acquire a working knowledge of the results of its prior use. There has been, therefore, a concomitant escalation in the extent to which educational institutions are beholden to their benefactors for this needed money. The sciences have become a higher faculty, but they have done so by adjusting their purposes to those of unenlightened public and private authorities rather than by teaching those authorities to shape their purposes rationally. Education has become a fettered servant of the public interest rather than a servant of unfettered truth. The methodists, it would seem, are no longer any different than the foundationalists they disdain. Both are lackeys of the status quo.

Chapter 4

Anti-Canonists

Egalitarianism

Foundationalism and methodism today are everywhere in disarray. Whether we look to particular academic disciplines or to common sense, the confidence is dissipating that some contents or procedures are beyond dispute. Our cultural and intellectual tradition, in the lingo of its Jacobin detractors, is being deconstructed. What the revolutions of the eighteenth and nineteenth centuries did to political privilege, the critiques of the twentieth century did to intellectual privilege. The cultural aristocrats who are the beneficiaries of an intellectual canon of substantial or procedural knowledge, with their elitist claims about what is the case and what is not, are cast out in the name of those who come proclaiming new and previously unenfranchised egalitarian understandings, practices, and creations.

We find ourselves committed to egalitarianism once we take seriously Kant's notion of the autonomous individual—if, that is, we interpret autonomy as a feature of human nature, a fact of our humanity, and not as the consequence of an educational process. We no longer believe that heteronomy is our natural condition and autonomy its transcendence, the subjugation of our appetitive nature to the discipline of reason. Autonomy, rather, is our natural state, and if we act heteronomously it must be because our natural propensities have been distorted by the artificial forces of societal compulsion.

As Rousseau puts it in that famous phrase near the beginning of *The Social Contract*, "Man is born free, and everywhere he is in chains" (paragraph 5). Rousseau claims that any social hierarchy is a structure of dependence: whoever is at a lower level of the hierarchy is subservient to everyone who occupies a higher level. For us to be free, our relationships to others must be reciprocal, an exchange among equals. Therefore, we cannot be free unless we are freed from our bondage to the status society has imposed on us, freed from dependence on another's command and on expectations grounded in the prestige accorded our family or tribe or nation, or grounded in the importance of the work we do.

Charles Taylor calls the contemporary demand for equality, the insistence on a whole cascade of rights and entitlements, a "politics of equal dignity" (38) based on the Kantian notion of autonomy combined with Rousseau's notion of freedom. For us to be treated as truly human, it is argued, we must all be treated with the equal dignity that is our birthright. No longer are hierarchies understood to be natural facts, our dignity found in fulfilling well the status to which we were born. Nor are hierarchies understood as necessary features of social organization, our dignity found in fulfilling well a status attained by our own lawful efforts. Rather, our dignity is independent of hierarchy and must be recognized and honored no matter where we are located along whatever arbitrarily constructed levels of social order happen to constrain us. The manual laborer and the social outcast deserve as much praise as the corporate officer and the aristocrat because they all have an innate equal dignity that trumps their social differences.

If all hierarchies are arbitrary constructs, the intellectual hierarchies that organize knowledge must be also. And if social status hierarchies put us in chains, snatching away our natural freedom and dignity, then so also our belief systems must be forms of imprisonment. The task of education should be to rescue us from what we have been taught, to free us from the iron maiden of claims about foundational truths and procedural conditions for assuring objectivity, for these are claims that undermine our autonomy. Universal and necessary truths are the tools tyrants use to justify their control over us.

This critique of objective knowledge is as old as Protagoras who argued that humans are "the measure of all things." He and his fellow sophists were referring to ethical norms, but their reasoning was readily generalizable: what we know is influenced by who we are. We stand somewhere in order to see; we think by means of culturally acquired ideas; our desires filter our beliefs. There are no universal truths or values, only what someone or some group at a particular time and in a particular place take to be true or valuable.

Michel Foucault gave these arguments contemporary salience when he showed, in *Madness and Civilization* and then in *Discipline and Punish*, that even something as fundamental as the essence of one's humanity is a social construct. He described how eighteenth-century Europeans, in response to changing societal conditions, invented a new definition of human nature. In order to justify removing growing numbers of undesirable persons from public view, the authorities needed to decide what counted as being essentially human so that they could derive from it a notion of deviance, of abnormal departures from that essence. They could then identify these deviants as strange, as other than truly human, and therefore as a public menace. Insane asylums and prisons were constructed to implement these novel ideas about human normality.

As Europeans became increasingly aware of other cultures, of other ways of being human, they used this same normalcy model to account for the differences. These other ways were pagan: hence they were deviations, due to ignorance or willfulness, from the modes of belief and practice appropriate to Christians living in Christian nations. As notions of progress and eventually of social Darwinism became popular, those who lived outside the pale of these rightful realms were taken as primitives, either as mere animals to be exploited or as childlike creatures to be cared for until they or their descendants might develop into civilized persons. The eighteenth century had seen timeless hierarchies of difference, ranging from the best to the worst. The nineteenth century, having turned the hierarchy on its side, saw the best as a historically emergent best, differentiating itself progressively from the worst. Foucault sees only difference. Natures and essences, good and bad, right and wrong, are all social constructs, expressions of the particular knowledge and values held by particular people at a particular time and place.

Barbara Herrnstein Smith, following Foucault, argues that "the prevailing tastes and preferences" of those in power "will always be implicitly threatened or directly challenged by the divergent tastes and preferences of some subjects within the community" and most subjects outside it or on its periphery: "exotic visitors, immigrants, colonials, and members of various minority or marginalized groups" (21, 22). Hence the perceived need for "institutions of evaluative authority" that will "validate the community's tastes, warding off barbarism, the collapse of standards." This "validation commonly takes the form of privileging absolutely—that is, 'standard'-izing—the particular contingencies that govern the preferences of the members of the group and discounting or... pathologizing all other contingencies" (22). But societies are thoroughly historical achievements, their valuational hierarchies based on nothing more than a contingent institutionalized consensus. Therefore, any attempt to transmute accidental successes into necessary ones, Smith argues, is pernicious and unjustified. No social hierarchy is truer than or better than or more satisfying than any other.

Those who attack hierarchies of human excellence and societal good must do more than expose the arbitrariness of their structures and the falsity of their claims, however. They must also account for them. The point needing to be made is not only that individuals have no preset natures and that societies stand under no transcendent norms regarding how they should be structured nor for what ends. It is also that all this apparatus is designed to legitimate those who benefit from a society so organized and so understood. The portrait of a human essence always looks very much like those who painted it.

In north European churches the statues of the Madonna show her with long blond hair, in Mediterranean churches her hair is brunette and curly, and in Ethiopia her skin is dark and her black hair kinked. Whatever the inalienable right proclaimed, it advantages the power elite who proclaim it. We Americans are partial to Jefferson's triad of life, liberty, and the pursuit of happiness only because and insofar as we are its benefactors.

These proclamations of what counts as truly human and as the normative conditions for genuine community manage to survive only by being constantly reinterpreted to suit the changing times. So the recipients of political rights nowadays are not limited to just the independent agrarian farmers Jefferson had in mind, and those still oppressed may someday gain these rights while others lose what they now think inalienable. It all depends on power: not simply force of arms, crucial though that be, but the power of education as well, the power of ideas, habits, and technologies, and also the accommodations forced by happenstance and environmental limitations. Those in positions of privilege are disingenuous: they hide their privilege behind a mask of objectivity. The value hierarchies by which they seek to justify their achievements are disguises. Their power is no more justified than anyone else's. The canon of highest truths, eldest wisdom, and best practices that they proclaim is really a tool of repression. Only a plurality of truths, judgments, and approaches, all of them unranked because unrankable, is warranted.

Jean-François Lyotard, accordingly, rails against the two "grand narratives" he thinks dominate Western civilization. One is that of science, which imposes "criteria of competence" upon those who would claim to speak the truth and so requires them to undergo "apprenticeships," to be taught a proper method and content of knowledge before they can be certified as its legitimate custodians and as contributors to the story of its ongoing success (1979: 20). The other grand narrative is that of liberty, which traces the triumph of the modern bourgeois nation-state, "its emancipation from everything that prevents it from governing itself" (35), and which prepares each new generation for its prescribed role in sustaining and expanding the nation's or the civilization's hegemonic scope.

The two grand narratives intertwine, says Lyotard, for it is through the inculcation of right thinking that the nation secures a supportive citizenry, and it is the nation that determines what will count as right thinking and how educational institutions should be organized to propagate it effectively. In this way a consensus is imposed and then internalized, a single way of thinking and acting that is taken as how things are and should be. These grand narratives are the self-justifying stories told by the University of Culture and the University of Reason. They are, for Lyotard, the iron hand of the Terror, gripping us with a velvet glove. He thinks they have lost their credibility, however, and so he calls us to the barricades, to a new storming of the Bastille for the sake of a different way to know and to be free. "The nineteenth and twentieth centuries have given us as much terror as we can take. We have paid a high enough price for the nostalgia of the whole and the one" (81).

Those who advocate this egalitarian tolerance of difference do so on historicist grounds. The keystone of their project is the metaphysical claim that there is no objective correlate against which to test our truth claims. Knowledge must be liberated from the idols of foundationalism and methodism. Hume said we could never know if there were an objective correlate to our ideas, but Kant assured us we need not worry since the forms of intuition and the categories of understanding that shape those ideas into meaningful experience are necessarily objective. Cassirer suggested, however, that these instruments for shaping experience are historical rather than a priori, contingent rather than necessary. If essences are made instead of found, then it is our wills and not our natures that are the arbiters of what should be taught and learned. We are all little gods creating our own essences *ex nihilo*.

In *Philosophy and the Mirror of Nature,* Richard Rorty applies Thomas Kuhn's distinction between "normal" and "revolutionary" science to philosophy and all other forms of inquiry: there are those who think and act within the boundaries of what everyone takes for granted, and those who call those boundaries into question. But, says Rorty, there are two sorts of ways to be revolutionary. "Systematic philosophers" are one sort. They "single out one area, one set of practices, and see it as the paradigm human activity." This is the canonical approach to things, whether in a content or a procedural mode. Impressed by some "new cognitive feat," by the "stunning success" of some body of truths or methods for attaining them, they generalize it. They attempt to "reshape all inquiry, and all of culture, on its model, thereby permitting objectivity and rationality to prevail in areas previously obscured by convention, superstition, and the lack of a proper epistemological understanding of man's ability accurately to represent nature" (367).

"Edifying philosophers" are revolutionaries of a second sort. They doubt that humankind's "essence is to be a knower of essences" and suspect that canonical truths are "no more than conformity to the norms of the day" (367). Their approach is "instinctively reactive" rather than constructive, "one that has point only in opposition to the tradition," to "the whole project of universal commensuration" (366). Rorty's litany of contrasts between systematic and edifying ways of thought and action makes it clear which sort of revolutionary he supports:

Great systematic philosophers are constructive and offer arguments. Great edifying philosophers are reactive and offer satires, parodies, aphorisms. ... Great systematic philosophers, like great scientists, build for eternity. Great edifying philosophers destroy for the sake of their own generation. Systematic philosophers want to put their subject on the secure path of a science. Edifying philosophers want to keep space open for the sense of wonder which poets can sometimes cause—wonder that there is something new under the sun, something that is *not* an accurate representation of what was already there, something which (at least for the moment) cannot be explained and can barely be described. (369–70)

The systematic philosopher struggles to "escape from humanity," hoping to know or even to experience something absolute, something "more than merely human," and thereby to put a stop to the ongoing conversation among humans about what they think might be true or good or beautiful, and what they should therefore do. "The point of edifying philosophy," in contrast, "is to keep the conversation going rather than to find objective truth" (377).

This historicist denial of objective knowledge is not merely a recognition that we are fallible, that our approach to truth is at best asymptotic. It is the denial that there is any objective correlate, that there exists a determinate reality which can gradually be approached. There is no nature for us to mirror. A theory about the world derived from data garnered through simple recording instruments and modeled by relatively simple, pure-case mathematical formulae defines reality as something external and objective with an essential core of structural relationships. Science in this traditional sense attempts to discover the truth of things, the world's reality, by picturing its essential features mathematically. Contemporary science, however, undercuts this traditional understanding through the very sophistication of its attempts to fashion and verify such pictures. For they are anemic when compared to what happens when the instruments of inquiry are capable of registering and retaining significantly higher powers of data, are able to take into account the supposed inessentials, the anomalies, the local variations, and can present models that articulate this sophisticated analysis in both numerical and visual format, along with relevant or interesting alternatives utilizing extrapolated, modulated, virtual, or outright invented data.

These far more sophisticated scientific models blur the familiar distinction between what is invented and what discovered, between the experienced and the experiencing, between the model and the modeled. And because these models are interactively responsive, they also blur the separation between observer and observed. Students, for instance, often come to regard the computer graphs they are able to generate—constructed in real-time from data they are gathering during a laboratory experiment—as parts of reality. They regard the graphs not as signs signifying something beyond themselves but as the signified itself. The "prepared data" of which Eva Brann spoke have come to be taken not as a way to mirror the real world but as what it is.

More information about the world; more information about the tools for gaining information; more concepts for defining the boundaries of knowability and the capacities of inquiry; more worlds of interpretation integrating all of this into a system of consistent, coherent, complete, and adequate theoretical understanding. More always breeding more, in an elegant feedback mechanism with exponential output. It should be no surprise that the result is the demise of the old, assured belief in a delimited, knowable, objective reality.

The Canonless Canon

Egalitarian historicists, invading the cathedral of learning, have wrought considerable damage to its traditional ways. Their edifying discourse has been as Rorty describes it: basically a destructive rather than a constructive enterprise. However, the critics of canonic learning do not simply direct their attack at the substance of the often conflicting proposals for what counts as the essential content or methodology for undergraduate education. That would be like shooting fish in a barrel. The absence of any significant consensus on what constitutes the educational canon can be embarrassing, but gleefully rubbing this fact in the faces of the canonists is a cheap thrill. It only implies that the canonists need to take more time in working through their differences. Often there is general agreement about the intellectual canon but considerable disagreement about the educational canon. What the educational canonists need, they say, is more time—a semester not a course, a baccalaureate not a core—to encompass everything that is crucial culturally. Their disagreements are not about the essentials but about what selection from that essence to teach under the constraints imposed by an academic curriculum.

What upsets both the traditional cathedral clerics and their methodological counterparts is not those critics who object to the substance or scope of the educational canon they defend, but those who object to its very nature. Because Western culture is essentially oppressive, this most radical kind of critic argues, the canon that marks out what is fundamental about it celebrates values that instead should be rejected. Those great Western souls, along with their great ideas, methods, and attitudes, are hegemonic, imperialistic, colonial, patriarchal, logocentric, and exclusionary. They need to be repudiated in the name of other more humane, more encompassing values, values respectful of ethnic difference and cultural variety, values of liberation, equality, and free association.

The content canonist Gertrude Himmelfarb quotes disdainfully one such critic for having the gall to insist that "the problem was not only that the 'Big Guys'—her variation on 'Dead White Males'—were guys, but also that they were big, thus 'privileging,' as she put it, big books, great books. This, she complained, was what was really offensive in the canon" (4). The view of these anti-canonists is not that the traditional educational canon offers a roster of repugnant ideas but that the very notion of a canon is itself one of those repugnant ideas. Canons, they argue, "are essentially strategic constructs by which societies maintain their own interests, since the canon allows control over the texts a culture takes seriously and the methods of interpretation that establish the meaning of 'serious'" (Altieri: 42). A cultural elite offers us the chimera of a "best self," a generic ideal that preexists us and is imposed on us as our goal in life. But we cannot personally realize anything so abstract and general; it therefore alienates us from who we actually are. We need to be free of such impositions. We need to be encouraged to make our own selves in our own way.

A canon is hierarchical, and it is hierarchy—not this hierarchy or that hierarchy, but hierarchy as such—that is the enemy of the multicultural and democratic ideals that the anti-canonists think it should be the goal of American education to inculcate in the nation's youth. Hierarchical thinking and action, says Mary Louise Pratt, is "monumentalist." It is "historically as well as morally distortive" (21) because it divides everything into privileged and unprivileged groupings, condemning some ideas, texts, and persons to the margins of a culture while exalting others to positions of primacy.

Barbara Herrnstein Smith finds it particularly irritating that canonists never argue for their hierarchies. Their "comparative estimates of value" are rarely more than fatuous appeals to self-evidence. They say, for instance, that it is "obvious" Milton's poetry is better than Blackmore's (whose epic *The Creation* is taken by "everyone" as "a topos of literary disvalue"), but the criteria for this judgment are never specified (12). "Beguiled by the humanist's fantasy of transcendence, endurance, and universality," canonists are quick to dismiss as unessential whatever is recent, "culturally exotic," or "highly innovative." For a canonist, recent works of literature have (by definition) failed the test of time, because insofar as they are novel—original as well as new—they lack (again by definition) the familiar characteristics of writings that have met that test. Clearly, therefore, their worth is ephemeral. But, Smith points out, the canonists thereby ignore "the most fundamental character of literary value, which is its mutability and diversity." Squeezed by "the narrow intellectual traditions and professional allegiances of the literary academy," they have "foreclosed from [their] own domain the possibility of investigating the dynamics of that mutability and understanding the nature of that diversity" (14).

Jean Ferguson Carr takes mutability and diversity seriously when she argues that literary studies should be renamed "cultural studies." The shift, she claims, "emphasizes the changed understanding of 'literature' and its relationship to society. Cultural studies moves away from 'history of ideas' to a contested history of struggles for power and authority, to complicated relations between 'center' and 'margin,' between dominant and minority positions" (25). Texts need to be seen within their cultural settings in order to be revealed as what they truly are, as one of the ways by which persons pursue their individual and collective interests. The sorts of books, ideas, and authors that make their way into an educational canon do so because they are taken to have been influential expressions of such interests. But this role they play will be misunderstood, idealized, and hence idolized, unless they are "set against a panoply of other voices" from that same cultural milieu, voices that exhibit other competing interests or the same interests from nontraditional perspectives. A popular broadside, the private diary or letters of an ordinary person, bureaucratic memos, subliterary or nonliterary artifacts, are all "productions worthy of study" because, just as much as literary texts do, they provide in their different ways access to a culture and to the play of interests that define it.

Cultural studies, Carr insists, is "not a game to play or a code to keep people out, but [is] a method of refiguring how we have gotten to where we are and how we can effect some significant change" (28). Canon-making, she implies, is an exclusionary stratagem, a way to define an elite. Privileged authors imply privileged readers, those who are like them with respect to background, experience, and interests, and who as a consequence respond appreciatively to what they have to say. To stop studying those authors as exemplars, to inquire instead into how they came to be revered and how others came to be reviled or ignored, is to find ourselves caught up in the moral and political question of why this should be so.

Carr envisions cultural studies, if so practiced, as having an activist outcome. She describes her own students as ethnically diverse "ordinary readers," people whom the canonists brand as having an unimportant past and a naive because canonically limited understanding of what they read. Her aim is to help these students discover that the supposed great souls, although different from them, are not their betters, that they too are fallible and biased human beings furthering their own interests rather than expressing universal truths. She thinks her students gain through this approach a new respect for their own ethnic heritage, for their own ideas and recommendations, and are emboldened to act within the wider culture accordingly. Thus, for Carr a decanonized cultural studies "tries to dispel the mystique surrounding authorized knowledge" and to empower marginalized people "to enter critical conversations at diverse levels and with the authority of their own experiences and knowledges" (28).

Sideways to Compaction

The content canonists propose that educators go back to teaching the great and enduring basic texts and ideas of Western civilization. The procedural canonists propose that educators go forward rather than backward, by encouraging an elaboration of the scientific method of inquiry into the full plenum of its specialized applications. There is a third approach, however, suited to a regime of anti-canonical egalitarianism where nothing, or at least no kind of thing, is intrinsically better than any other. The educational strategy that makes sense in this context would seem to require us to affirm the diversity of worthwhile ideas and methods by enlarging the traditional roster of course topics to include new and once marginal ones. The problem is that this enlargement is supposed to be accomplished without enlarging the number of courses offered.

So faculty attempt to go on teaching the same introductory physics course they have taught for decades, somehow managing to cope with more and more topics needing to be covered, and with the need to integrate the use of computers and other high-tech instruments into the strategies for dealing with those topics. They set about integrating the new appreciation of feminist and minority authors into their American literature survey while still teaching all of the traditionally important figures. Miller's *College Physics* now runs 896 pages; the current *Norton Anthology* is nearly as lengthy. Faculty recognize, of course, that these additions must be balanced by corresponding deletions, but the textbook authors and their publishers leave that choice to the individual instructor. They provide enough material for four or five semesters, from which an instructor is supposed to choose what the students will study during a one or two semester course. Yet this selection can only be done in arbitrary fashion, given the absence of an agreed core of concepts and methods able to function as the criterion for such selectivity.

Course syllabi operate under the iron law of hydraulics. The pipeline of learning has an opening that is inelastic: one course means three class hours and, say, nine hours of student preparation each week. If we have expanded the content of our canon, we are faced with a greater volume of material needing to pass through the pipe. Since the pipe cannot be enlarged or lengthened, this material will have to be moved along more rapidly. This acceleration can be achieved by compaction, packaging the information more densely, or by simplification, omitting details or other complications. But breathless nonstop lectures and superficial summaries both lead to the same consequence for our students' learning: a loss in their appreciation for the subtlety of things, a dilution of their familiarity with the texture of inquiry that has defined any given subject matter, a casual dogmatic confidence reflecting their insensitivity to the limits of theory, their willingness to substitute labels learned by rote for an understanding of how the relevant concepts and methods in a field function to build up an interpretation of what is experienced.

A procedural response to the egalitarian growth in what should be learned is to give priority in the pipeline to matters of method and to limit content to illustrative material. We think that a few good courses in writing and speech will prepare us to communicate effectively whatever subject matter someone at any given point might wish us to explicate, proclaim, or criticize.

We expect management courses to train us to manage any business enterprise and so to be taught without our needing to learn about particular businesses or business sectors. As we have seen, however, basic methods quickly proliferate into their kinds and each species lays claim to parity with what was once its genus. The anti-canonist can offer no prophylactic assistance, and so the pipeline is soon as clogged by methods as it had been by contents.

The one remaining option is to insist upon a greater share of the student's time. The pipe will need to be lengthened after all. So a one-course survey expands into a year-long survey, and soon the department is arguing that a nine-course major is insufficient. A putative accrediting agency for undergraduate liberal arts computer science programs once demanded that a minimum of half the student's baccalaureate work be in the major. Most majors in technical and preprofessional programs insist on the same minimum. The extreme of aggrandizement of the speciality is the elimination of general education altogether, which is the European model for higher education. But this is only the specialization solution decked out in imperialistic garb.

We are left on the horns of an intolerable dilemma, having to choose between the superficial and the parochial. So we end up trying to do everything, but more efficiently. This classic Type-A behavior strategy may work for a while, especially if there are, indeed, inefficiencies in the system that can usefully be squeezed out by the press of more and more things to be done. But eventually the piper must be paid by watering down the course, the major, or the balance of depth and breadth in a student's program of study. Because this is the solution for which most faculty have opted these days, it is no wonder that teaching makes them increasingly ill at ease, that burnout is a popular faculty malady. We can catch the hints of an impending curricular coronary but are at a loss for what to do about it.

The tension between pinpoint narrowness and paper-thin breadth cannot be long sustained. On the one hand, it yields students who have no sense of how to apply the empty formalisms they've been taught, except arbitrarily, quartering the chicken without regard for its actual anatomy. And on the other hand, it yields students who have no historical and conceptual ecology within which to locate what few things they do know well. They are aware of the subtleties of texture, flavor, and nutritional value of drumsticks without knowing that unbutchered chickens use them as instruments of locomotion, forage, and defense.

Thus, anti-canonical education is as troublesome as the two versions of canonical education it aspires to replace. The old cathedral foundations may be so rotted as to be worthless, but attempting to fashion a cathedral without foundations is a quixotic alternative. The blistering exposé by the anticlerics of the deficiencies of the cathedral's traditional approaches to education has not led us toward anything better.

Unagonized Academics

Santayana identified Transcendentalism as a second strand of the Genteel Tradition. It is what happens to the agonized conscience when its sense of sin has "totally evaporated," when the world is thought to be all "beauty and commodity" and the individual self "victorious and blameless" (191). We usually think of Transcendentalism in terms of its claims about the nature of the universe and the relation of each individual self to its totality—Emerson's "Oversoul," for instance, "a universal soul within or behind [each person's] individual life.... This universal soul he calls Reason: it is not mine, or thine, or his, but we are its" (1836: 33). But Santayana dismisses these metaphysical assertions as "chimera," as so much "transcendental myth." What is important about Transcendentalism, and what makes it a sunshine version of the darkly overcast agonized conscience, is its notions about a "transcendental grammar of the intellect" (195).

Transcendentalism, says Santayana, is "systematic subjectivism. It studies the perspectives of knowledge as they radiate from the self" (193–94). The self is the center of its universe, with everything defined by its relation to that center: "The past and the future, things inferred and things conceived, lie around it, painted as upon a panorama. They cannot be lighted up save by some present centrifugal ray of attention and present interest, by some active operation of the mind" (194). Since past achievements and future possibilities are thus taken to be functions of the self, it must occupy a sort of timeless here and now, a present moment that never passes away, that is always determining its world in the bright light of its immediate interests. Autonomous and free in just the way Rousseau and Kant wanted it to be, it asks "all things to show their credentials at the bar of the young self, and to prove their value for this latest born moment" (196). It should therefore come as no surprise that the Transcendentalist conscience is unagonized: it is beholden only to itself—"No wonder, he says to himself, that nature is sympathetic, since I made it" (200).

The two modes of conscience, agonized and unagonized, are genteel in the sense that both are closed systems. For both, the self is at the center of things and is the bearer of an ideal of human perfection, in the one case subjected to its demands, in the other case its author. Both with dogmatic assurance organize their world in terms of dichotomies: inclusivists and exclusivists, saints and sinners, great souls and mediocre ones, hard-nosed scientists and soft-headed humanists, egalitarians who celebrate difference and hegemons who repress it. The anti-canonists, although seemingly inclusivists, are exemplary dichotomizers, repudiating every criterion of selectivity except the one that identifies selectivists as unredeemable and so excludes them from its supposedly inclusive embrace.

The embrace of an unagonized conscience can nonetheless be wide, encompassing at its most exuberant not only humans but creatures of all sorts, even the whole of the natural order. Although Santayana interprets Walt Whitman as a successor to the Transcendentalists, as one of the early voices challenging the Genteel Tradition, I think this is a mistake. Whitman is still practicing the Transcendentalist's grammar of the intellect when he presumes that if every self is at the center of the universe then all souls must be great souls. Radical subjectivism and radical egalitarianism are mutual implicates, obverse and inverse of the same coin. For Whitman, as Santayana rightly characterizes him, "the slightest sights, moods, and emotions are given each one vote" (202). He refused to discriminate: "He simply felt jovially that everything real was good enough, and that he was good enough himself" (203). Even hegemons, he would think, once they have been cured of their hegemonic behavior, once they realize that autonomy is no one's prerogative but everyone's natural right, should be invited to take their rightful place among natural equals.

The problem with a reality that is only horizontal is that it is unavoidably superficial. Where there is no discrimination of relative worth because no standards that make such discrimination possible, there are no longer any developmental pathways. Unless we have some ideal of a better self to guide us, our present self will have no place to go except laterally. But since any place is as good as any other, we have no motive to make even that move. At least as agonized consciences, our sense of our sinfulness gives us depth: a pit of perdition into which to fall and out of which to climb, a heaven for which to yearn and for which to strive. The canonists' sense of their failings gives them a goal worthy of their allegiance.

Santayana, in his elliptical way, sees the anti-canonist's problem clearly. If we are the source and authority for our world, we have no way to be "unhappy." There is no way for us to judge how adequately we have become who we could be, how well we have fulfilled our potential. Only by recognizing our limits can we hope to reach them. So in blatant denial of what they seem to have been affirming, subjectivists turn away from the concreteness of daily life to such things as "music" and "landscape," hoping to find there the guiding ideals they cannot find in themselves. Their "imagination is driven for comfort into abstract arts, where human circumstances are lost sight of, and human problems dissolve in a purer medium." The egalitarian celebration of the individual ends in a romanticized and empty utopianism. "In the presence of music and landscape human experience eludes itself" (200).

This eluding of oneself, this escape from the problems—the challenges and opportunities—of the concrete world of limited alternatives and partial successes, is at the heart of the attitudes that Bill Readings thinks have transformed both the University of Culture and the University of Reason into what he calls, derisively, the "University of Excellence" (ch. 2; see also Allan 1997: ch 4: "The College as Resource Center"). What do we do when the familiar standards of education are everywhere under attack, where there is no agreement about canonical texts and canonical methods, much less about the curricular features essential for an arts and sciences baccalaureate? How can we know if a particular school's general education program is adequate or inadequate if any criterion for making such an assessment is considered as yet another example of hierarchical—and therefore arbitrary and hegemonic—thinking? When accrediting agencies created by the colleges and universities they accredit are taken to be hegemons no less tyrannical than governmental or ecclesiastical agencies, there is no objective way to measure educational success. "Excellence," as a name for such a putative measure, ceases to have any definable meaning and hence any identifiable referent.

Readings likens this understanding of excellence to money. It is a quantity into which specific things with their unique qualities can be translated for purposes of comparison. By assigning a certain dollar value to a bushel of red pippins and another dollar value to a crate of clementines, we can compare apples and oranges. Their value is no longer a direct measure of their qualitatively differing tastes, however, for tastes are fundamentally incomparable. Instead, what is measured is their exchange value, their relative worth under supply and demand market conditions as objects for customers to purchase.

Similarly, if we assess a college or university in terms of the excellence of each of the several parts of its educational program, we can arrive at a relative measure of the school's excellence. The excellence of each component is assessed: each academic major, the general education offerings, study abroad options, internship opportunities, student life programming, counseling services, student housing arrangements, library acquisition rates, admissions application-acceptance ratios, alumni/ae giving percentages and amounts, endowment growth, debt payment schedules, Moody's financial risk ratings, the extent of deferred maintenance, new construction schedules. These several measures are then summed in some appropriately weighted fashion and can be compared to similarly determined summaries for other institutions. The comparisons can be ordered on a scale from lowest excellence score to highest and published by *Barron's* or *U.S. News and World Report* as guides for students and their parents to use when shopping for the college or university most likely to meet their needs.

"Excellence," says Readings, is supposedly how "the pre-modern traditions of the University" are exposed "to the forces of market capitalism" (38). But it is a measuring instrument without any objective calibration, as though the carpenters in a particular woodshop were each using their own arbitrarily marked rulers to size and cut the lumber needed in building a cabinet to specification. The units each carpenter uses are quite precise, but they are not coordinated with each other nor with the calibrations that appear on the design instructions they are following. All the more is this absence of meaningful units of measure a problem when what is being measured is qualities rather than quantities, pedagogic skill and departmental reputation instead of a pine board's length and breadth. The "dubiousness of such quantitative indicators of quality" should be obvious (25). It is blatantly wrongheaded to measure the quality of a classroom learning experience by the number of students in attendance, by the grades the professor gives out at the end of the semester, or by the student course evaluation averages. The quality of a college's curriculum has only a very indirect connection to the number of volumes added to the library's collection in a year, the number of books checked out, the percentage of faculty with the highest degree in their field, or the school's average class size.

These kinds of quantified measure are selected because they produce information that is readily collectable, comes in additive pieces, and can be comparatively scaled. No matter how suspect it may be to translate into abstract units of excellence the concreteness of a Tuesday morning discussion in a Religion and Literature course or a Wednesday night scholar's insight into how best to interpret the third line of a particular poem, once the translation has been effected the rest is a simple matter of arithmetic calculation and statistical analysis. But the results do not provide comparison data about what they purport to measure if there is no standard of translation. If a dozen linguists translate Dante into English, each under no requirement to be literal or to preserve word order or rhyme scheme or meter, the resulting translations can be compared with respect to their relative stylistic merits but not with respect to their appropriateness to the original text. "As a non-referential unit of value entirely internal to the system," Readings argues, "excellence marks nothing more than the moment of technology's self-reflection" (39).

Where there are no canons of excellence based on criteria that capture essential substantive features of the educational ideas to be measured, we fall back on essential practices. Where there are no canons of excellence based on criteria that capture essential formal features of the educational practices to be measured, we fall back on a nonessentialist inclusiveness. If differences in both content and procedure are unrankable, if they are all objectively good, then our preference for one over the other can only be a subjective determination, a choice without any objective grounding. And where all choices are gratuitous, all are equally acceptable. Richard Shweder quotes from Kurt Vonnegut's *Slaughterhouse Five:* "I went to the University of Chicago for a while after the Second World War. I was a student in the department of anthropology. They taught me that nobody was ridiculous or bad or disgusting." Vonnegut, Schweder adds, "never wrote a book with a villain in it because that is what they taught him at college. They taught him there are no villains. They taught him that whatever is, is okay" (14).

We do not want students to be choosing their colleges and courses of study for no good reason. We are reluctant to agree that it makes no difference which school we pick because they are indistinguishable in respect to the education they offer. So we cook up an ersatz standard based on nothing objective: an unjustifiable ranking instrument, one that locates schools on a scale of excellence where what counts as excellent is undefined except by the measures utilized. College A is ranked in *U.S. News and World Report* as superior to college B because it has a lower application-acceptance ratio, this ratio reflecting the judgments of potential applicants that it is more excellent than its rival. These judgments of greater excellence are not based on the firsthand experience of the potential applicants, however, but on their sense of the institution's reputation, which means on information about its relative excellence derived from *U.S. News and World Report*. The circularity is vicious in the logical sense, and otherwise ridiculous—except that the success and failure of most colleges and many universities is to a significant degree dependent on their ranking on these scales of excellence. And, of course, there is no objective appeal from a ranking decision because there is no standpoint outside the evaluation system from which to call its measurements or its measuring instruments into question.

The University of Excellence, notes Readings, is trapped—ironically—in precisely the sort of self-enclosed, self-defined, arbitrary system Foucault warned against in *Discipline and Punishment*. There is no way out of a cultural system that takes deviance as a pathology needing to be cured. Criminals are understood to be normal people who suffer from an illness that requires their temporary removal from normal society in order that they can be cured; normal people are potential criminals, safe from imprisonment as long as they remain socially healthy. The dominance of the socially constructed reality is complete: everything, both normal and deviant, is defined relative to everything else. No one can choose to be other than to be part of a system that determines their social location within it, for to rebel against the system is merely to indicate that one's location is closer to the periphery than the center.

"Is it surprising," Foucault asks, "that prisons resemble factories, schools, barracks, hospitals, which all resemble prisons?" (228). When all institutions are defined with respect to their cultural meaning, their societal function, by reference to the same internal system of relative truth, they are all going to look and function somewhat alike. For they are all modalities of a single inescapable system. Readings therefore paraphrases Foucault: "Is it surprising that corporations resemble Universities, health-care facilities, and international organizations, which all resemble corporations?" (29). It is ironic that the anti-canonical egalitarian revolt against hierarchical hegemonic systems should have ended up a helpless pawn of the hierarchical hegemonic system known as national capitalism. But as the anti-canonists have insisted from the first, when there are no objective standards of value then whoever controls the levers of social power gets to define those standards, including the educational standards. And the rest of us, educators and educated alike, have no grounds left us for gainsaying that definition.

Chapter 5

Relative Canonists

Contextualism

The anti-canonists overstate their case. By rejecting the claim that all things are elements of one overarching system, understandable ultimately in terms of a Unified Theory of Everything governed by a single normative method of inquiry, we are not compelled to reject a belief in systems or unified theories or normative methods. "All" and "none" are logical contraries: both are denied by "some."

Arthur Lovejoy points out that the notion of a Great Chain of Being, which we argued in chapter 2 was a presumption of the content canonists' foundationalism, rests on a "principle of plenitude": "It is this strange and pregnant theorem of the 'fullness' of the realization of conceptual possibility in actuality, . . . that no genuine potentiality of being can remain unfulfilled, that the extent and abundance of the creation must be as great as the possibility of existence" (52). This principle entails a second one: the "principle of continuity," which asserts that there are no breaks in nature, no disjunctions or ruptures. Given any two kinds of things, if there is a way to exist that is in any sense intermediate between the two, then there must exist some third kind of things that exemplifies that difference (58). Two further principles then follow, says Lovejoy. One is the "principle of gradation," which indicates that the key continuity among kinds of things is with respect to their perfection, resulting in a hierarchical arrangement of kinds from the least to the most perfect, from the transient to the permanent. The "principle of sufficient reason" then asserts that the reason why anything exists can be explained by indicating the role it plays, the place it occupies, in this hierarchy.

Lovejoy quotes Alexander Pope as summing up these four principles in "two neat couplets":

Of systems possible if 'tis confest
That wisdom infinite must form the best,
[then] . . . all must full or not coherent be,
And all that rises, rise in due degree.

A hierarchy of this sort, however, a system in which "everything is so rigorously tied up" with its Source or Apex, which in turn "is so rigorously implicative of the existence of everything else," allows no room for "conceivable additions or omissions or alterations" (328). Such a world is thoroughly deterministic, and hence is timeless with respect to its structure, with respect to the nature and pattern of the kinds of things there are.

Yet, argues Lovejoy, the world is obviously not that way: it is "a world of time and change" (329), "a world of impossible contradictions" (331). "It is, in short, a contingent world; its magnitude, its pattern, its habits, which we call laws, have something arbitrary and idiosyncratic about them" (332). If there is no great chain, however, there are nonetheless plenty of little chains. Contingency and idiosyncrasy are not modes of chaos. The world has laws and patterns even if they change over time, and even if the laws are not all compatible nor the pattern of the patterns coherent.

William James walks this same middle road. A system, he says, is any collection of things that "hang together," that are linked by "lines of influence." In some cases, those influences may be purposive, so that the ways of the hanging together "work out a climax," go together to "tell a story." Were there no such "conductors," the "parts of the universe" would be like so many "detached grains of sand." Were there nothing but conductors, never any "non-conductors," the parts would comprise a totality—the universe would be a solid "block" of things.

"In point of fact," however, James contends, "all stories end."

The world is full of partial stories that run parallel to one another, beginning and ending at odd times. They mutually interlace and interfere at points, but we can not unify them completely in our minds. . . . It is easy to see the world's history pluralistically, as a rope of which each fibre tells a separate tale; but to conceive of each cross-section of the rope as an absolutely single fact, and to sum the whole longitudinal series into one being living an undivided life, is harder. (67)

There are hierarchies, but the claim that they fit together into a single overarching hierarchy is problematic. Any such unity is certainly not a given, a precondition for what we experience. It is, at best, something to be attained, a hope informing our experience. James would have us "abjure absolute monism and absolute pluralism," a world filled full of connectors or a world with no connectors at all. "The world is One just so far as its parts hang together by any definite connexion. It is many just so far as any definite connexion fails to obtain" (71).

Relativists do not denigrate hierarchies in the way historicists do. They recognize that it is because systems have centers and peripheries that they can generate criteria for distinguishing better from worst. By insisting that such differentiations are bad, historicists accept the monist presuppositions of the foundationalists and methodists while transvaluating their values. They agree that systems are necessarily totalizing, but see such structures as disvalues needing to be repudiated rather than as positive values needing to be embraced. For a relativist, in contrast, order is a necessity, which is why it is omnipresent, but any specific order of things is contingent and partial. An order is a function of the things it orders, a manner of their relatedness, and so it comes to be naturally or artfully as they come to be, altering or perishing when they alter or perish. Some orders are repressive, some liberating. A systemic structure can be adequate, efficient, elegant, or just; it can be irrelevant, antiquated, ugly, or unfair. What is at issue is not the system but its character.

Foundationalism and methodism identify a timeless essence, an unchanging normative character of entities or processes, an ideal against which to measure any particular thing's nature or behavior and so to rank it on a scale of its approximation to or deviation from that ideal. For each kind of thing, there is a proper place along the hierarchy of approximations to the ideal, and the task for each particular thing is to attain as nearly as it can that proper mode of ideality, fulfilling to that extent its nature. With Hegel and his ilk, this hierarchy is temporalized. Approximations and deviations to the ideal become phases of the ideal's concrete realization, stages along the way to an ultimate fulfillment of the nature of all things. This view of history is progressive, the divisive diversity of things eventually overcome, dialectically integrated into a single harmonious whole. Relativism accepts the Hegelian temporalizing of hierarchy but then pluralizes it as well. The diversity is endemic; conflicts may get resolved but new ones will always arise. There is no attainable final harmony—no actualizable ultimate fulfillment—no such thing as an ultimate best character for all systems. Each way of ordering things is unique to those things in their unique context. Adequacy and relevance, elegance and justice, are relative judgments.

Although, as we saw in chapter 4, Jean-François Lyotard attacks the "grand narratives" of Western civilization, his intent is not to leave us without systems able to order our experiences meaningfully. Instead of yearning for one overarching story, he argues, we should revel in a multiplicity of differing ones. Consensus should always be local: a temporary game of shared talk or coordinate action "agreed on by its present players and subject to eventual cancellation" (66). These "little narratives" suffice, for they alone are how we can come to appreciate that the presuppositions of what we know are a function of our standpoints. The contexts for our action are a function of our interests and so what today leads us into confederation may tomorrow turn us into enemies. There are no underlying basic truths or goods, only those that different people on varying occasions fashion to suit their needs. We need our narratives, but they are always limited accounts of things, relative to the local conditions they interpret.

With respect to human history, Oswald Spengler provides a vivid illustration of this relativizing shift. For Hegel, cultural worlds are ranked in terms of their distance from the ideal, each realization from the Chinese world to the European an improvement on its predecessors, bringing closer to concreteness what was initially only an abstract possibility. Spengler turns the intercultural connectors into nonconnectors, transforming the progression of Spirit toward a utopian apotheosis into a random sequence of unrelated cultures. He retains a generic pattern governing the development of cultures, but this pattern applies to each culture in a unique way and dies with the death of that culture. No pattern governs the whole process: cultures develop but the history of the rise and fall of cultures has no development.

> I see, in place of that empty figment of *one* linear history . . . the drama of a *number* of mighty Cultures, each springing from primitive strength from the soil of a mother-region to which it remains firmly bound throughout its whole life-cycle; each stamping its material, its mankind, in *its own* image; each having *its own* idea, *its own* passions, *its own* life, will and feeling, *its own* death. (17)

Not one history but a number of histories, not one essence or image of what it means to be human but each culture with its own essence, arising in some particular geographic location at some particular time, flourishing for a while in some specific manner, and then in its own distinctive way perishing. Spengler's metaphors are biological: cultures "grow with the same superb aimlessness as the flowers of the field," and like those flowers each "has its peculiar blossom or fruit, its special type of growth and decline" (17).

What this relativizing does for objective knowledge is obvious. "Every thought lives in an historical world and is therefore involved in the common destiny of mortality," Spengler argues. "There are no eternal truths. Every philosophy is the expression of its own and only its own time, and . . . no two ages possess the same philosophical intentions" (31). Spengler's conclusions are similar to those that were coming to prominence at the time in cultural anthropology as it shucked off its lingering social Darwinist presuppositions. Primitive cultures are not to be understood as inferior to European cultures but merely as different from them. Hottentots and South Sea Islanders are not less developed kinds of humans than British gentlemen, apelike primates to be used as farm animals or childlike innocents to be protected. They are adults who inhabit a culture every bit as sophisticated, as rationally and emotionally satisfying, as any Western culture. The differences among cultures are not rankable. They each have their own hierarchical structures, but there is no hierarchy among them.

The anthropologist Clifford Geertz reflects this interpretive shift in his explication of the biological basis of cultural relativism, turning Spengler's metaphors into literal scientific assertions. He brands the quest for universal cultural values, for behaviors or beliefs that are culturally invariant, as a chimera because rooted in the assumption that there is an "essence of what it means to be human." If there is such a human essence, it would be "most clearly revealed in those features of human culture that are universal rather than in those that are distinctive to this people or that." But where people are most genuinely human, most distinctively themselves, is in their "cultural particularities." As he asks rhetorically, "Is it in grasping such general facts—[e.g.,] that man has everywhere some sort of 'religion'—or in grasping the richness of this religious phenomenon or that—Balinese trance or Indian ritualism, Aztec human sacrifice or Zuñi rain-dancing—that we grasp him?" (43).

Geertz argues that our genetic inheritance does not determine our behavior. We are born with generalized indeterminate capacities, which then need to be completed by the "extragenetic, outside-the-skin control mechanisms" culture provides. We have a linguistic capacity, for instance, that a given culture completes by teaching us a specific language, a concrete structure of sounds, marks, rules, and meanings. In the absence of a completing culture, this linguistic capacity withers away. A child raised in isolation from humans, cut off from an environing culture, loses its humanity. Obviously there could be no culture without human beings to create and sustain it, but it is equally true that without culture there would be no humans. "We are, in sum, incomplete or unfinished animals who complete or finish ourselves through culture—and not through culture in general but through highly particular forms of it: Dobuan and Javanese, Hopi and Italian, upper-class and lower-class, academic and commercial" (49).

Who we are essentially is inherently relative, tied to a specific place and time, because our essence is as much cultural as biological, and cultures are always temporally and spatially specific.

Our ideas, our values, our acts, even our emotions, are, like our nervous system itself, cultural products—products manufactured, indeed, out of tendencies, capacities, and dispositions with which we were born, but manufactured nonetheless. Chartres is made of stone and glass. But it is not just stone and glass; it is a cathedral, and not only a cathedral, but a particular cathedral built at a particular time by certain members of a particular society. To understand what it means, to perceive it for what it is, you need to know rather more than the generic properties of stone and glass and rather more than what is common to all cathedrals. You need to understand also—and, in my opinion, most critically—the specific concepts of the relations among God, man, and architecture that, since they have governed its creation, it consequently embodies. It is no different with men; they, too, every last one of them, are cultural artifacts. (50–51)

Thus, there are as many essential kinds of human being as there are cultural systems, each kind of societal ordering of things a contingent accomplishment, neither necessary nor universal nor inherently superior to the other kinds.

The Contemporary Canon

If cathedrals are cultural artifacts and each cathedral is important because of its unique way of expressing its culture's meanings, it should be no surprise that there are some among its clerics, squabbling about the whether and what of an educational canon, who are ready to argue that canons can be foundational without being timeless. The problem, they argue, is that the traditional content canon, along with its procedural surrogate, is no longer suitable, that it has been undermined by alterations in the cultural terrain. Times change and educational canons must change with them: we need a contemporary canon, one suited to this contemporary world of ours. Our current understanding of the requirements for a firm foundation indicates the old one is too narrow or too rigid. It has become outdated and is in need of serious repair or simply in need of replacement.

Richard Rorty, whose rejection of eternal truths seemed to put him in league with the anti-canonists, insists on "the inspirational value of great works of literature." He disparages egalitarians, who seem to be following Horace's advice "to stand in awe of nothing" (1998: 125). Their "knowingness" is "a state of soul which prevents shudders of awe," which "makes one immune to romantic enthusiasm" (126). Romance, in contrast, involves an appreciation of "charisma" and "genius," a delight in works of art and literature—and of philosophy and science—that "make people think there is more to this life than they ever imagined" (133). Inspirational works provide "excitement and hope" rather than understanding, "self-transformation" rather than information. They "recontextualize" our previous knowledge, temporarily sweep us off our feet, catch us up in a "wild, unreflective infatuation" akin to what happens when we fall in love. Sobersided criticism, debunking skepticism, analytic "deromanticizing" have their place, to be sure, but they need to be balanced to inspiration.

An intellectual canon for Rorty should be composed of the works people find inspirational. The roster of these works is "as changeable as the historical and personal situations of readers" (137), but this does not mean the works are not great. The criterion for membership in a canon should not be that a particular work offers us a link to some kind of eternal truth, from which it follows that our indifference to that work indicates a flaw in our character, our refusal to commune with things that are ultimately significant. The sole criterion should be that the work has inspired a number of people and that it might possibly inspire us as well. "We should see great works of literature as great because they have inspired many readers, not as having inspired many readers because they are great" (136). The intellectual canon should vary as the culture varies of which it is an expression.

Ralph Waldo Emerson, even though located by Santayana among the anticanonists, can be taken, like Rorty, to be a canonical relativist. He advocates canons that are relative to a particular cultural context, insisting that any proposed definitive list of the best books, best methods, and brightest minds amounts to what Amy Gutmann calls "intellectual idol worship." She quotes from his famous essay on "The American Scholar" where he argues that no book is ever "quite perfect":

As no airpump can by any means make a perfect vacuum, so neither can any artist entirely exclude the conventional, the local, the perishable from his book, or write a book of pure thought, that shall be as efficient, in all respects, to a remote posterity, as to contemporaries, or rather to the second age. (Emerson 1837: 87; cited by Gutmann: 17)

The imperfection of any author's achievement, its inescapably conventional and local character, does not mean it should be read only as a way to learn about the author's era, about times past and cultures long since perished. The best among the older books also speak to our time and our culture, but not definitively nor even adequately. They are useful stimuli to thought and provide helpful context, but we need—not merely also but more importantly—our own authors, inspiring us by their interpretation of our own situation, its limitations and its possibilities. "Each age must write its own books" (Emerson 1837: 87; cited by Gutmann: 17).

Barbara Herrnstein Smith notes that a canonical text able to meet the test of time, to retain its importance from generation to generation, does so for constantly changing reasons. It is valid initially because it "may perform certain desired/able functions quite well for some sets of subjects." It does so by virtue of certain "properties" attributed to it, "as they have been specifically constituted—framed, foregrounded, and configured—by those subjects under those conditions and in accord with their particular needs, interests, and resources" and under the influence of what have previously been taken as valued properties (30). Over time, however, "under the changing and emergent conditions of that subsequent time, the functions for which the text was earlier valued are no longer desired/able." Nonetheless, the text may continue to be revered because it "continues to perform *some* desired/able functions particularly well, even if not the same ones for which it was initially valued" (31). In an important sense, it is not the same text it once was: new times and a new standpoint have made it into a different text, one valued for new reasons. This survival power does not make the reevaluated text superior to a newly authored text. If both are now valued as canonical, it is because they are both appreciated for their relevance to current cultural concerns.

Leon Botstein agrees. He rejects as "self-serving" any claim that a canon should be, or can be, objective, timeless, "apolitical": "The organization of knowledge and certainly the modes of its transmission are inherently part of a fabric of social ideas and action" (52). An educational canon is a "tactical decision" we make about how to introduce students to the "larger questions" and "to forge some agreement about an answer." What we think worth teaching is thus a function of what we decide "would help any undergraduate student deal with central issues whose substance outstrips the limits of journalism—issues that are undeniably unavoidable and central to the existence of each of us" (54, 55). Botstein poses ten such issues (56–59; selectively quoted):

1. How does the individual define himself or herself in terms of identity? Who am I? What am I? How do we understand differentiation in the definition of identity?
2. How does my conception of my own identity help me conceive of who someone else is? The definition of the other in terms of nation, race, religion, or any other category, is a crucial problem.
3. By what rules should individuals conduct their lives? How should we resolve the age-old issue of the conflict between so-called natural rights and societal obligations and rights?
4. If in our personal lives we embrace a religious faith defined as commitment to transcendent truth, how does that faith square with any notion of civil society?
5. Are there procedures and rules with which we can agree in order to avoid an unacceptable obliteration of the boundaries between truth and fiction?
6. Is the generalized use of the victim status, whether applied to individuals or groups, ever justified?
7. In today's United States, we encounter an extraordinary amount of bad faith with respect to our capacities for thought. Why is the quality of public discourse so low?
8. In an age of enormous technological dependence, why is the percentage of people who have any idea or notion about science and technology steadily declining? What will be the future of memory and written language?
9. What does an American need to know about the world that is different from what previous generations needed to know?
10. What do we make of the fact that the intimate has become public?

Botstein does not claim that what makes these issues canonical for twenty-first-century Americans would also have made them canonical or even relevant for fourth-century B.C.E. Athenian citizens or sixteenth-century English gentlemen. Nor does he claim they are necessarily relevant to people elsewhere in the world or that they will still be relevant for twenty-second-century Americans. They are our important issues, right now, and so it is the responsibility of our educational system to help students recognize what these issues are and how to go about dealing with them.

Howard Gardner's approach is similar to Botstein's, although his focus is on primary and secondary education. He contends that we need to replace the aim of education as "the need for students to master certain basic texts and certain core disciplines" with a "less directive," more "progressive" approach, one that "encourages students to develop interests and to pursue them in ways that are personally meaningful" (92–93). The educational canon becomes a matter not of great books and great souls, not even of great methods, but of "essential questions" (94–95, quoted selectively):

1. Personal identity: Who am I? Where do I come from? What will I be?
2. Group identity: What group do I belong to, in terms of family, community, nation, religion? What does that mean?
3. Group relations: How does my group resemble or differ from other groups? How do groups relate to one another? How might they get along better?
4. The physical world: What is the world made of? How did it get to be that way? Where is it going?
5. The natural/biological world: How did the world of nature—of plants, animals, other living things—originate? How do humans relate to these other entities?
6. The world of symbols: What is the status of those entities that are created by human beings—poems, songs, histories, myths, dreams, language? How do they relate to the supernatural?
7. The true, the beautiful, the good: What patterns exist in the world? Where do they come from? How do these realms relate to one another? Is there a Higher Being?

Gardner's questions are more traditional than Botstein's, but they agree in taking a student-centered approach. The value of an idea or a text is its usefulness, its relevance as a tool of analysis and interpretation, and since relevance is situational so is value. The great books that should compose the educational canon to be taught in one cultural context are not those appropriate for another, but for any culture during any period of its history—for each generation—there are great books that reflect and shape it.

For Martha Nussbaum, colleges and universities need to fashion curricula that respond to the most salient feature of the contemporary world: globalization. Technology has made it easy to communicate with people anywhere in the world, to travel anywhere quickly and easily, and therefore to exchange goods and services, ideas and attitudes. We need to learn how to live in harmony with these new neighbors whose histories, hopes, and current practices are different from our own, to become citizens with them of the same world. "Education for world citizenship requires transcending the inclination of both students and educators to define themselves primarily in terms of local group loyalties and identities" (67).

Multicultural education—a mode of cross-cultural inquiry that leads students to understand, appreciate, and respect cultural difference—means freeing them from a life dependent on the authority of their parents or of "an idealized image of nation or leader" serving as "a surrogate parent who will do our thinking for us." It means, argues Nussbaum, helping students discover "the beauty and interest of a life that is open to the whole world," a life "of questioning and self-government." Much is at stake: "We had better show them this, or the future of democracy in the nation and in the world is bleak" (84).

Nussbaum identifies three conundrums that plague attempts to design such an education for world citizenship, and proposes ways to overcome each of them. First is the question of how to balance a global and an American perspective. Does it make sense to study other cultures, including our own minority cultures, unless we first know our own mainstream culture? Nussbaum affirms the importance of "local knowledge," insisting that curricula "strongly emphasize," for example, American constitutional traditions, Western political philosophy, and Anglo-American literature (68). But she argues that "this material be presented in a way that reminds the student of the broader world of which the Western traditions are a part" (68–69) and that this "infusing" strategy "pervade the curriculum as a whole" not just a few courses here and there (77). She suggests beginning with courses on "topics that invite a global perspective," such as hunger and famine, free speech, climatology, religious and ethnic violence (78).

Second is the question of how to balance breadth and depth. Requiring students to take a course or even a sequence of courses that covers all the world's cultures would be as unhelpful as expecting them to learn all the world's languages in a course or two. Yet to avoid this superficial skimming of surfaces by requiring that students focus in on a single culture, indeed on a single aspect of that culture, is to achieve depth at the price of meaningfulness. A pile of specific but unrelated courses on topics in a non-Western area—"an amorphous elective diversity requirement"—is no way to teach diversity: it would be "as if the grasp of any part of any one of them would somehow yield a person the breadth of learning that could be yielded only by some grasp of each area" (71). Nussbaum favors a well-designed single basic multicultural course or course sequence, ideally one that acquaints students with "five categories of diversity: race, gender, ethnicity, social class, and religious sectarianism" (73).

Third is the question of how to provide firsthand experience of other cultures, given the usual constraints of time and money. Nussbaum recommends study abroad programs, particularly those integrated with on-campus courses in the target culture. However, tourism in foreign lands for academic credit is not a preparation for becoming persons able to live meaningful and productive lives as members of a global community. "To become world citizens we must not simply amass knowledge, we must also cultivate in ourselves a capacity for sympathetic imagination that will enable us to comprehend the motives and choices of people different from ourselves, seeing them not as forbiddingly alien and other, but as sharing many problems and possibilities with us" (85). The arts foster this sympathy, especially storytelling, the cultivation of "narrative imagination" through reading novels and other fictional presentations of specific people in specific circumstances. "Empathy" and "compassion" are "an essential preparation for moral interaction," for the "sympathetic responsiveness to another's needs" that creates genuine community (90).

Of course, Nussbaum is quick to point out that the need for an education suited to a complexly pluralistic world is as old as civilization and was, for instance, defended in particularly apt fashion by the Roman Stoics. They advocated, as we should now, a curriculum that calls into question the comfortable parochialism of traditionalists. Education for world citizenship "is in its way a radical political agenda":

The current agenda is radical in the way that Stoic world citizenship was radical in a Rome built on hierarchy and rank, in the way that the Christian idea of love of one's neighbor was and is radical, in a world anxious to deny our common membership in the kingdom of ends or the kingdom of heaven. We should defend that radical agenda as the only one worthy of our conception of democracy and worthy of guiding its future. (112)

The Progressive Canon

Relativists typically find it difficult to remain Spenglerians, to affirm the unique canonical needs of their own time without at the same time denigrating previous canons. The temptation is to become Hegelians—to see the present as an improvement on the past, as having passed beyond its limitations. The first step down this progressivist road is to recognize that we can only understand today's great souls by seeing them in the light of the great souls who preceded them and influenced them.

Most core curricula, following the Columbia University model, recognize this fact by organizing their educational canon historically. Even if, following

Bennett and Bloom, we think Plato or Shakespeare speak timeless truths, we nonetheless assign them places in the Hall of the Greats that are located on a timeline. By arranging canonical authors chronologically, by studying them as predecessors and successors, as voices in a historical narrative or stages of a journey, their timelessness is put in question. The judgment concerning what constitutes the best that has been said or written is always made from a particular standpoint, and as that standpoint changes so will the judgment.

When Eva Brann, one of the strictest of the content canonists discussed in chapter 2, explains her criteria for a book's greatness, she emphasizes its "self-sufficiency." A great book, she insists, has "independent interpretability," so that students and their tutors "need no background preparation" in order to be equipped for their exegetical tasks (1999: 165). To insist on providing a historical context "begs all the questions, for if the text assumes, as do most major works, a radical originating power of thought, then to offer to explicate it by providing its historical setting is simply to deny the truth of the text before making it read"—it is "a way of saying that the teacher does not believe in [the book's] intelligibility" (1979: 115).

"Except," Brann goes on to add, "perhaps the earlier books" have background value (1999: 165). She says immediately thereafter that the St. John's curriculum uses "no comparative or interpretive schemes" for organizing their canon of readings, that the curriculum's chronological arrangement is the "hermeneutical null principle" that mere dates carry no interpretive implications (165). Why then the "except"? Perhaps understanding the earlier books is important to understanding the later ones. Perhaps their mutual "quarrelsomeness" is due in part to differences in their cultural contexts, differences that need to be appreciated in order to understand why—rather than merely that—their ideas are different. Perhaps where authors stand is not irrelevant to what they see. Brann is disingenuous in calling chronology an interpretive null principle, for she would surely think it inappropriate to organize the readings in the curriculum by a genuinely null principle: for instance, to organize them alphabetically by author.

Likewise, Allan Bloom's content canon is not a collection of timelessly great books. He looks to the past not for a standard that transcends time but for ancient exemplars to be emulated. What we need today, he argues, is to recapture Plato's world, to reproduce in our own thinking and sensibility "that magic Athenian moment." Brann acknowledges that an "original" book is not only one with "indefinitely rich interpretability" but also one that is "at the origins or foundations of human knowledge" (164). Bloom simply gives that origin a temporal and spatial address. His educational canon is the content canon shrunk to a privileged era. The great souls of enduring significance are all from one particular cultural period, an apotheosis of the human spirit to which all of us should turn for inspiration and guidance.

Whitehead's descriptive observation that all Western thought is but a series of footnotes to Plato becomes for Bloom an educational ought.

Bloom is thus a relativist, for he insists on the importance of cultural eras as the nurturing contexts in which great authors flourish. He differs from standard relativists such as Emerson and Rorty, however, because he repudiates their belief in self-reliance. He rejects their argument that each new generation must create its own unique canon, arguing instead that the canons of old are the foundation on which the canons of today should be built. There is, and there ought to be, a continuity of influence from culture to culture and hence from canon to canon. Whereas progressivists see these influences as culminating in present achievement, Bloom relocates the developmental apotheosis in the past—his Golden Age is an Eden rather than a Utopia. He makes Athens in the fifth and fourth century B.C.E. the paradigm for canonical importance: we should lean on the cultural judgments the Athenian canon makes possible. Bloom's progressivism is inverted—we begin with the best and cannot get beyond it, rather than working our way beyond the ancients toward the best.

Frank Wong is a recent voice speaking on behalf of the progressivist canon. The present is normative; the past must pass muster before its court of judgment. Wong contends that the reason the traditional educational canon is outmoded is because of its "failure to confront the contradictions between the aristocratic basis of Anglo-European approaches and the democratic, scientific, and technological realities of American life" (66). Bloom's and Bennett's canons—and Rosovsky's as well—have become outmoded. The Great Souls lived in a preindustrial nondemocratic age; their ideas are simply antiquated. The Great Methods of scientific inquiry are a myth of the Enlightenment, having little to do with how science really works. Our world is incomparably different, its central concerns unimaginable to our ancestors. What is needed is "a distinctively American approach to liberal education," Wong argues, one that takes seriously "the contemporary needs of a pluralistic America" (69).

Progressivist relativism is always in danger of slipping into a triumphalist mode. When the explosion in knowledge makes it impossible to teach everything, the progressivist's criterion for selecting what to retain favors whatever is best suited to present concerns. As W. B. Carnochan points out, the nineteenth-century tropism in American higher education toward a free elective system in which students rather than their professors decide what courses they should take meant that personal choice came to define what is educationally valuable. The curriculum began to take on a Darwinian look, with courses functioning like biological traits and student preferences playing the role of natural selection. "In the environment of free election the fittest would survive best: the fittest student would succeed, the fittest teachers and the fittest courses would attract the best students, the fittest subjects would dominate the intellectual scene" (14). The works of the ancients have no intrinsic value; their ability to stand the test of time is their ability to survive by adapting to shifting senses of perceived usefulness.

The application of Darwin to education, is, of course, a form of social Darwinianism. It misuses Darwin's ideas by equating adaptive success with moral and intellectual improvement, so that survival of the fittest is taken to mean survival of the best. The racist and jingoist implications are legion. Emerson, for instance, advocates self-reliance but presumes that those who are not Anglo-Saxon will be unable to learn the practice of that virtue, for they lack the "genius" and the "excess of virility" needed for command of self, and hence for command of others. Cornel West says that unfortunately we must conclude "that Emerson's conception of the worth and dignity of human personality is racially circumscribed; that race is central to his understanding of the historical circumstances which shape human personality; and that this understanding can easily serve as a defense of Anglo-Saxon imperialist domination of non-European lands and peoples" (34).

Progressivists thus end up every bit as elitist and universalist as the content and method canonists they repudiate. They shift the standard of educational value from a timeless objective norm to a historically developing one, and from disinterested reason to interested choice as the method by which that standard can be known. But the distinction remains between a privileged center that knows and in some sense embodies that standard and a delegitimated periphery that lacks those capacities. A progressivist approach to the canon is the traditionalist wolf in grandma's relativist woolens. Lean in too close to hear its comforting words about the need for change and about the inclusive fairness change seems to promise, and we are likely to feel the bite of the new absolutist claim those words are masking.

The Ethnic Canon

So relativists, advocating a contemporary canon, can easily slip into a progressivist version of it, their relativism absolutized by turning a pluralism of canons into stages on the way toward the realization of some one true canon. They can absolutize their relativism without abandoning pluralism, however, by retaining the importance of historical continuity but limiting it to a particular strand of human beings—a people, a race, a nation, an ethnic group—and insisting that its invaluable canonical ideals cannot be judged by any standard external to it. We have returned to Lyotard and Spengler, but without their evenhanded attitude. One of the little narratives, one of the myriad flowers of the field, is special—because it is ours.

An *ethnos* is a particular cultural world, a group of people, with or without political sovereignty or historical continuity, that takes itself as one entity, its members sharing the same basic values, the same heritage and aspirations. An ethnic canon is constituted by works an *ethnos* finds uniquely emblematic of what it is fundamentally. The American canon is not the British canon nor the Greek, and the American people are the sole judges of its content. Construed ethnically, human history may spin golden treads but it does not weave them into a single tapestry.

The ethnically monochromatic character of the Western canon is what upsets Henry Louis Gates Jr., whose rhetoric is adequate to his anger:

> These two men [William Bennett and Allan Bloom] symbolize for us the nostalgic return to what I think of as the "antebellum aesthetic position," where men were men, and men were white, when scholar-critics were white men, and when women and persons of color were voiceless, faceless servants and laborers, pouring tea and filling brandy snifters in the boardrooms of old boys' clubs. (95)

The "us" is African Americans. At a time in American history when blacks and other minorities have finally gained some modicum of visibility and influence, have finally had their demands for political, economic, and educational justice taken seriously, even if these demands have hardly yet been adequately addressed, Gates is incensed that those in positions of public and academic importance would be attempting to turn back the clock. "The return to 'the' canon, the high canon of Western masterpieces, represents the return of an order in which my people were the subjugated, the voiceless, the invisible, the unrepresented, and the unrepresentable. Who would return us to that medieval never-never land?" (111).

Gates is not interested in expanding this canon, however, adding some color to its whiteness, nor is he interested in abolishing it. He thinks canons are crucial for all the foundational and methodological reasons that motivate the promulgation of the traditional Western canon. A canon is a means of self-identification, a way to organize the experiences of a collection of people into a meaningful story, to give them a sense of their unity, their common origin, purpose, and destiny. Therefore, African Americans need their own black canon so that they might have a tangible social identity: "We can't become one of those bodiless vapor trails of sentience portrayed on that *Star Trek* episode, though often it seems like the universalists want us to be just that" (112). Maybe there will be a time when it is appropriate to talk of an American canon or even a Western canon that includes blacks and other minorities, but what black Americans need right now is their own canon.

The publication of a *Norton Anthology of African American Literature* is as good a starting place as any, Gates argues. Such an anthology "functions in the academy to *create* a tradition, as well as to define and preserve it.

A *Norton Anthology* opens up a literary tradition as simply as opening the cover of a carefully edited and ample book." Gates is aware that this canon, as any canon, is hardly objective and definitive, that it is "one possible set of selections among several possible sets of selections." What is important is that it exist, that it be available for blacks as an ethnic resource of values and possibilities for emulation. Its function is to provide a "Sears and Roebuck approach," as it were: "the 'dream book' of black literature" (107).

An African American canon needs to include more than texts, however, for "the vernacular, or oral literature, in my tradition, has a canon of its own" (108). Therefore, the Great Books canon for African Americans should be complemented by a cassette tape of "sermons, blues, spirituals, R&B poets reading their own 'dialect' poems, speeches—whatever" (109), and so the Norton anthology comes with an appropriate "Audio Companion CD" (for a listing of its contents, see http://www.wwnorton.com/english/naaal/cd.htm). A canon is for a people in a historical context, relevant to their needs. It is relevant not in any reductive or simplistic sense, however, but because of its function in their ongoing efforts to create and preserve a shared identity of their own making.

There is no way to gainsay Gates's contention that every *ethnos* deserves its own canon, once the relativism of cultural values is acknowledged. If lacking a "strong principle of selection" means, as Carnochan argues, that "little or nothing can be excluded from categories of the relevant and the important" (121), then where ethnicity provides that needed strong principle the categories of selection become the relevance and importance of the text or author for some identifiable cultural group. The function of an ethnic canon is twofold. First, it teaches the members of a group about the great souls and the great books in their past, reaffirming and perhaps even helping to create what they take to be their common heritage and shared hopes. Second, the ethnic canon teaches members of other groups that this group is also important, that it deserves their respect, that it is a culture every bit as great as theirs.

This cultural self-affirmation is what Charles Taylor calls a "politics of difference" (38). As we saw in the previous chapter, Taylor contrasts this attitude with what he calls a "politics of equal dignity" in which everyone is said to deserve respect because everyone has the same natural capacity, a "universal human potential" for achievement (41). For the anti-canonists, there are no standards by which to rank some individual or group achievements better than others except ones that artificially distort this natural equality. The celebration of ethnic difference, however, is based on a shift in the basis for respecting persons and their communities. Their dignity is a matter of the particular ethnic identity they and their ancestors have achieved, the incomparable way of life in which they participate. The key value for ethnic relativists is originality—each ethnic tradition has something special to say, a unique cultural history it has invented, and this accomplishment ought to be recognized by others for its incomparable and unrepeatable value. There is no external standard for judging such a group identity, since it is obviously sui generis. The only response possible is to acknowledge it. As long as the members of a group—a culture or nation or *Volk*—are true to their inner sense of its possibilities, its ideals of authenticity, we should respect and admire the group and its representatives for what they are, for what they have made of themselves.

An identity understood in this way, even though unique, is not solitary—as Taylor perceptively notes, it requires that others recognize it. We need others who are not members of our group to show us that we have achieved something distinctive, something that matters not just to us but to everyone. "Recognition forges identity" (66). We know that our difference matters to others not just by what they say, however, but by how they act. "Where the politics of universal dignity fought for forms of nondiscrimination that were 'blind' to the ways in which citizens differ, the politics of difference often redefines nondiscrimination as requiring that we make these distinctions the basis of differential treatment" (39). Consequently, whoever withholds recognition, whoever refuses to treat us differently, in a manner befitting the unique way in which our group has differentiated itself from other groups, is engaging in a form of repression. Not to credit the worth of a group's ethnic canon is as hegemonic an act as to have imposed one's own canon in place of it, for in either case what is distinctive about the ethnic canon, and hence what is distinctive about the *ethnos* itself, is denied importance.

The politics of difference is what that label implies: a political activity. In Charles Altieri's words, it turns canons into "ideological banners for social groups: social groups propose them as forms of self-definition, and they engage other proponents to test limitations while exposing the contradictions and incapacities of competing groups" (43). Rorty's edifying conversation among the proponents of differing judgments concerning what is admirable becomes a struggle among special interest groups, adversaries each demanding that it be admired and that this admiration find expression in the privilege appropriate to its special needs and accomplishments.

Respect on demand is an oxymoron, however (Taylor: 70). Either the respect we are commanded to provide will be condescending, granted to a group on condition that it cease pestering us, or it will be cowardly, extorted from us out of our fear of reprisal for failing to grant it. What is missing, what makes the relationship among the differing *ethnoi* and points of view merely political, is any trans-ethnic standard for judgment. Yet such a standard is precisely what respect requires. Instead, we are asked to respect other *ethnoi* in the same way we respect our own *ethnos*—yet we are to do so not because they measure up to some ideal of cultural worth we and they all share, but rather because they measure up to their own variously self-defined criteria of worth.

It is impossible therefore that there would be an achievement that fails to measure up, that does not deserve our respect. There is no ethnic educational canon that is not the equal of our own, not because our experience with them all has led us to an appreciation of their varied modes of greatness, but because they are each by definition of incomparable value. But this lack of critical judgment is precisely the same valuational dead end into which egalitarian standardlessness leads. Ethnic canonists are hierarchical with respect to the character of their own canon, but they are forced to be egalitarian with respect to the significance of that canon among the multitude of other ethnic canons. They affirm the necessity and objective significance of a temporally and spatially circumscribed content canon, for reasons that can be judged as warranted only by those it already encompasses.

Chapter 6

Canonical Dynamics

Polarized Academics

Relativism turns out to be foundationalism or methodism with the essential taken as temporal and particular rather than timeless and universal. Contemporary canonists locate that essence in the present, progressivists locate it in the future, ethnic relativists limit it to the history of a tribe or a people. Because they have restricted the scope of the community for which certain ideas, texts, and persons are canonical, relativists are anti-canonical egalitarians with respect to whatever lies beyond the scope of their canon's relevance—trans-ethnic or global or historically inclusive intellectual and educational canons are at best fanciful constructs, at worst attempts at hegemonic imposition by a momentarily dominant era or *ethnos*. The anti-canonists are the only ones who take a thoroughly deconstructivist approach to canons, seeing them all as arbitrary and self-serving—to be avoided or, insofar as they are unavoidable, to be divested of any objective, much less any transcendent, aura of significance.

It would seem, therefore, that our journey through the differing senses of an educational canon and the metaphysical presuppositions undergirding each has ended up with a simple polarity. Either there is an objective hierarchy of importance that undergirds a rationally defensible standard by which to rank things as essential or unessential, as central or peripheral. Or there is no such hierarchy, and in the absence of any objective standard all judgments of importance are subjective, situationally biased, and probably self-serving. Either the quest for a viable educational canon is justified, however difficult such an undertaking might be, or it is a chimera that we would be better off to avoid.

We are back to the dichotomy that Bruce Kimball argues is as old as Western civilization: the competing traditions of the "philosopher" and the "orator" (1986). On the one side, he argues, are those who propose a *methodus,* a method or set of standards which if adhered to will lead us to objective truths that are independent of cultural biases. On the other side are those who offer a *modus,* a way to articulate our personal and cultural values clearly and to come to a consensus about our differences concerning them (1995: 102). Although these two traditions share similar concerns about the importance of education for attaining truth and for becoming good persons and responsible citizens, they "are fundamentally divergent in their respective views that either language or experimental method is the primary conduit and source of knowledge and values" (1995: 56).

On the right side of the chancel, the traditional canonists are arrayed, foundationalists and methodists alike. Across from them sit the critics of tradition, advocates of a plurality of canons or of no canon at all. Each side fires cannonades of assertion and invective across the aisle separating them, each outraged at the refusal of the other to acknowledge the obvious, each muttering about the dark reasons that clearly must constitute their opponents' real motivation.

John Searle, for instance, chides the "cultural left"—his label for anti-canonists—because they confuse epistemology with ontology. "All investigations are relative to investigators. But it does not follow, nor is it indeed true, that all the matters investigated are relative to investigators" (sec. 3). Metaphysical realism, contends Searle, is presumed in the sciences, indeed "everywhere except in English, French, and cultural studies." An objective reality independent of our interpretations of it is the presupposition of all linguistic communication, and so even in attempting to argue against realism its opponents only end up exemplifying it. Searle dismisses the anti-canonists as philosophically muddleheaded and their views on education, therefore, as not worthy of serious consideration.

Francis Oakley goes further. The problem with the critics of a canonical *methodus* is their "intellectual malfeasance and moral confusion." Without some standard of judgment, a "morality of process" against which our intellectual claims are measured, we are "severely compromised" as a community, our quest for disinterested truth and social justice at the mercy of those who are most effective in appealing to our momentary passions and interests (1992a: 165). Even Rorty attacks the cultural Left, distinguishing his own activist "reformist Left" politics from its unremittingly negative petulance, accusing its adherents of being unpatriotic. They imagine themselves to be a "saving remnant" s truggling against entrenched powers and principalities they despise unbearably. So "it becomes increasingly difficult for members of such a movement to think of themselves as fellow citizens, to say 'we' when they speak of the country in which they live" (1992: 235; see also 1998).

The nontraditionalist Left replies in kind, vilifying the cultural Right for its confusion of ontology with epistemology. Simply because a group of people or even all people share the same common sense, and so take the same things as objectively the case, it does not follow that there is some reality external to themselves on which their agreement rests. Intersubjectivity is a sufficient presupposition for linguistic communication, whether in the sciences or in the humanities, and those who fail to acknowledge this limit to our knowledge must be doing so for self-serving reasons.

Mary Louise Pratt speaks disdainfully of "the killer B's"— Bloom, Bennett, and Saul Bellow—whom she accuses of attempting to close the American university to those they consider cultural riff-raff, "to all but a narrow and highly uniform elite with no commitment to either multiculturalism or educational democracy" (15). As Gerald Graff puts it, canonists proclaiming their essential truths and values are "educational fundamentalists" who can manage to get their views "institutionalized in the curriculum only by shoving them down dissenters' throats" (1992b: 59). If these traditionalists are not taken to be antidemocratic elitists, they are judged to be simply out of date. They are, says Oakley, who is as much displeased by them as he is by the anti-canonists, "philosophical Canutes bidding the tide of history to stand still"— adding, somewhat smugly, that "emulators of King Canute tend to emerge from the experience with their feet wet" (1992a: 135).

Both sides in the dispute over the nature and reality of an educational canon seem simply to presuppose the truth of their predetermined views concerning the nature of reality and hence of how best to learn about it. Unsurprisingly, the claims and arguments of one side are nonsensical if grounded in the other side's assumptions, and so are rejected—without giving any consideration to the possibility that there might be some other grounding for those opposing views, one that would render them plausible and hence formidable. Both sides, says Amy Gutmann, "express mutual disdain rather than respect for their differences. And so they create two mutually exclusive and disrespecting intellectual cultures in academic life, evincing an attitude of unwillingness to learn anything from the other or recognize any value in the other" (21). Richard Shweder sees both approaches as forms of Puritanism, a Puritan being understood as "someone who exegetes a virtue until it becomes a vice" (18). George Kennedy provides the appropriate Latin tag for this unremittingly shrill exchange (230): *"Si natura negat facit indignatio versum"* (If nature denies, indignation composes the verse: Juvenal, *Satires* 1.79).

Two different human temperaments, committed to two different ontologies—canonists of various stripes insisting on the importance of certain fundamental truths, anti-canonists insisting on the value of a plurality of contingent truths. One side tenderly enraptured by the notion of a few great sacred texts or methods to be preserved against the ravages of time as a precious resource without which we shall surely perish as a people. The other side tough-mindedly open to the incredibly diverse and divergent ways of belief and practice composing the human adventure through time, that very pluralism a precious resource without which we surely shall perish as a people. Anti-canon to left of us, canon to right of us, into what deadly valley are we riding when we try to decide how best to improve higher education?

It is as though we were once again with William James's camping party in the mountains (1907: 25). After a day of hiking and hunting, the campers gather around the fire for supper, and their casual conversation slides into an increasingly angry argument over an incident they have all witnessed. When one of them approached a squirrel, it had scrambled part way up a tree on the side farthest from the camper. Trying to get a better view of the squirrel, he starts around the tree toward the side where the animal is located, but as he does so it shifts its location so as always to be on the opposite side of the tree from him. Eventually the camper has circled the tree, returning to his original location, but without ever seeing the squirrel. So has the camper, having walked around the tree, thereby walked around the squirrel? Or since that creature has always had his belly toward the camper, should we insist that the camper has failed to walk around the squirrel? Red-faced from shouting down their colleagues, our canonists and anti-canonists seem to be engaged in a new version of this old wrangle.

The American pragmatists thought of their philosophy as a method designed for use on such occasions, evoked in such disputes as an instrument of reasonable good sense and creative imagination, one that could take the engines roaring in heated opposition and put them back into gear, that could shift the argument and so get things running smoothly once again. As James expected the camping party to get back to the useful business of chopping firewood and cooking supper once he had "assuaged the dispute" by his pragmatic observations, so the application of pragmatic thinking in reference to the canonical wars should be the means by which faculty and students on our college and university campuses, in collaboration with academic administrators, government officials, and opinion leaders throughout the nation, might be led back from endless idle arguments to their real and proper work of providing—and providing for—a properly educated citizenry.

William James proposes the measure of success or failure in this endeavor through his famous criterion for the resolution of metaphysical disagreement:

There can *be* no difference anywhere that doesn't *make* a difference elsewhere—no difference in abstract truth that doesn't express itself in a difference in concrete fact and in conduct consequent upon that fact, imposed on somebody, somehow, somewhere, and somewhen. The whole function of philosophy ought to be to find out what definite difference it will make to you and me, at definite instants of our life, if this world-formula or that world-formula be the true one. (27)

An Open-Ended Canon

Defending the old educational canon or imagining we can do without a canon, emptying it of content or multiplying it into features of a myriad historical eras, ethnic groups, or disciplinary traditions—all of these responses offer little more than recipes for disaster because they are all, in their differing ways, based on an inadequate social ontology. They are impractical ways to resolve our problems about education because they misunderstand how problems arise and why canons are both their cause and crucial to their resolution. The educational canon needs our attention because of the devastation to the foundations of our culture that has been going on these many years. Remortaring the old stone will not suffice, nor will it help to ignore the hard fact that without strong foundations there can be no cathedral of learning and hence no culture that it makes possible. Yet structural repairs to a foundation are not something readily effected. It is easy enough to accelerate the damage in an ill-considered effort to correct it.

Our society needs some broadly defined consensus regarding what is important, regarding personal virtue and practical value, the good life and the common weal. And we need citizens able to embody that consensus concretely in their daily practices, in their quality of life and their realistic expectations for the future. The function of our society's educational institutions should be to inculcate such convictions and skills in its young people and to sustain or rekindle them in its adult citizens. But the necessary condition for any intelligent use of skill in the service of value, for the application of knowledge to the resolution of individual and collective problems, or to an appropriate recognition of their insolubility, is a clear sense of the way to go about distinguishing truth from falsehood, right from wrong, meaningful order from incoherence. A capacity for sound judgment, for being able to use our cultural consensus prudently, derives from the canonical orientation that defines our culture, that delineates its integrity and character. It is by respecting, learning, and creatively utilizing the canonical conditions of our cultural life that we can make it an instrument for achieving the goods to which we aspire.

Times change, however, and they render old truths uncouth. The world of this twenty-first century—the world of the information society and the global village—has made things important that before were thought trivial. It has altered our sense of what it means to be virtuous or clever. These changes force us to revise our attitudes and habits, requiring of us skills and learning different in important ways from those required in the twentieth and the nineteenth centuries, yet also similar in important ways. So the old canonical orientation will need to change if we and our children are to achieve the capacity for sound judgment so crucial to our survival. The inadequacy of last century's intellectual canon, however, is no argument for denying that we need one or for shattering it into a thousand separate fragments. We cannot do without a common world, a basis for the common good that gives sense and lasting import to our individual strivings. We need a canon fit for our times, neither the tarnished old one repolished nor a lot of bright shiny little parochial ones. We need, rather, a thoroughly reconstructed canon, one made from the old but not reducible to it.

Paulo Freire recognizes that the Puritanical excess of those who believe in a governing intellectual canon leads them to turn the value they give to certainty and stability into a metaphysical absolute. They take past achievement as "something given and immutable," then link it to the present as a way to "domesticate the present," in the expectation that by doing so "the future will reproduce this domesticated present." However, those who find the past repulsive, along with the canons that have dominated it, because these hierarchies distort human possibility, are led with an equal Puritanical excess to take the future as "decreed beforehand." They insist that our emancipation from the errors of the past is assured because it is based on a fundamental truth about our natural equality, a sort of "inevitable fate, fortune or destiny" that it seems outrageous anyone would resist. But, says Freire, "this rightist and this leftist are both reactionary because, starting from their respectively false views of history, both develop forms of action which negate freedom" (22, 23). The dichotomy between hierarchy and equality is the product of a static absolutistic worldview. Either what is great is timelessly great or nothing is great, either previously marginalized achievements must always be included on an equal footing or they are not genuinely being included. In a dynamic world, however, there can be no always—except the always-changing character of things. Greatness is neither self-evident nor a sham: it is a crucial although perishable cultural attainment.

The intellectual canon, and consequently the basis for an educational canon, is by its very nature in dispute. The canonists and anti-canonists of various sorts all seem to think that disputes need to be settled, that there is or is not some canon, whether grounded in the past or future, whether narrowly elitist or generously inclusive, that needs once and for all to be affirmed or denied. But if hierarchies of importance, both cultural and natural, are dynamic, then they need constantly to be reformulated. If the old wine bottles are not suitable for the new wine, we still need wine bottles—a different sort of bottle, but a wine bottle nonetheless. And this need will be recurrent, for the new will slowly become the old and so also eventually will prove to be inadequate. If it is in the very nature of intellectual canons that they should be in dispute, then, although a canon will always be needed, the one we have will always be in need of reformulation.

Those historians who have investigated previous disputes over the question of an educational canon are usually aghast at the ahistorical tone of today's arguments. There are no books or authors, no methods or topics, that educators have considered essential from the first, whether this be defined as when Plato founded his Academy, when medieval scholastics organized the University of Paris, or when Puritans established Harvard College. What seems to have endured has done so only if we consider it abstractly. Plato may be one of the great souls, but for medieval students it was his *Timaeus* that was key, for their successors in the modern West it was *The Republic* and the other middle works that were crucial, and many contemporary students find Plato's importance to lie in the early dialogues with their inconclusive explorations and enigmatic dramatic settings. And, of course, even where a single book has retained its canonical importance over long periods of time, its reason for being read has changed. The stability of the hierarchy of worth is an illusion.

As Lawrence Levine puts it, educators have always been "vigorously debating the orthodoxies of prior days, or supplementing and replacing canonical texts and subjects, or altering and experimenting with curricula, or using abstruse theories and complex language, or constructing courses to accommodate the changing nature of the student body, or responding to the major social, cultural, and political forces of the day" (25). Indeed, the very notion of a course on the Great Books, to serve as the centerpiece to an arts and sciences curriculum, is "a specifically American creation," and one of comparatively recent vintage—a reaction in the period between the two world wars to "the more egregious excesses of the free-elective system" (Oakley 1992b: 286).

So we should revel in these disputes, rather than finding them an embarrassment. The notion of canonical reconstruction is an ideal worthy of our commitment because a culture depends upon its intellectual canon. The creative, critical, constructive thinking requisite for societal adaptability involves people being able to apply a repertoire of conceptual framing devices to experience. It involves them constantly modulating what is relevant in that repertoire until it can provide the standpoint needed to grasp a situation adequately, interpret it coherently, and project its consequences accurately. Thinking, in short, is not simply a matter of following the established rules, not a method of systematic analysis and synthesis governed by taken for granted categories of understanding. It also involves the use of a cultural reservoir of perspectives, aperçus, and concept patterns that those categories presuppose. By means of analogy, metaphor, and affective symbiosis, this reservoir can be used to modify traditional ways of thinking, its protean potency put to the service of reconstructing extant scientific and humanistic theories, bending them to new purposes, fashioning novel alternatives.

If this be so, then a culture's intellectual canon is the parent of effective thinking. Without the repertoire it provides, we would have no way to discern or impute meanings other than those given by external authority: by the traditional and the acceptable. We would be blinded by such a limitation, prevented from seeing the need for change and the resources by which to effect it. An education suited to a dynamic society, a society adaptively related to a dynamic world, must focus on inculcating not only a heritage of facts and methods, beliefs and practices, but also the intellectual frameworks they presuppose. The defenders of a static educational canon—whether the community it serves be an *ethnos,* a civilization, or all humanity—and the anti-canonists who find it stifling are both mistaken. In their differing ways, they both overlook the transformative power of a society's canonical materials not only to liberate the individual from unthinking custom but also to question thinking custom. The educational canon is a resource, the only resource, for reforming a culture's intellectual canon. It is both the source of a community's stability and a key destabilizing impetus.

This understanding of canons as essentially dynamic is in keeping with the ideals of a democracy. Frank Wong advocates "some standard that transcends particular cultures," but he sees it as "aspirational rather than presumptive" (70). In a democracy, ideally, the plurality of views about educational worth should not be measured against a preemptive procrustean standard of unity. But neither should the question of worth be measured by a protean standard in which nothing is judged expendable, nothing taken as worth compromising or giving up for the sake of a possibly broader or deeper unity.

"The democratic way," Steven Rockefeller argues, "means respect for and openness to all cultures," to the variety of *ethnoi* any community encompasses. But it does not give those ethnic groups "any rigid idea of, or absolute right to, cultural survival." It requires that they "abandon those intellectual and moral values that are inconsistent with the ideals of freedom, equality, and the ongoing cooperative experimental search for truth and well-being" (92). Accordingly, Francis Oakley sees the college campus as a "privileged forum" in which this democratic way of dealing with canonical differences should be modeled. The campus should be "a sort of dialectical space wherein the complex and testing issues of the day can be vigorously debated and tenaciously explored in an atmosphere distinguished above all else by its openness, its rationality, its civility, its generosity of spirit" (1992a: 165). The educational canon is a procedure and a content that sets the conditions for debate and exploration, even though these conditions are themselves among the proper subjects to be debated and explored. It is a hierarchy forever putting itself in question, so as constantly to retest its validity and so constantly to reformulate its scope and shape and integrity.

Realities and Processes

We should pause a moment to consider what might be meant by saying that the world is "dynamic." One of the key hypotheses of pragmatism is that its methods are successful because the world is amenable to them. Pragmatism's adaptive opportunism works because that's how the world works. The modalities of effective learning, the manners of genuine human development, the proper shapings of a democratic society, and the ways of biological and physical evolution: these are all dynamic processes that echo one another. The echoing should not be a surprise, however, for they are all natural processes. Although Alfred North Whitehead is usually not thought of as a pragmatist, the basic features of his interpretation of the world as we find it in experience explicate the ontology implicit in Dewey's and James's philosophies.

The title of one of Whitehead's books is *Process and Reality*. It makes a convenient bumper-sticker summation for a perspective that makes process its central category but does not then lose itself in a maelstrom of ontological fluidity. Everything, says Whitehead, is in process, either in the process of coming to be or in the process of perishing. This process is not a steady ongoing flow, however, but is rather one that moves toward closure, attains it, but then loses what it has attained and so once more must move toward closure. William James says somewhere that reality is like the flittering of a bird among the trees: it flies toward a branch, alights there and perches for a moment, then flies off to another branch. Movement and rest, rest and movement, movement and rest.

So process is fundamental, but so is reality. Processes are actualizing impulses—impulses that have products. Whatever exists does so because it was realized through a process, because it came to be this or to be that. But thises and thats are short-lived achievements, and so soon they cease to be, although each perishing then calls forth the need for a fresh becoming. Time is like Penelope working at her loom all day and then at night undoing what she has done, returning to her loom the next morning to weave her fabric anew, yet once more undoing this handiwork after the sun has set. And so on and so on, world without end.

Now add this further thought. These momentary achievements, insofar as they recur in similar fashion, give rise to enduring structures. The same thing repeated is two things but one form, by which form we identify them as expressions of the selfsame reality. The separate images received by each eye are seen because of their formal congruence as a single three-dimensional image. The movie projector turns a sequence of discrete still pictures marked by certain structural similarities into a dramatic action sequence. We sustain across a sequence of momentary deeds a single enduring character, a distinctive personality, a disposition to act or think or judge in certain ways. And by this consistent way of our being, by these recurrent forms of our varied actions, others know us, and we know ourselves, to be the same person now who yesterday did such and such.

What Robert Bellah, borrowing from Tocqueville, calls "habits of the heart" are these dispositions and attitudes that define what is important about us because they compose a pattern that recurs again and again in our actions. This pattern is essential to who we are, for without reference to it we would not adequately be described. If I habitually see issues in terms of flights and perches, if *Process and Reality* is a text I have practically memorized, then something fundamental to understanding who I am has been omitted if these habits of my head and heart are not mentioned, if it is not said up front and bold that I'm essentially a process philosopher. An essence is something achieved; it does not precede our existence. Yet it is not just a laundry list of our choices but the pattern immanent in them, a pattern that grows through use from a vague, peripheral feature of our life to a central, definable characteristic.

Groups have habits, too, patterns of behaving and believing that are reiterated from individual to individual. The folkways and mores of a community, its customs and laws, its traditions and socially available roles, its cultural treasures and communication structures, are all iterated features that characterize it. It is *this* community rather than *that* one because it manifests the patterns that it does. Its essence—its genius or spirit or character—is found in the way its people live. And the same holds also for the biological and physical orders of things: their distinctive features, articulated by us in terms of laws of nature, are the typical ways in which species evolve and chemicals interact, the habitual manner by which the atoms run.

The laws of nature, the customs of a people, the character of an individual. If these are patterns of regularity abstracted from the welter of becomings and perishings, then three things need to be said about them.

First, a pattern comes into being insofar as mere flux takes on a determinate coordination. Movements cease to be random and idiosyncratic, but are lined up in replicating ways, lured or compelled by their environment to mimic predecessors and neighbors. British colonists, frustrated by taxation policies, argue among themselves and with the king's ministers and parliament, and angrily throw bales of highly taxed tea overboard in protest; eventually they begin to focus their frustrations by proclaiming their intention to sever the bands connecting them to Britain and to institute a new and more just government; they fight skirmishes and major battles, and reorganize themselves as a confederation of states; having won the war, they seem to be losing the peace, and so decide to craft a more perfect union; they ratify a federal constitution, elect a president and congress, and begin to function as citizens in a United States of America.

Second, this coordinate accomplishment is a pattern that can be expressed without reference to the actualities upon which it rests. It is a structure of relationships more stable than its relata, and it serves to explain them, perhaps to predict them, to make sense of them. Americans are born and grow up, become eligible to vote, and eventually die; they vote or fail to vote for the nominated candidates; the politicians win high office, are defeated in the next election, or retire after long years in power. The voters and politicians come and go, but these election procedures change only occasionally, usually at regional levels in response to specific abuses, and the constitutional rules for elections change hardly at all. And so throughout its history, America has remained the republic its founders created. Hence, general patterns are the meanings of particular things, the source of their importance, of their place and role and destiny within the ongoing course of time.

And third, patterns perish when the habitual behaviors of the actualities manifesting them destabilize, become erratic, break down. A specific order of things, a pattern dominating an environment, has achieved its stable structure by dealing with incompatibilities in some effective way. It might have eliminated certain contentious elements, or subordinated them, or interpreted them under one aspect rather than another. Determinate order is the result of selectivity, and so the price paid for order is that some things must be excluded or taken as peripheral. What is ignored is nonetheless still there, haunting the order that has consigned it to irrelevance. Under new conditions, however, what was excluded might turn out to be more aptly included instead, what was trivialized might now need emphasis. The Constitution of the American republic legitimates slavery in those of its states that decide to countenance it, but disputes arise concerning the federal government's authority to ban the extension of slavery in all newly admitted states; a civil war is fought over the right of states to reject such exercises of federal authority and withdraw from the union; in the course of that war, the emancipation of slaves in the slave states becomes a practical opportunity and then a reality first by presidential proclamation and then by constitutional amendment; henceforth people of any race are included among the nation's citizens, the republic proclaimed as having really originated in support of liberty and justice for all. So the established order adjusts, adapting itself to the requirements of the changing times. Or it might continue to ignore what cannot be ignored, but in doing so it will stultify, begin to falter, and eventually collapse under the weight of its own irrelevance.

In *The Function of Reason,* Whitehead captures this dynamic by making a distinction between practical and speculative reason. Practical activities are those we engage in when struggling to create and sustain patterns of order. For, as we have already argued, it is by means of stable structures that we understand our selves and our world, control things to serve our purposes, and discern what purposes are worth being served. But the success of every practice lies in its selective focusing power, and it is therefore vulnerable to what it has ignored. So the achievements of practical reason—a lifestyle, a methodology, an established way of doing things, a mythology of aspirations, a cultural form of life, a scientific worldview and the technologies it supports—need constantly to be critiqued. We need to confront our practical achievements with alternative orderings, with what from our current perspective seems unimportant, fantastical, or simply false. This invention of alternatives, says Whitehead, is the work of speculative reason, which is any activity we engage in that seeks to be original and comprehensive even at the expense of practicality. Speculation, by being unsystematic and untested, is in its turn vulnerable, however, for when we are being imaginative and experimental we often blur the difference between appearance and reality, the important and the trivial, relevance and irrelevance.

Whitehead recommends a mix. Practical reason can be saved from narrowness, rigidity, blindness to changing realities, by the broadening vision of the speculative. The effort after synoptic vision and unexpected relationships can be saved from silliness, flaccidity, a shallow disregard of stubborn fact, by the methodical realism of practical concerns. Either by itself, Whitehead says, leads to a loss of viable order: speculation by its lack of interest in what will work, practicality by its indifference toward what isn't required by what now works. Collaborating, however, and correcting the other's vulnerabilities, they comprise a way by which our ways of living can be both sustained and improved.

Because anything must be made in order to be, we humans in our own makings need the practical skills by which to organize available resources into concrete achievement. Because anything made is vulnerable, soon suffering its inadequacies, we humans need the speculative skills by which to imagine alternative achievements and ways of attaining them in order to turn the loss of what we had made into a new making. We need to learn how to perch and how to fly, how to create a sustainable world and then as it becomes unsustainable how to recreate it. We need to acquire the canonical tools for each—a canon of content and method that is adequate to the needs of the day and, so that it can be adequate to the next day's needs, a canon that is also self-transcending.

The Human Serpent

Every philosophy that talks about fixed essences, that claims there are objective truths about timeless realities, argues that the task of education is to be sure that students learn those truths and live in accord with them. It says that we possess knowledge about something if we have a mental picture of it, a conceptual replica of its essential features. We act rightly if what we do replicates in the specifics of our context the essential features of a good person.

We are educated if our thoughts and our behaviors mirror—are in harmony with—the physical and moral laws of nature. This interpretation of what is true or right in terms of adequation to a timeless standard has been described in the chapters on foundational and procedural understandings of a canon. As we saw, the anti-canonists replace these standards with an egalitarian standard, insisting that the absence of objective hierarchies is objective truth. Thus, canonists and anti-canonists alike embrace what William James calls the "copy theory" of truth and goodness. They differ only with respect to what they propose should be copied: a world governed by a universal and necessary hierarchy, or one on its way toward the actualization of such a hierarchy, or a world composed of a plurality of necessarily local hierarchies, or one universally and necessarily nonhierarchical.

The pragmatic critique of all such copy theories is twofold. First, there is no apparent reason for wanting to create a mental copy of an antecedent physical or moral reality. James likens wanting to do so to the Irishman being carried to a banquet in a bottomless sedan chair—were it not for the honor, he might just as well have walked. Whether or not anyone copies reality would seem to make no real difference (105). The world remains the same either way, and so do we. Second, reality can never simply be copied anyway. "The trail of the human serpent is ... over everything" (33). Elements of human perspective, concern, and interest are inextricably mixed with the elements of reality. "Does a man walk with his right leg or with his left leg more essentially?" James asks. "Just as impossible may it be to separate the real from the human factors in the growth of our cognitive experience" (113).

James readily meets the conditions for being a metaphysical realist, for insisting with the canonists that the truth of our interpretations is measured against something other than our desires. But he agrees with the anti-canonists in arguing that we know these measures and what they interpret only in our making them. "Reality" is composed of what we experience and of our ideas: the facts our sensations disclose and the abstract patterns by which we think. The human factor has to do with fitting the two together, making judgments about which abstract patterns obtain among the sensations, subsuming facts under theories. A workable fit is not easily achieved. The fitting must conform to the necessities of what is given, to both the brute obduracy of the sensations and the logical demand for coherence and consistency inherent in the patterns of relationship by which they are ordered. "Between the coercions of the sensible order and those of the ideal order, our mind is thus wedged tightly. Our ideas must agree with realities, be such realities concrete or abstract, be they facts or be they principles, under penalty of endless inconsistency and frustration" (96).

No matter how tightly we may be wedged, however, there is still wiggle room. If it is misleading to say, as F. C. S. Schiller did, that reality is indeterminately "plastic" to whatever fittings of its elements we might choose to make, we nonetheless still make additions to suit our purposes, and reality quite often "tolerates" the additions. Reality is like a client who has given his case to a lawyer and then must listen passively "to whatever account of his affairs, pleasant or unpleasant, the lawyer finds it most expedient to give" (111). The lawyer's case is constrained by the need to be adequate to the facts, but the constraint is only partial; he still has to argue the case and quite a bit rides on whether he does so effectively. "We receive ... the block of marble, but we carve the statue ourselves" (112).

James calls these fittings "perspectives" or "hypotheses," sometimes "frameworks" or "editions of the world." He complains that the copy theory of truth presupposes an absolutist perspective, an *édition de luxe* above and beyond all finite, fallible editions (116). It can do so only by neglecting the human factor, the presence of which necessarily relativizes all perspectives into working hypotheses, necessarily turns the claim about an absolute version of the world into one among the many fallible claims about the world proposed by fallible human beings. Truth is always a framed work, and all frameworks are temporary expedients.

Canons, taken in this Jamesian sense, are thus framing devices. In Erving Goffman's phraseology, they are "schemata of interpretation" (21), "principles of organization which govern events ... and our subjective involvement in them" (10). A "primary framework" is one "seen as rendering what would otherwise be a meaningless aspect of the scene into something that is meaningful" (21), and the frame for all such primary frameworks, the understandings shared by a group regarding interpretive schemata, their interrelationships, and "the sum total of forces and agents that these [schemata] acknowledge to be loose in the world," constitutes that group's "belief system" or "cosmology" (27).

What Goffman call a "natural canon," such as a scientific theory, frames the "unguided events" of inanimate nature, and the canon for such canons sets the boundary conditions for scientific inquiry in general, the conditions for what count as empirically verifiable facts or rationally intelligible concepts. A "social canon" differs from a natural one in that its framing also includes "guided doings," events that involve human agency. A social canon provides for the "serial management of consequentiality" by intentional agents (22). An intellectual canon, even when it is about elements comprised by the natural canon, is a framework of this latter social sort. Its function is to make sense of human interactions, to advise us regarding how properly to act with respect to any situation framed by that canon and how by such a framing to understand properly our own and others' actions.

In saying that a knowledge of certain facts, concepts, or methods, of certain books and certain authors, is indispensable to an educated citizenry, advocates of an educational canon offer to provide us with a guidebook for living effectively within the culture that defines what it means for us to be citizens. The educational canon teaches us what to feel, what to think, and what to do. It teaches us how; it teaches us why. It instructs us in what it means to be a human being dwelling, interacting, living and dying, within the horizons of time and space that encompass us. A culture's educational canon is an orientation program for membership in its community. Without it, we would be left to founder in a sea of confusion—our emotions alienating, our thoughts unintelligible, our actions strange.

Plato is one of the great souls. One or more of his dialogues is typically high on the list of any traditional educational canon for American undergraduates to ingest. *The Republic,* for instance, provides an aesthetic standard for us to emulate. It is a well-crafted work of art, well worth studying for the formalistic criteria it suggests for identifying and evaluating dramatic structure, literary composition, conceptual coherence, and affective import. We learn from a close reading of the text about the formal conditions for aesthetic enjoyment and symbolic significance.

The Republic also offers a moral standard. Its subject matter explores the question of justice as it relates to persons, communities, and the whole of the cosmos. It offers positive and negative role models for this virtue through its portraits of Socrates, Thrasymachus, and their friends, and in the action of the dialogue it offers exemplary insight into how such virtue might be best acquired by an individual or a state. By attending carefully to what Plato has to say, we learn about the conditions for right understanding, action, and sensibility.

In addition, Plato's dialogue proposes an epistemic standard, a method for acquiring knowledge. It formulates a theory of levels of comprehension, from the play of perceptual images, memories, and fancies, through the practical know-how of our everyday purposes and the general principles by which these flickering purposes are organized, to the timeless values that indicate and judge their significance. There is also an account of the ways a person or a state can progressively improve what it knows, what ends it seeks, and how best to pursue these things. Furthermore, the dialogue sketches an educational curriculum for making it possible for young people to undertake this progressive improvement, and offers a theory of human differences that tailors their progress to their capacities. We learn from *The Republic* a model for attaining truth, and find how closely truth is linked to morality and aesthetics.

Plato's dialogue also teaches a critical standard. It invites extrapolation of its exemplary ideas, agents, and procedures. It lures readers into applying its aesthetic, moral, and epistemic standards to other situations, to step out by metaphor, analogy, or generalization beyond the dialogue's parochial limitations in order to bring its truths to bear upon matters of current relevance, and so perhaps to find that those matters are actually instances of endlessly recurrent concerns. Plato even offers the tools for criticizing his claims about these standards, by presenting issues through a dialogue rather than didactically, exhibiting the importance of questioning and answering, of the ways in which disagreement can lead to insights that would likely not be available to a solitary thinker.

As this example suggests, the materials composing an educational canon should teach three things about the culture for which they are canonical: the basic or characteristic elements of its content, the best methods for validating and expanding that content, and resources for critiquing and reforming both content and methods. This third function is crucial, for it is why cultures are able to endure, simultaneously adapting to changing conditions and changing those conditions. The canonical standards of any group are ideals against which what has actually gone on can be measured. The possibilities for change—for improvement, retrenchment, reform, revival, even radical transformation—are an implicit aspect of any given situation. A culture's canon offers possibilities for devising an alternative to what it has accomplished, interpretive tools for refashioning the stable world it once fashioned. The canon is always pointing us beyond the imagined to the unimaginable, beyond truths we clearly know to mysteries that might harbor a more adequate truth, beyond the comfortable goods we find fulfilling to a better possibility we find unsettling because attainable.

James says that extrapolation of this sort is the way that new cosmologies, new cultural worldviews, arise. It must therefore be the way old ones arose as well. "Our fundamental ways of thinking about things are discoveries of exceedingly remote ancestors, which have been able to preserve themselves throughout the experience of all subsequent time" (79). A certain way of framing a situation provided people with useful guidance on some occasion long, long ago. That idea or affective mood or procedure was subsequently brought to bear upon another situation, and here also it led its utilizer prosperously. Many such ways were similarly invented and, proving useful, were repeated. Some turned out to be only of limited value, their usefulness short-lived or restricted to narrow or trivial situations. Those ways that continued to be useful—that were valuable in contexts that never seemed to change, but that could also be put to new uses in new contexts—eventually became canonical. They became rules of thumb for dealing successfully with certain kinds of situations, or rules for determining the kind of situation a given situation is in order to know what rules of thumb are relevant.

Intellectual canons of this sort eventuate in learned habits, in accustomed practices of such long-standing and unquestioned relevance that they seem natural rather than acquired. The cosmology of a people, its common sense, is thus foundational for it, the solid ground upon which its meanings, its presumptions about reality and its sense of purpose, rest. Yet there is nothing timeless about this cosmology—precisely the opposite. The frameworks fundamental to a culture have survived the test of time by retaining their relevance. They were worked out by people "whose names the night of antiquity has covered up," says James. They were kept for reuse, whereas other framing devices were cast aside, because "verified by the immediate facts of experience which they first fitted," and then treasured by successors for these same utilitarian reasons. And so "from fact to fact and from man to man they may have *spread,* until all language rested on them and we are now incapable of thinking naturally in any other terms" (83).

Flights and perches. A culture survives when its canonical standards are able to guide it along a flight path of change, winging it away from where disruptive forces have unloosed it from its accustomed branch and bringing it to a new stability where it can once again safely roost. The disruptions are inevitable; no perch is more than momentarily secure. So if the culture has no guidance, if it fails to recognize its problem, fails to interpret the signs of its disintegration, or if it has no sense of the alternatives whereby it might reintegrate, nor any clue as to how to make the transition to one of those alternatives, it will not survive. The world is a dynamic place. Only dynamic cultures can succeed in such an environment, and only cultures with self-transcending canons can function dynamically. Those always in flight will too soon grow weary; those always clinging to some perch will too soon find themselves without support. Those cultures that endure encompass, on the one hand, processes that are trajectories from perishing realities to their new-made successors and, on the other hand, realities that are emergent reformulations of their predecessors and relevant resources for their successors.

Chapter 7

Canonical Dialectics

Masters and Apprentices

The purpose of a canon for education is that it be able to define what must be done in order for a society to teach its members the cultural cosmology that frames it and makes it work. When a society is functioning properly, commonsense beliefs are taught in family and peer group interactions, imbibed in the language and attitudes of the people, in the taken-for-granted everyday assumptions of their social intercourse. Schooling serves to make commonsense explicit where this is thought necessary, but also to correct commonsense with respect to the technical beliefs and institutional practices that constitute the community's reigning scientific, moral, and legal systems. From cradle to grave, cultural guidance must be endlessly inculcated and reenforced if a society is to survive. Its principles of order, the foundations for its reality, are solely cultural.

The necessity for such a canon, however, does not entail that its rules simply be copied, that the world it frames be mirrored accurately and fully in the beliefs and practices of each citizen. To claim so is to presume regarding acculturation precisely the same absolutistic perspective James warns us against regarding objective truth. It is to embrace the claim that there is no human factor in what needs to be mirrored, or rather that the presence of any such human factor distorts reality and so should as far as possible be transcended.

There is a half-truth to this demand for slavish imitation, this insistence on the direct *mimesis* of cultural norms. Novices to a group are well advised to begin by attempting to emulate its veteran practitioners—to learn its ways, its affective, effective, and cognitive dimensions, from the inside, empathically. This copycat strategy is what apprenticeship is all about, and in modern

Western nations formal schooling is the standard way by which young people are apprenticed in the skills of citizenship required of adults. We learn to think well by thinking about an issue while utilizing the concepts a great thinker once fashioned when struggling with some similar issue. Education in this sense is akin to learning how to make good cabinets by utilizing the techniques and tools a master craftsman has used, by copying one of the master's cabinets as exactly as possible.

But these are training wheels. When a cabinetmaker's apprentice thinks she is ready to be a master, she must demonstrate her readiness by making her own master piece. She must cease replicating what her teacher does and make instead a cabinet of her own design and workmanship. Whatever the value of imitation, mature accomplishment means moving beyond our mentors, developing our own voice, a personal style, a distinctive mode of operation. The aim of education is to outgrow the need for training wheels, to gain the maturity needed to pedal on our own. We yearn to write books and not just read them, to become leaders rather than memorizing tips on leadership, to actually love and work and even suffer rather than to do so only vicariously. Without instructors to mimic faithfully and prefashioned tools to utilize properly, we would never be able to function on our own. But when that time comes, the old slavishness is put away and a new distinctive version of the old becomes at last a viable reality.

Charles Altieri calls this process "self-subsumption": "a process of projecting images of the self and then adapting one's behavior to them." An intellectual canon is "curatorial" in the sense that it provides us with a "rich, complex, contrastive" reservoir of "frameworks, which create a cultural grammar for interpreting experience" (51). A linguistic grammar is a canonical imposition, but one that is liberating rather than stultifying. It separates the patterns of sounds we can make into those that are able to convey meaning and those that do not, thereby freeing us to articulate whatever meanings we might wish or, if we choose, merely to babble nonsense. By analogy, an intellectual canon is a grammar for interpreting experience, a set of guidelines for making sense of our lives.

The novelist Christa Wolf agrees: "Mere life—life undescribed, untransmitted, uninterpreted, uncontemplated—cannot come to terms with itself directly" (23). We learn the grammar for describing and interpreting our lives by acquiring a collection of "medallions," little scenarios that show us how to find meaning in our experiences. Fairy tales, for instance, offer young people such a grammar. A child can apprentice herself to Cinderella: she will see her world as marked by a struggle between good and evil, and she can find in Cinderella's triumph over her wicked stepmother the confidence to believe that if she is good she too can prevail against the world's temptations.

Pulp fiction, popular magazine stories, hagiographies, and television soap operas also all provide such medallions. But these merely reenforce current cultural stereotypes: the forms for emulation they offer are cliched and superficial. Wolf protests against both the totalitarianism of the communist East German regime under which she once lived and the consumerist conformities of Western Europe and the United States under which she now lives because they encourage such medallions. She argues for the importance of a special sort of medallion, the kind provided by great literature, by that genuine sort of fiction she calls simply "prose." Prose functions canonically. It articulates a grammar of self-interpretation that allows us to "tackle a new reality in a new way" (35). It does not mirror things as they are, but fashions from old realities and vivid imagination a unique world for the reader to explore, a world in which she can find fresh possibilities for who she might be, for ways by which she might extend the story of who she has been in a more meaningful direction. Genuine prose is a grammar that gives people a future, that invites them to undertake the "daring and hazardous expedition" of creating their own personal identity (40).

Altieri captures this distinction between mere fiction and prose in his second function of an intellectual canon. It is not only curatorial but also "normative": it provides not only a repertoire of useful exemplary frameworks for interpreting our lives but also "modes of wisdom," models of ways in which ideals could guide us in deciding "what we can make of ourselves" (51). We need to learn that we need ideals for how we might live, in order with their help to break out of the "narcissistic circle" (53) in which everyone emulates everyone else. We need to realize how important it is for us to find in our past heritage a way by which "to gain distance from our ideological commitments" (44), to hold off the embrace of present conformities so that we might glimpse new possibilities for realization. An educational canon, celebrated as culturally normative and so thought to comprise the essential core of what an arts and sciences curriculum should teach, plays the role of "institutionalizing idealization" (52): it is "an institutionalized form for exposing people to a range of idealized attitudes" (46).

Altieri identifies three criteria that a book or work or art needs to meet in order to be canonical in a normative and not just a curatorial sense. First, it must not only provide model ways of interpreting human experience but also show itself self-referentially as being capable of that modeling. Second, it must represent fully and powerfully the models it exhibits. And, third, the ideals to which its models point must clarify and cultivate those powers of action found in beauty, truth, and goodness. A work that meets these criteria—a whole "theatre" of such works richly different and mutually contentious—is a key cultural instrument for "capacitating autonomous individuals" (60).

The wisdom of the traditionalists lies in realizing the heuristic necessity for interpretive frameworks and the prudential value in having canonical ones. A Great Books or Great Ways core course requirement presumes the importance of selective valuation. It frames for students the need for frames, reminds them of the silliness in reinventing wheels, shows them the further sights to be seen by learning how to stand on another's shoulders. Our concern may be with axles instead of the wheels that were our mentors' concern, and our seeing may turn in another direction than was intended when they invited us to use their shoulders for our vantage point. But without the wheel we would never have thought of linking them in pairs, and without our predecessors' invitation we would not have thought a further seeing possible, perhaps not even conceived of it. We outgrow the truths of our cultural heritage only by first growing into them.

So we definitely need durable resources, canons composed of works each of which has, as Eva Brann told us, "infinitely rich interpretability" (1999: 104), each of which is what Italo Calvino called a classic, "a book that has never finished saying what it has to say" (128). But "infinite" and "never" are hyperboles. What is durable is not eternal. Over the decades and the centuries, its riches of interpretability are eventually spent and what it has to say does in fact reach its end. Although any master's piece may not survive, her many apprentices, whose work has earned them a mastership as well, are ready and eager to take up what their master has laid down. Traditions are canonical powers for making and sustaining cultural values because they are self-transforming.

Strangers and Rebels

No item in a canon, however, was ever created to be a norm for others to emulate. The problems any particular idea is fashioned to address, the reasons a specific book is written, an experiment conducted, a policy approved, is always thoroughly situational. There is therefore something too self-conscious, too mannered, too artificial in a work that is undertaken with one eye on its likely place in history. Its author is all too likely to modulate purposefully her distinctive voice in order to blend in better with the voices of her heritage. Yet by doing so she sacrifices her own mastery, settles for being nothing more than a permanent apprentice of the cultural norms. Such an author's work has lost what she sought to gain by her very attempt to gain it.

Concretely, amid the rough and tumble of the real world, there are no canonical happenings, no higher truths or normative ideas, except those that are self-proclaimed. Genuinely canonical achievements thrive best in the murk of an ancestral past, and stand in stark contrast to contemporary candidates for the canon, which are always notoriously suspect when paraded in the bright light of peer criticism. No one can agree who the greatest thinkers or artists or leaders of the present generation are. No new idea strikes us as equal in stature to the great, world-shaking concepts of former times. The problem, however, is not that we are too hidebound to appreciate the value of new things; nor is it that familiarity breeds contempt. Our difficulty in discerning the worth of recent achievements is that up close, our perspective limited to the immediate, the seemingly timeless truths and universal norms that compose the frame for our value judgments disappear. We bring norms to the present; we do not find them there.

This is the wisdom of the anti-canonists: that there is no natural hierarchy to things, that people, deeds, and ideas are all born equal. Each concrete thing is just what it is. What it is, to be sure, is not something atomistic, self-enclosed. Anything is related to other things in complex, intertwining ways, but no thing is reducible to its relationships, nor adequately defined by them. Each is a distinctive integration of its relations and relata, a one-time-only this-not-those accomplishment. The equality among all these particular achievements should be celebrated, each of them recognized for its uniqueness, its special voice adding a new melodic line to the ongoing and unending chorale of the world.

To see Plato through fourth-century B.C.E. Athenian eyes as just another young aristocrat, his dialogues a way to attract a following by which to further his own political agenda or feather his nest financially, is to strip away the later accretions of canonicity and to see him for what he was rather than for what the Western world has made of him. This Plato is best understood by studying other young Athenian aristocrats, by piecing together information about highborn men and women of that time, by investigating the character of slavery, the status of foreigners, the dynamics of commerce, war, and demographics in the Hellenic period. There is an egalitarian and pluralistic bias to such inquiry because what makes a given voice distinctive is best shown through comparison with other voices, including those that share with it all but its most subtle aspects.

The value of this approach to pedagogy is obvious. It strips away our blinders, pulls down the idols of the tribe, debunks the status of the proud and powerful, desanctifies the saints and desecrates the holy places. As the blinding sunlight of their glory fades, the gathering dusk reveals a hundred thousand points of lesser light, each with a glory of its own. Ideas, authors, methods, books that the canon has neglected or vilified come into view in this way. Each has its proper framing concepts to offer, its perspective, its cosmology. Each models its own version of a grammar for interpreting experience. Each struts and frets its fifteen minutes on the stage of Altieri's theatre of ideals. They are no longer lunar frameworks, valued only as reflections, supplementary or distortive, of a greater canonical light. They shine by their own glory now, in contrast or complement to other accomplishments.

Hence, Shakespeare's sister, writing in a world where gender did not debilitate, would have written plays the equal of her brother's plays (Woolf), and Vermeer's daughter, had her father responded to her pleas to be taught his craft, would have made paintings as profound as his (Vreeland). The Harlequin romances are the equal of Faulkner's fiction as expressions of American culture. The critique by a young freshman in the back row of Jean Carr's class can hold its own against the critiques of Michel Foucault or Richard Rorty, for the one no less than the others provides a fresh reading of the text. America is a congeries of ethnicity, and each deserves its equal due in any educational curriculum devoted to transmitting our nation's heritage to a younger generation.

Anti-canonists argue that affirming an intellectual canon is like deciding to play a game together. A canon, like any moral or political system, is governed by a set of rules two or more people agree upon as the frame within which to carry on their social intercourse. These language games, as Lyotard told us to call them, go on for as long as those who invent them wish to keep their relationship in play. Each story that traces the history of one of these associations exhibits values important to that story: originating moments, nodal turning points, major crises, plans and dreams, heroes and villains, saints and sinners. So the little narratives generate little hierarchies of significance. They frame a grammar nesting a clutch of medallions, just as the master narratives do. But their reach is limited and their power noncoercive. A language game stops when those who have devised it decide to go their separate ways. The canon they made of their commonality is thereby unmade, dispersed in order to make way for some new game with its novel canon.

If intellectual canons are merely the foundations for brief compacts of association, however, our focus will eventually shift from a celebration of their various uniquenesses to the difficult question of how such canons are sustained and how they interact. If there are no natural frames, if each group is created by virtue of the willful framings its members have agreed on in order to integrate the elements of their differing experiences, it is not clear what happens when conflicts arise. Does a group have any right to prevent some of its members from seceding whenever they wish? If two groups have agreed to cooperate, can either abrogate that pact at will? It would seem some sort of encompassing frame needs to be fashioned, a canonical set of rules governing how the canonical rules of groups should be made, a language game about how language games are to be played, a canon for the mediation of conflicting canons. But there is no such supergame, objective and ready at hand, on which we can rely if precisely what has been denied is the legitimacy of anything more general than the particular language games.

Under these anarchical conditions, a group need not be limited to securing or retaining its members by their consent. There are no grounds for objecting were a framework, and hence a canon, simply imposed by force—perhaps the force of an argument, which presumes there are reasons that are not functions of an individual's preferences or a group's history; perhaps the force of rhetorical persuasion, which includes propaganda, intimidation, brainwashing, and the like; perhaps the force of military armament. These nonconsensual methods of group formation and interaction are canons of integration that present themselves, whether we like it or not, as organizing principles available for other groups to use for whatever self-serving or self-aggrandizing purposes they might choose. Just because our group values parliamentary debate and majority votes as the way to settle disputes does not mean another group need respect those values, neither for how its internal differences are resolved nor for how it should comport itself toward us. The Cherokee may have been one of the "civilized tribes," but if a value is applicable only to the group that makes it a value, then they had no grounds for complaining that their forced resettlement in the Oklahoma territory was uncivilized; the Trail of Tears violated no Jacksonian canon. But surely these are unnerving and unacceptable conclusions. To avoid them, education in an anti-canonical or ethnically canonical mode must do more than celebrate difference. It must come to terms with its inability to restrain the necessarily hegemonic consequences that result from delegitimizing all trans-group hegemonies.

William James was always willing to agree with the tough-minded egalitarians and relativists among his critics that "the world we live in exists diffused and distributed, in the form of an indefinitely numerous lot of *eaches,* coherent in all sorts of ways and degrees" (118). But he also saw the need to bring those diffused little collections of eaches together into larger unities. His name for the ideal of increasing the number and scope of such unities was "meliorism," an ideal the realization of which is neither necessary nor impossible—hence one inviting our commitment and courage on its behalf.

The unities James sought were physical as well as conceptual, interpretive frameworks for organizing experience that would work precisely because reality was suited to accept those framings:

Our acts, our turning-places, where we seem to ourselves to make ourselves and grow ... [:] Why may they not be the actual turning-places and growing places which they seem to be, of the world—why not the workshop of being, where we catch fact in the making, so that nowhere may the world grow in any other kind of way than this? (129)

James argues that the existing unities important for us, both physical and cultural, are not preestablished timeless conditions. They are achievements, harmonies wrested from previous collocations of lesser groupings. Therefore, notions of yet other more encompassing unities are viable ideals for realization, future possibilities to be achieved or not depending on opportunity, creative skill, and persistence. James presumes the greater value of the wider harmonies: order is an improvement over chaos, peace a better social arrangement than war, cooperation a greater good than isolation. But they are ideals not actualities, standards by which to measure our limited frameworks and to suggest how they might be improved, lures and goads for meliorating the conditions and hence the quality of our lives.

The anti-canonists are correct to point out the ways in which a hegemonic framing marginalizes a considerable number of people, ideas, and practices to the benefit of a comparative few. It is important for us to go back constantly to the basics, to the raw truth of things, and through a close reading of the original realities to recover or gain a genuine appreciation of those things in all their uniqueness. But it is naive to imagine that we can dwell forever in a world that is no more than a random pile of parochial "eaches." Sophistication comes as we learn the hegemonic skills by which communities are build up—by which one and one become a pair, pairs become families, families are gathered into a gens, the gentes become a state, the states form a united nations of the Earth, and (dare we even dream it?) the planets are linked in a galactic federation.

This creating of wider and deeper unities need not be an imperial effort. Language games can be fashioned, as Lyotard wants them to be, through mutual give and take rather than by fiat. But if this is so for the little narratives it is just as much so for the master narratives: they too can be woven rather than imposed. Power can be an agent of empowerment, and self-interest need not be merely self-serving. An educational program aiming to nurture citizens of the sort Martha Nussbaum envisions, citizens who can function justly within the mosaic of American culture and within the world's multicultural pluralism, should teach students the dynamics of various hegemonic orders, the reasons for their emergence, the conditions of their continuance, the factors that lead to their decline and fall. There is abundant learning here, ample for helping young people see both the value and the vice of intellectual canons, their intertwined necessity and risk.

Paula Rothenberg captures the practicalities of this dialectic between an established canon and its challengers in her distinction between the "oppositional" and "empathetic" approaches to the study of difference. She thinks it quite appropriate for a course on "Race, Class, and Gender" to be confrontational. Nonminority students, "smug in their own sense of superiority," need to have the framework justifying that attitude deconstructed. What they have been taking as acceptable modes of human interaction need to be reinterpreted as "various forms of oppression," as rationalizations for "the domination of some and the subordination of others" (195–97). Without this sort of a critique, a course on cultural diversity—either a multicultural approach to American culture or one dealing with the world's varied cultures—will more than likely "teach about difference within a context that defines what is different as inherently inferior" (296).

Once the smugness has been wiped off their faces, however, once these latterday Menos have felt the humbling Socratic sting of a critique that makes them painfully aware of their prejudices, students should be ready to approach cultural differences neutrally. Both the judgment that American ways are superior to other cultural ways, and the counterjudgment that they are blighted and perverse, should now be set aside. Value judgments of any sort should be deferred, put out of gear, "until we have engaged with the [different] culture on its own terms," asking not whether a particular practice is good or bad but how it developed, what needs it serves, whose interests it promotes. This shift into judgmental neutral teaches "appreciation, respect, and critical awareness rather than contempt" (297). The deconstruction of our taken-for-granted value judgments, judgments we thought natural and hence transcultural, opens us to the possibility of appreciating the intrinsic value of cultural frameworks for interpreting experience that are other than our own, prizing them merely for their difference, for the effective varied worlds their internal coherences afford.

However, Rothenberg does not leave us in that relativist mode. The horizon of our experience thus pushed out, deparochialized beyond our imagining, we are ready to put our capacity for making value judgments back in gear. The varied cultures we have come to appreciate for what they are can now be appreciated for their usefulness, as aids for improving the character, scope, and intensity of our own cultural hierarchies of value. We can use "the wisdom and culture of previously marginalized people to transform history and knowledge for us all" (295; see also Banks 25). The point of studying cultural difference is not simply to expose our shortcomings, nor merely to celebrate the richness of the grammars of interpretation humans have crafted for themselves. Both have their own intrinsic pedagogical value as learning experiences, but they need to be cashed in as preparations for transforming how our students frame their lives. They need to become a part of the meliorative process by which American culture can achieve that greater sort of unity captured by the ideal of a multicultural culture, by which we can fashion a master narrative of the diverse narratives its citizens are able to contribute, without losing the distinctive textures and flavors of those narratives. Our ideal should be to create what James envisions by his metaphor of a stew: something that is tasty and nourishing because of the way in which its variety cooperates to produce a result greater than the sum of its constituent elements.

This way of framing the aims of education would provide students with an appreciation for the historical process, discussed in the previous chapter, by which particular perspectives, working hypotheses, and dumb guesses manage to be prized for more than their momentary usefulness, how they come into general use, are embedded in habits and commonsense, generalized into legal conventions and scientific theories, questioned for their inadequacies, and then reformed or cast aside. A justified pragmatically rooted philosophical appreciation of intellectual canons can be taught through a pedagogical strategy that begins with the *mimesis* of established canons of greatness and that when this foundation is solidly established encourages the critique of those canons—a pedagogical strategy that calls into question the claim of any canon to be among the natural given furnishings of the immediately real, in order to rediscover it as one of the inherited cultural accretions by which we transform the immediately real into a world of enduring meanings and human significance.

Curricular Rhythms

Those responsible for an academic discipline need to organize their subject matter so that there is some operative principle of selection they can use to determine what is important to teach in a single course and in a full major program of study. As more and more things pile up that should be studied, as more ways are developed to study them, as even what count as these "things" and "ways" increases, the experts need a way to winnow the embarrassment of riches. This culling cannot reasonably be done by sorting through the pile of what should be learned and arbitrarily saying yes or no first to this and then to that. Attending only to the particulars will not do. Disciplines can only accomplish their winnowing adequately by means of theoretical constructions: the introduction of some categorical structures, an interpretive paradigm, an appropriate method. Think of the impact the categories of comparative phenomenology made on what religious studies should encompass, the impact of the plate-tectonics paradigm on how geology is taught, the impact of the thick description method on the appropriate data for anthropology.

Disciplines change as new information and ideas call old interpretative frameworks into question, but they also change under the impact of changes in other disciplines. The invention of calculus made Newtonian physics possible, Darwin's biological paradigms spilled over into the social sciences, deconstruction was born as a philosophy but became important as a theory of literary criticism. Just as a specific course content needs to change under the impact of general changes in the discipline, so the disciplines need to change as they suffer the impact of other perspectives. Sometimes these are competing perspectives on the same subject, as when historians and sociologists both concern themselves with popular culture. Sometimes the relationship is an imaginative leap, applying what was designed for one specific use to a quite different area, as when theories about the stages of individual cognitive development are applied to civilizations or when literary hermeneutics takes the physical world as a text.

These borrowings and cross-fertilizings lead to synoptic integrations, to disciplines that pull together the work of other disciplines and fashion distinctively new approaches. Biochemistry, women's studies, and semiotics are recently emerged disciplines; so, not all that long ago, were geology, psychology, and art history. Thus, principles of organization that transcend the disciplines are also needed, ones that address the question of which disciplines are important and which derivative, that ask about the relation of specific subject matters to the more general subjects of nature, society, and self, and to those broadest of human concerns: the meaning of life, the origin of the universe, the ideal community.

Students need opportunities to confront the great issues, to muck around in them, to sink knee deep in vague generalities and felt importances. Something with definable shape eventually should be made of this wallowing, however. Students must acquire the potter's skills, learning after considerable and diligent practice how to purify the muck into a workable clay and then throw it into forms that have beauty and utility. The techniques for fashioning viable results make one forgetful of the reasons for doing so, however, and hence students should also learn how to bring their expertise back into relationship with those broader concerns from which it arose, those having to do with what is great and general and important.

Students, in other words, need to experience the pattern of learning Whitehead proposed in "The Rhythm of Education": a journey from "romance" through "precision" to "generalization." They need broad liberal arts courses before they decide upon their majors, lest they have no sense of what it is about the world that would lead people to want to organize it in the manner that the majors insist on. And students need to test the assumptions, applicability, and worth of their majors by bringing them into alliance with other academic and nonacademic ways of making sense of things. This last step, Whitehead's generalization phase, is when the shift from apprenticeship to mastery occurs—when fresh perspectives and novel integrations are imagined and tested, when the springtime seeds are sown that may some autumn permit a harvest of adaptive practices, a harvest of the innovation a society needs in order to cope successfully with the many wintry challenges to its viability. Students who have grown from excited romantics into experts in the conceptual and methodological precision of a craft or profession, and then have gone on to become masters in creative generalization, will be those citizens ready and able to help fashion the new grammar of learning we need in these perilous times when our familiar sense of our society's canon is in disarray.

Not just disciplines and students, but likewise faculty need to be open to canonical transformations. Faculty should teach courses in which they can take their intellectual tools for granted and initiate students into the power and the wonder of what results when those tools are put to work. But faculty need also to teach courses in which those canonical tools are put in question, their limits probed, novel uses for them explored, cooperative ventures undertaken. This questioning might transpire in the form of a naive freshman's question—but why can't "p" and "not-p" both be true?—but I don't always seek to optimize my interests, so why assume I do?—but why should he be punished if it was fated anyway? Or a faculty member's confidence in her competence can be challenged by teaching interdisciplinary courses with other faculty, or by participating in conferences where papers are discussed with those whose fields are other than her own.

The academic disciplines should all aspire to being sciences, although not just quantitative sciences, by insisting on greater and greater precision in their methods of inquiry. Yet they need just as much to aspire to be philosophies, although not just humanistic ones, by insisting on greater and greater integrative generality in the principles from which they work, until all their assumptions have been grounded in self-evidence. The canonical should always be in place but always also in question, every use of a method or principle a test of its adequacy and of its comprehensiveness.

No technique should be taught as a mere abstract skill, but always first learned within a particular discipline for which it functions as an expression of that discipline's canonical principles of organization. For there are no canons-as-such but only particular and very concrete ways in which a person expresses a point of view framed by a set of concepts, actions, and language taken as canonical. Conversely, no content picked out by a canonical framework should be taught as a self-contained subject matter, but always by setting it within a context that discloses the governing framework. For there are no canons complete in themselves but only ones that are salient local features of a wider experiential environment. So the practical no-nonsense effectiveness of disciplinary accomplishments needs to be leavened by wide-eyed concerns that lie beyond its purview or even its ken. And the speculative revel of synoptic insight and creative imagination needs to be sobered by beady-eyed concerns for verification that seem to it nit-picking and trivial.

What this dialectic between the practical and the speculative demands of faculty and students is what Charles Anderson terms "creativity": an ability to recognize when the old is inadequate, and when it is not, to imagine viable improving alternatives, and to test them out. It means "not resistence to discipline, but an effort to perfect it." Creativity as an educational virtue is "the master dissatisfied, who becomes critic. It is the critic, inspired, who becomes creative. But in reverse, it is the critic who must judge the worth of the innovation. And it is the master who must discover how well it performs" (113). The creative transformation of the educational canon expands "the boundaries and possibilities of a system of activity," but it does so for profound reasons, for reasons that remain rooted in what is recognized as needing to be pruned, grafted, and even transplanted. The proposed changes "emerge out of a deep understanding of a way of doing things, out of that perception of pattern that enables one to say 'Now I can go on' " (85–86). Educational creativity is the perception of new patterns, new grammars, that are adequate to changes in facts, ideas, and methods that have made old patterns and grammars inadequate.

Eva Brann understands the need for this sort of creativity with respect to canons. She considers both those who exhibit "perfect piety" toward a canonical tradition and those who "admire a clean slate" as "problematic extremes" (1979: 69). Somewhere in between lies an approach she calls "renovation," the one "most essential to the life of the tradition" (74). The great ages of canonical renovation or renewal—her exemplar is the Renaissance—are times in which the old is not repudiated but transformed, respectfully and lovingly "refurbished." She quotes Petrarch, who likens the old and the new to fathers and sons: "different in every detail; and yet 'a shadow, as it were, and a something our painters call an air' is common to them." Brann adds, with respect to our current situation, that "we are so situated as to be capable of no other novelty" (74). New grammars cannot be invented de novo; they are always, insofar as they are viable, old grammars refurbished.

Even Leo Strauss, that most encrusted of traditionalists, the deaconal canon of the content canonists—even he notes the need for a continuing reinterpretation of the works of great minds. "Since the greatest minds contradict one another regarding the most important matters, they compel us to judge of their monologues; we cannot take on trust what any one of them says. On the other hand, we cannot but notice that we are not competent to be judges" (7). Strauss claims that it is the collapse of "authoritative traditions in which we could trust" that has forced us into this active but unjustified role as judges attempting to reconcile the divergent views of our great-souled mentors. I have been arguing, however, that we should reject his presumption of a lost but maybe someday to be recovered absolute canon of great works, a conversation of ultimate voices speaking in timeless harmony. In its place, the dialectical reading of the educational canon I propose is one that sees the great minds of the tradition as always in need of present-day judges. We may be incompetent insofar as we cannot claim to be ourselves great-souled, but it is we alone who can judge between the canonical voices and the new-sprung experiences. And in doing so, we create new canons by virtue of which the old ones do not perish but are continually renewed.

What all this means is that an academic curriculum and its component disciplines require a governing educational canon. But this canon can be only relatively permanent. It must change under the nurturing influence of internal criticism and the stimulus of different perspectives. An educational canon insulated from change, isolated in its imperial splendor, is stultifying and therefore barren. The hurly-burly formlessness of a canonless curriculum where anything goes, where there are only appreciations and never choices, is hopelessly diffuse and therefore also barren. A canon-in-process, a canon of perches resulting from and leading toward flights, is one that requires the sort of creative interdependency that is educationally fruitful. Learning should be a conversation among those who bring their disciplined and undisciplined perspectives into an ongoing relationship in which they give and they take, and in which they together discover and invent what no one alone could have ever found or made. Education apart from this community of interdependent perspectives is a waste of time—and of history.

Fusing the Horizons

A culture's intellectual canon, and therefore its educational canon, ought always to be put in question. Like an ancient king or a contemporary CEO, it should have to defend itself constantly against younger challengers. But for such struggles there must be rules, just as much as there must be rules for the placid periods of uncontested authority. Every bit as much as we require an educational canon of great works and great ways, we require also a canon for continually assessing, updating, reforming that canon.

These rules of refurbishment are themselves subject to change, however, although never routinely and only when the broad foundational consensus shared by the members of a culture begins to disintegrate. As Thomas Kuhn has taught us, the governing paradigms for a specific academic discipline, or for the sciences more generally, indeed for a whole culture's worldview, change when the facts they command prove recalcitrant to interpretation, when anomalies become too prevalent to be ignored or explained away. The grammar of learned discourse is no longer able to frame a way by which to speak the whole truth about what is happening. The available medallions tell stories that seem to skip by the things that most need telling. A tune-up no longer suffices, and so not only is the canon in doubt but the established methods for its reform as well.

The fundamental rethinking of the nature of the liberal arts during the twelfth and thirteenth centuries is an example of this process in which foundational paradigms change. Bruce Kimball rightly insists that "this reformulation was not a mere shift in Christian apologetics. It involved a sea change in conceiving the significance, the nature, and the source of knowledge, of method, and of inquiry" (1996: 15). The traditional grammar of interpretation, an eight-century-long educational canon, was set aside because it was increasingly thought to be inadequate as a framework for knowledge. As is typical in these situations, an explosion in the scope and kinds of knowledge was the trigger: new texts of Hellenic and Hellenistic origin, in particular Latin translations of the whole Aristotelian corpus, plus commentaries on these texts by Arabic scholars.

This wealth of new ideas and information could not simply be dismissed as irrelevant, for instance by branding it as pagan or heretical—although this strategy was certainly attempted and for a time was even successful. A more generous approach, in the long run more effective, was to encompass the raft of new works, to take them seriously as contributors to knowledge potentially the equal of the traditional sources, and then to devise a canonical hierarchy within which they would find a proper place. The resulting reconciliation, the ordering of both old and new knowledge into a coherent system, involved important changes not only in the roster of canonical materials but also in the criteria for determining a work's canonical status and a method by which those criteria should be applied.

An interesting example of what was happening is the contrasting responses of Bonaventure and Thomas Aquinas, thirteenth-century contemporaries at the University of Paris. They both needed to come to terms with the fact that Aristotle's views seem at important points to be in conflict with the teachings of the Church. Averroes in his commentaries on Aristotle, for instance, argues that Aristotle denies that the world is created, that God has foreknowledge, and that individual souls are immortal. The key to the last denial is Aristotle's claim that forms are generic, that what differentiates one oak tree from another is not the common oak form they both exhibit but the material substance in which that form is instantiated. If so, then the form that survives a person's death is not unique to that person. As Thomas puts it: "Take away from men diversity of intellect, which alone among the soul's parts seems incorruptible and immortal, and it follows that nothing of the souls of men would remain after death except a unique intellectual substance, with the result that reward and punishment and their difference disappear" (19).

Bonaventure's reaction is straightforward: "The water of philosophical science is not to be mingled with the wine of Holy Scripture merely so that the wine is transmutted into water" (420). There is always a danger in reading original texts without proper guidance. Even when the texts are those of the saints, "some studying them have fallen into many errors and heresies." All the more so, then, "beware of the multitude of writers" and recognize that the "greatest danger lies in descending to philosophy" (419). Since what Aristotle says is false to the teachings of the Church, reading him will lead us into error. Therefore we should ban the reading of Aristotle's texts. There is no place for them in the intellectual canon of Christian civilization, and therefore no place for them in the educational canon of the universities, because what they teach is contrary to its foundational truths.

Thomas takes a quite different approach. Instead of rushing to condemn a philosopher of Aristotle's stature, we should make sure his ideas are in fact incompatible with revealed truth. Thomas argues they are not, by citing the places where Aristotle indicates that intellect is not a substantial form but, in Thomas's words, "a part or power or faculty of the soul, which is the form of body" (79). Each individual body has its own individual form or soul, and each soul has certain powers. It does not follow that the soul perishes when the body perishes, however. Although the soul enforms the body, some of its powers, in particular the power of intellect, are not dependent on a body. Hence, an individual soul, able to exercise active powers, is capable of surviving the corruption of its body. Thomas goes on to demonstrate that the view he has just articulated is Aristotle's, that Averroes gave a false reading of the Aristotelian texts, and that if Bonaventure and his followers had gone back to the originals, as they should have done, they would have known this. He then systematically disposes of a number of objections to his reconciling interpretation, and challenges his opponents to propose further arguments in their defense: if anyone "wishes to say anything in reply to what we have written, let him not speak in corners nor to boys who cannot judge of such arduous matters, but reply to this in writing, if he dares" (145).

Thomas's "penchant for ligature rather than rupture" (McInerny: 251) is backed up by an explicit method for reconciling differing texts and authorities. He not only is willing to make changes in the content canon; he has a transformation procedure for doing so. His predecessors and contemporaries constituting the various university arts and sciences faculties had been developing a style of learning that involved dialectical exchange: the *quaestiones disputatae*. Contrasting views, culled from relevant authorities, were debated, some kind of common ground or principle sought, and the contrasts then shown, insofar as that was possible, to be compatible rather than incommensurable. Thomas exhibits this method in its most formal rigor in his *Summa Theologica* where a thesis is proposed, a host of views on the thesis are marshaled, a key text is cited as definitive, and the marshaled views are then disposed of one by one in the light of that text (see my discussion of this method, 1997: 54–56). Aristotle and Averroes—the one a pagan, the other an infidel—are taken as sources for the key authoritative texts on a par with the church fathers or St. Paul. The words of The Philosopher or The Commentator (despite his error in the case just mentioned!) are as definitive for Thomas as those of the Blessed Augustine or The Apostle.

Kimball draws the moral of the story for us: "We modern masters have our own pagans and infidels, of course. Those who argue that teaching them would invigorate the liberal arts need only look [for support] to the tradition that those excluding them sometimes claim to defend" (1996: 16). The traditional canonists, instead of pretending the canon as it now stands is somehow timeless, should recognize not only that it is all the time undergoing modest changes in its specific content but also that on occasion it undergoes significant reformulation. The anti-canonists, instead of attacking past canonical values as repressive, should see them as dynamically open to alterations resulting from the inclusion of previously marginalized values, and as occasionally undergoing sea changes of revolutionary proportion.

One obvious way to make this dialectic explicit within our contemporary arts and sciences curricula is for courses to undertake what Gerald Graff calls "teaching the conflicts" (1992a). He argues that "the mistake of traditional educational thinking has been to assume that schools and colleges have to resolve disagreements in order to teach effectively, that without a consensus on what to teach and why, the curriculum will be chaotic, confused, and without direction" (1992b: 58). But Graff does not really mean to celebrate disagreements and conflicts as intrinsically good. The goal should always be the resolution of conflict, the building of a viable consensus. What he objects to is the attempt of "educational fundamentalists" or "ideological factions" to use Bonaventure's strategy, imposing their exclusionary views unilaterally, "a dogmatism that wants its voice to be the only one in the discussion."

The pluralist approach Graff advocates is one suited to a democracy, in which ideally different methods and values are respected, diversity judged good, and "public discussion of and reconciliation of conflicts" taken as the presumed way to proceed. "No educational proposal is worth much that has no strategy for dealing with disagreement" (70). So teaching the conflicts means not presupposing how the conflicting differences should be resolved, but making the experience of the conflicting materials the occasion for exploring the character of their differences—their respective critical, epistemic, moral, and aesthetic value—and inventing a workable means for their resolution.

The conflicts taught should be not only those among the currently accepted canonical thinkers, as Strauss would have us do, but also those between canonical and currently noncanonical authors. To teach Milton's *Paradise Lost* alongside Mary Shelley's *Frankenstein* is a way to ask if the latter can be read as a reply to the former. The question is not which is better in its use of language and its power of insight—Milton would easily win that sort of beauty contest—but why Milton has been the more important for our culture and what we can learn about the value and the limits of both canonical writings and their challengers through this interesting juxtaposition. To read Shakespeare's *Tempest* in tandem with a contemporary black Caribbean writer's retelling of the play, framing both tellings in their respective contexts of self- and world-understanding, is to appreciate aspects of meaning available through Shakespeare's version that are easily overlooked and to hear resonances in the contemporary version otherwise drowned out by its overtly political agenda. The canonical texts are taught, but not as a set of isolated finalities. They are taught in conversation with other texts, other framings, some merely different, some once or presently contending with them for canonical relevance. The dynamics of the classroom thereby models that of the culture, teaching tomorrow's citizens the knowledge and appreciation they need of both ancient authorities and fresh sassy pretenders to authority, and thereby also teaching them the dialectical skill of canon transformation.

The presumption of a pedagogy and a scholarship of dialectical reconciliation is that the values about which we differ are indeed valuable. In Charles Taylor's words, "all human cultures that have animated whole societies over some considerable stretch of time have something important to say to all human beings" (66). This presumption of importance should be the "heuristic device" with which we approach different cultures and our own differing subcultures. We should presume that our own culture's part in the human story is limited and that other stories are likely to have "something that deserves our admiration and respect, even if it is accompanied by much that we have to abhor and reject" (72–73). Our presumption should not be, as the politics of recognition insists, that all cultural values are undebatably of equal and incomparable worth. Just the opposite: we should begin presuming that all cultures are valuable in some ways, with respect to some of their features, but we should leave it to our shared experience—to our interactions, our debate about the character of our conflicts, the creative imaginings by which we explore the limits of our differences and the opportunities they provide for novel senses of communion and even commonality—to determine what is of equal worth and what incomparable.

Our presumption that the parties in a canonical conflict all have something worthwhile to contribute is prophylactic: it prevents one party from insisting that the harmony sought be cast in its mold or not at all. We have already encountered in chapter 2 an example of this presumptuous attitude: Cardinal Newman's claim that Hottentots are intellectually inferior to Westerners because they have not produced texts that meet the standard set by Plato's. Taylor reports a similar attitude on the part of Saul Bellow who is supposed to have said, responding to a complaint that Westerners are insufficiently appreciative of the great works produced in other cultures, that "when the Zulus produce a Tolstoy we will read him" (42). Bellow presumes that the Western standard for what counts as greatness is unquestioned and that no Zulu author has met that standard. Any alteration of the canon will be in accord with Western criteria of selection, and so far there are no southern African candidates worth considering for inclusion. But as the Thomas Aquinas example makes clear, when different cultural canons come into conflict and it is presumed they each must be taken seriously, new methods of reconciliation are required if the new canon is genuinely to effect what Taylor, borrowing from Hans-Georg Gadamer, calls a "fusion of horizons." Zulu standards of artistic expression are different than Russian standards, African than European, so a transcultural standard needs to be developed, and by a method for doing so that is not already implicate in one of the two competing standard systems. "Real judgments of worth suppose a fused horizon of standards ... ; they suppose that we have been transformed by the study of the other, so that we are not simply judging by our original familiar standards" (70). They suppose it is possible to ligate the rupture caused by a clash of incompatible differences.

Steven Rockefeller echoes Taylor when he argues that "we need a new, deeper appreciation of the ethnic histories of the American people, not a reduction of American history to ethnic histories" (95)—nor, it should be added, a reduction of ethnic histories to American history. What Rockefeller calls "the moral meaning of democracy" is a constant effort at fusing the horizons of the multiple cultures of its people, reconstructing its institutions so that—each in its distinctive way—they all "become instruments of human growth and liberation" for all Americans (91).

Only insofar as the nation's colleges and universities operate on the basis of a self-transforming educational canon of this sort, will they be able to nurture the maturing of citizens able to live and flourish in a culturally pluralistic environment. American higher education's twenty-first-century master piece will need to be wrought dialectically from dynamic materials. Appropriately so, since the reality it normatively interprets is an iterative sequence of dynamic flights from which temporary perches are dialectically attained and then put to flight.

Chapter 8

Pragmatic Canonists

Pragmatism

Santayana argued that the Genteel tradition, in both its objectivist and subjectivist forms, provided a grammar of interpretation inadequate to the novel character of the American experience. He contrasted its closed and cramped systems of understanding with the pragmatism of William James, which he said has three distinctive features.

First of all, because James had a generous, inclusive heart and mind, he was willing to give serious attention to things others dismissed as merely odd. He sought "to recast what the learned world has to offer, so that as far as possible it might serve the needs and interests of ... those groping, nervous, half-educated, spiritually disinherited, passionately hungry individuals of which America is full" (205). Secondly, says Santayana, James believed that "intelligence has its roots and its issue in the context of events." It is an instrument for identifying and solving concrete problems, for coping with particular events in their unique contexts. It provides us with "a local and temporary grammar of action; a grammar that must be changed slowly by time" (206). And lastly, James held a "vitalistic" theory of nature: it was a matter not of "static harmonies, self-unfolding destinies," but rather of purposes, of "concrete endeavors," of "finite efforts of souls in an environment." The universe was unfinished, "an experiment," its laws "a description *a posteriori* of the habits things have chosen to acquire, and which they may possibly throw off altogether" (208).

These three features are closely entwined, according to Santayana. Because nature is an unfinished experiment, our ways of dealing with it will always be local and temporary. And since no one is protected against the risk of failure inherent in such a world, our endeavors should be cooperative. We will all at times be the odd ones left out by shifting circumstance and in need of help. James's mood is upbeat. Our methods may be temporary, today's well-grounded achievements needing to be set aside tomorrow, but this is good. Passionate hunger, nervous groping after knowledge and fulfillment, is what gives our lives their savor. As Santayana summarizes this pragmatist mood, "eternal vigilance is the price of knowledge; perpetual hazard, perpetual experiment keep quick the edge of life" (209).

Bruce Kimball turns to pragmatism—which he expands in the usual way to include Peirce and Dewey as well as James—for the framework of interpretation he thinks is needed if we are ever to resolve the current debilitating standoff in education between canonists and anti-canonists. It is not enough to decry the mutual vilification of the contending factions: we must find a philosophical standpoint able to effect, and to justify, a reconciliation. So Kimball surveys the views of the various American pragmatists and distills them into six basic claims (1995: 29–83, summarized 29, 83):

1. Pragmatists are fallabilists: they recognize that any possible assertion about what is true or right might well be in error.
2. They advocate the experimental method of inquiry, a method they take as having egalitarian implications since it is a method anyone can be taught to utilize.
3. They understand judgments of truth or right to be intersubjective, assertions that are warranted by the judgment of a community of inquirers not by any single individual's judgment.
4. They argue that human beings are part of the natural order, organisms in dynamic interaction with their environment.
5. They think purpose is intrinsic to thought and inquiry: truth is a matter of habits that guide us successfully toward the attainment of our ends.
6. They believe inquiry is inherently normative: thinking cannot be separated from preferring and choosing.

As with Santayana's short list, Kimball's longer one needs to be seen not as a series of discrete points but as facets of a single interpretive system. Pragmatism's theories, after all, should exemplify what they claim is the case: they should be experimental and therefore tentative, intersubjectively warranted and contextualized, serving purposes worth accomplishing. For Santayana, the underlying motive for pragmatic theorizing is to find a way to deal with a dynamic interconnected world. Kimball's hope is for that dynamic interconnectedness to become an accepted quality of American education, for arts and sciences curricula to reflect the character of the world for which the learning they offer is supposed to prepare students.

Kimball thinks that a number of recent cultural developments have made the current educational environment more than ever before open to, and more in need of, a pragmatic perspective. He sees a growing "convergence" between liberal education and the ideas of James and his ilk, for these cultural changes all "find a principled rationale in pragmatism" (97). So Kimball provides another list, this time of seven alterations in our educational context and how he thinks pragmatism addresses them (89–97):

1. Pragmatism's insistence that knowledge is perspectival and contextual—affirms the importance of multiculturalism in constituting a student population and fashioning a curriculum.
2. Pragmatism's emphasis on the centrality of value considerations—supports the recent attention on college campuses to student involvement in service projects.
3. The key role pragmatism gives to intersubjectivity in the determination of warranted belief—justifies campus efforts to help students develop a sense of community and citizenship.
4. The way in which pragmatism underscores the importance of social and historical contexts in the search for knowledge and the formation of values—puts general education at the core rather than the periphery of a student's course of study.
5. Pragmatism's egalitarian approach to education—gives salience to the need for educators at all levels, from kindergarten to graduate school, to understand themselves as part of a common enterprise: habits of learning developed early are the key to later success.
6. The primacy pragmatism gives to experimental inquiry—justifies a learner-centered pedagogy, one that emphasizes discussion, collaborative research, and hands-on activities.
7. Pragmatism's insistence that learning something must make an identifiable practical difference—is consistent with the recent focus on standards and assessment.

The engine driving Kimball's list, making sense of all these particular virtues of pragmatism, all these many modes of its relevance to the current educational situation, is a double critique of traditional presuppositions about the world. Pragmatists and Whiteheadians, as we have seen, understand nature, and hence human nature, as both dynamic and dialectical—that is, as both vital and interconnected. These two features are intimately related, and when they are denied the impact on education is immediate. When the material flux of the world is thought to be grounded in immaterial fixed principles, and when the basic elements of the world are taken to be individual material atoms and individual immaterial souls, the result cannot but be educational theories and practices that are profoundly flawed. A dualism that denigrates change and valorizes what is claimed to be unchanging, and an atomism that ignores the fundamental relatedness of things, will be translated with respect to teaching and learning into what Pete Gunter calls the "bifurcation of education" (28).

Gunter notes that the traditional distinction, still evident in many British universities, between natural philosophy and philosophy of mind, or the nineteenth-century Germanic distinction between *Naturwissenschaft* and *Geisteswissenschaft,* has been updated in the current distinction between, on the one hand, mathematics, the natural sciences, the quantitative social sciences, engineering, and the technological applied sciences, and on the other hand, the fine arts, the humanities, history, the various forms of culture studies, and untechnological applied fields such as social work and education. The depth and scope of this dichotomy precludes either side of the division having anything intellectually important to say to the other. Uncriticized because presumed to mirror the way the world is, this separation, says Gunter, has become "hardened into operative prejudices" of each discipline that are "oblivious to subtle interrelatedness" among the disciplines (26).

The division of education into the sciences and the humanities faculties is an abstraction, a piece of human artifice that was designed to serve a particular purpose. No matter how legitimate that purpose, however, when it is taken as an objective fact, a necessary feature of the natural landscape, its boundaries become intellectual habits that cut deep and seemingly unbridgeable grooves in the surface of our ways of thinking. Gunter quotes Whitehead: "Now to be mentally in a groove is to live contemplating a given set of abstractions. The groove prevents straying across country, and the abstraction abstracts from something to which no further attention is paid. But there is no groove of abstractions adequate for the comprehension of human life" (26).

Extricating ourselves from the established grooves of academe requires finding a background of assumptions that the separated worlds of scientific and humanistic learning share, even if those assumptions are unacknowledged. For it is only on the assumption that there are some common assumptions that the two sides of the bifurcation will think mutual comprehension possible, much less engage in an exchange of views. Only by calling in question the dualistic metaphysics they both presuppose will there be a chance of any emergent reconciling beliefs and principles, of what Jeffrey Stout calls a gap-bridging "schematism for understanding" (163).

Another bifurcation immediately rears its ugly head, however: the one between our familiar antagonists, the canonists and anti-canonists. This bifurcation is not the same as the disciplinary bifurcation. There are both scientists and humanists who count themselves among the canonists, although, as we have seen, canonists of the humanistic kind tend to be content canonists, scientists procedural canonists. Similarly, both scientists and humanists are to be found among those opposed to canons, scientists emphasizing the contingency of theory formation, humanists emphasizing its egalitarian implications. Nonetheless, both the disciplinary and the canonical differences are rooted in the same dualistic metaphysical schema: a belief that there is an ontological gulf between the concrete tangible things that come to be and perish and the unchanging principles that govern those changes.

A reconciling schema for understanding, therefore, cannot beg the dispute over the nature of nature in an attempt to settle the dispute over the nature of disciplines and canons. The proposed schema cannot be presumed to have roots in some sort of deep transcendental structure, but neither can it be composed of principles and purposes presumed to be merely an arbitrary concoction for solving an essentially political problem of accommodation. Affirming either pole of an ontological dualism in order to overcome the differences to which that dualism gives rise would be incoherent if not downright silly. We cannot build a holistic interpretation of education on a nonholistic foundation.

Stout proposes that we not hurry too quickly to settle the question of metaphysical underpinnings. We should simply begin where we are—*in media res*—accepting the historical context in which we find ourselves, one seared by the incommensurability of conflicting viewpoints. Our initial approach to the clash of canonical and anti-canonical educational schemata should be to presume as our working hypothesis that they share a nondualistic common background. On that assumption, we should be open to the possibility of a reconciling schematism of understanding—even though we have no idea what it might be. "The possibility of responsible criticism and cross-cultural understanding" does not depend on "the existence of an invariant set" of ontological beliefs and principles (163). "There is no 'pure' basis on which to begin a project of reconstruction" (195), so we should proceed impurely, on little more than the hope that such a basis might eventually be developed. Confronted with clashing schemata, we can begin by temporarily setting them to one side. We can "avoid both transcendental method and metaphysical speculation without succumbing to relativism simply by abandoning all the traditional dualisms, including that of scheme and content. This would leave us with a thoroughly holistic historicism consistent with the best in American pragmatism" (218).

Stout's "holism" is the dialectical interdependence, his "historicism" the dynamic openness, that are the key features of pragmatism's alternative to a dualistic ontology. Stout asks us to presume that the principles by which disciplines and canons are constructed, whether they be egalitarian or hierarchical, are perspectives. We cannot do without them, but no one of them is definitive. Our perspectives are not arbitrary: they are ways to organize our experiences of a reality independent of us, constraining our interpretations of it. In ordering the world in some particular way, however, we necessarily leave something out, and as the world changes more and more is left out as some of what has been included becomes irrelevant or inappropriate. Our perspectives are the most important aspects of who we are, as individuals and as societal groups, for they provide the frameworks by which we find and give significance to our lives and our world. But we cannot be dogmatic about them because they are, by their very nature, incomplete and so always needing to be altered.

Stout's explanation for why a dualistic way of thinking came to predominance in modern Western thought points to the Port Royal logicians, contemporaries of Descartes, who like him struggled to develop a strategy for freeing people with divergent religious beliefs or scientific interests from the control of those with the power to command assent to the established societal truths and values. "The 'autonomy' of the [private personal] sphere, then, like that of science, was something that had to be carved out by the threatened minorities and weary peace-makers of the sixteenth and seventeenth centuries" (237). Their strategy, Stout argues, was to substitute "probable reasoning" for deduction from self-evident first principles, thereby allowing dissenters to avoid having to make any direct challenge to those principles when defending their own perspectives.

This strategy, unfortunately, was pushed aside in favor of Descartes's alternative—which retained self-evident first principles, but located their justification in an individual's powers of reasoning. As a result, global absolute principles are replaced by regional ones—autonomous scientific principles, autonomous humanistic principles. This parochializing of principles leads, at the extreme, to each individual becoming his or her own region of autonomy. But principles are methods for adjudicating disagreement: if each individual is the final authority on what the relevant principles of truth or value are, then there are in fact no normative principles at all, only personal viewpoints. So Stout invites us to return to the Port Royal technique of probable reasoning as a route back toward holism from the various regional autonomies that are now our established authorities on value and truth. He has no clear goal in mind, certainly no pocketful of encompassing principles to lay on the table, but he has a pragmatic heuristic to guide us: the evidence, slim though it sometimes is, of mutual comprehension between the opponents.

If our working presumption is that we share a common nondualistic background as the resource for any reconciling schemata we might be inventive enough to fashion, then the simplest proof of its presence is that we can find ways to communicate our differences, that the two sides of the dualism can understand what the other is saying—not agree with those views, not even appreciate them; just comprehend them. And so Stout proposes this test: "Whenever neither of two rival programs of research can explain the common history of their competition to the satisfaction of the other, this is itself an objective indication of weakness in the theories thus far proposed" (268). The followup to this discovery should be a rethinking and reformation of one or both of the theories, enough so that they then meet the comprehensibility criterion. More likely, however, the situation will take a dialectical turn in the form of a "third program" that will displace both the others "by the power of its theories and the persuasiveness of its narratives" (268).

When that middling third way emerges, "holding out for an old theory becomes a sign that reasons have ceased to be the most significant causes at work in determining judgment" (268–69). But insofar as theorists and educators behave intelligently, Stout's criterion will set in motion a dynamic and dialectical process of reconciliation—of refurbishment, renovation, renaissance. We do not need to know in advance where we will end up to know that the journey is important, and that only in the journeying will we ever begin to see where we should head.

The Workable Canon

The attack on the American educational system by the anti-canonists of the cultural Left, their diatribe against its promulgation of beliefs and practices that are hierarchical, hegemonic, and exclusionary, presumes that it is possible for people to live without shared canonical frameworks. Since, they argue, cultural canons are historical constructs and are as multiform as the cultures and subcultures relevant to a given context, they should be desanctified. Any particular canon should be taken as a reflection of the power equation characterizing some group at a particular time and space, and so all canons should be demoted from being the centerpiece of the arts and sciences curriculum into being just one among many of the topics available for consideration. Counterattacking, the content canonists of the cultural Right presume that no social order can be built on the shifting sands of the politics of recognition, that American society is tethered to a single natural canonical framework for the regulation of a good and just society, and that it should be the core of any arts and sciences curriculum.

The educational radical thinks that since there is no natural canon the best society is an unregulated one, and that the design of an undergraduate curriculum should therefore be the responsibility of each individual student. The educational reactionary thinks that since there is a natural canon the best society is one regulated by its norms, and that the design of an undergraduate curriculum should therefore be the responsibility of those who best understand that canon. On the one hand, we have the Marxist classless society, each member without benefit of state supervision making anew each day the place that best serves his needs and exercises his abilities; on the other hand, we have the Kantian kingdom of ends, each member assigned her proper place by the state and fully consenting to the role defined by that place. Between the rock and whirlpool of these absolutes, a constructive postmodern pragmatic philosophy offers us an uncertain but navigable passage.

When James characterized "reality" as made up of the strands of eaches and suches we experience, finite stretches of concrete particular facts and abstract relational concepts, he added a third element: reality is also composed of "the whole body of other truths already in our possession" (96), the "ancient stock" of truths constituting our cultural heritage. For "the most violent revolutions in an individual's beliefs leave most of his old order standing. ... New truth is always a go-between, a smoother-over of transitions. It marries old opinion to new fact so as ever to show a minimum of jolt, a maximum of continuity" (31).

The ancient stock, if absolutized, sets rules that eventually prove inadequate to the ever-changing eaches of the world. That stock was canonized because of its relevance to worlds past, and even then its relevance was partial, its adequacy approximate, its flaws not fully appreciated. Things change, and old truths become uncouth because no longer able adequately to frame the world. But new truths, if designed solely by reference to their immediate relevance, have all the limitations that result from inexperience, expedience, and the absence of thoughtful criticism. Designed to solve a particular problem, their usefulness may not be generalizable. In healing one wound they may, absolutized, cause a hundred others. A schema tailored to the moment of its need is only momentarily helpful. Another schema is soon needed, and another, the daily disconnected replacement of one organizing principle by another growing into a general incoherence of things.

Thus, a community functions viably insofar as it can marry its traditional frameworks for thinking and valuing with the novelty of present experiences. We educators and advocates of education, like it or not, are the clerics responsible for the cathedral of learning: its gatekeepers, liturgists, and janitors. But if our cathedral is somehow to encompass dialectically both the preservation and the constant transformation of our cultural heritage, a delicate question arises. Who should be allowed to take part in this crucial enterprise?

An inclusive vision would say that every living person, whatever their characteristics and qualifications, everyone from canon idolaters to canon iconoclasts, should be a part of the cathedral community. The voices in the educational conversation it carries on among its members should even include the dead, persons whom we bring back to life by studying them, finding ourselves influenced by their ideas and imaginings, by the stories of their achievements, and by the customs and institutions to which they contributed their often anonymous lives and unsung loyalties.

In contrast, an elitist vision would say that the educational community, just like any community, must have a hierarchical structure, the higher reaches of which need to be restricted to those who have acquired its necessary conditions for membership. For everyone cannot be learned, cannot contribute to the shaping, refining, and critiquing of the perspective from which they live. Many people lack the self-control, the mental powers, the energy, to be leaders, to contribute actively rather than passively to the perfecting of a way of life or a disciplinary perspective. Of course, the separation of wheat from chaff should not be pre-restrictive and hence unfair. But education can only do its job if it has levels, each higher platform of learning building upon lesser ones, each of them calling for specific prerequisite qualifications, admissions standards, appropriate credentials.

Here again lurks the danger of a false dichotomy. The elitist approach tends to cook up an educational stew able to nourish a narrow self-perpetuating few in their privileged roles while failing to meet even the barest minimal daily requirements of everyone else. But an egalitarian approach tends to make of learning such a thin gruel that those who consume it will be unable to develop the bone and muscle, the sophisticated expertise, required by a complex nation and the complex world of which it is a part. We need both—both cooks who know what makes an educational stew nourishing and consumers who know whether it is nourishing them. We need educational clerics to run our various kinds of cathedrals, both professional experts and their aspiring novitiates, but who these people are cannot be left to the experts alone to decide. Our conversations must therefore be among those who meet some specific canon of acceptability, those who meet another, and those who find neither or none acceptable. Our conversations must ask the difficult questions about intellectual canons and their curricular implications without begging these questions. The one question that must always be on the table during such conversations is which of the range of possible educational standards are best and under what conditions or why at all.

It is a different question, a different topic for the conversation, when our concern is with the proper uses to which this learning should be put. The canons of the cathedral need to find workable answers to such perplexing questions as these—Is the aim of education self-development, community service, or knowledge for its own sake? If for the improvement of our individual selves, is that a goal each person decides alone or is the educated self an ideal that a community should define? What is the community for whose service we prepare? Is it our family, our neighborhood, a political party, a special interest group, our nation, the United Nations, a transnational corporation, an international NGO, spaceship Earth? What is this service we prepare to offer it? Is it a particular profession or trade that has standards of excellence it holds sacred, or is it one that conceives its social role as providing its members with an instrument for income maximization?

The educational mission of a college or university or of a whole nation cannot be so encompassing, so protean, that it simply answers all these questions in the affirmative. Canons of acceptability are needed, ones that set expectations for young people, that channel how the flow of resources into education will go, that formulate the parameters of a people's future. But such canons must be constantly challenged by tracing the losses accompanying each gain, by venturing boldly beyond the horizons of concern and relevance that define the value of the existing canons, returning home with neglected truths and unimagined possibilities requiring serious consideration.

Of course it would be silly to presume that any assembly of educators and educational advocates could ever sit down together and intentionally construct an educational canon for a statewide university system or for a confabulation of private liberal arts colleges, much less for the nation or for an emerging worldwide human community. But we can work at devising lesson plans and course syllabi, standardized tests and general education requirements, public or private school budgets and mission statements that draw their justification from our sense of what is essential to any student's education. And we can insist that our personal sense of what is essential take its justification in turn from ongoing debates with our colleagues and neighbors in our local communities and on our home campuses.

Society is the author of such things as canons, but society is us. The social reconstruction of our reality can be carried on nowhere more appropriately than in civic and campus arguments about course content and graduation requirements. It is a good enough beginning that we bring our good sense and our pedagogical artistry to bear on these matters of seeming detail. The greater task of refashioning a canon, difficult or impossible as it might be, will come about only by means of such interactions. For like all ideals, this one is accomplished only by those who pursue it confident of its importance, doubtful about the best means for its realization, but persistent nonetheless in the effort to imbue the reality they know, however parochial it be, with traces of something better, truer, more beautiful. Educational canons change incrementally as individuals, trying to make their own or their children's learning conform better to the ideal of an existing canon, end up remaking it.

Every college and university has a motto that in some manner or another points to the ideals that make possible an objective, workable, culturally affirmed, educational canon. The motto of my own institution is *pietate et doctrina tuta libertas:* "through commitment and learning, we make safe our liberty." Not by succumbing to an easy relativism with respect to the problem of what is worthwhile educationally, but by a disciplined commitment to the ideal of a knowledge that is both objective and adequate to our experiences, are we freed from intellectual and political bondage. Not by knowing only what we want to know in order to satisfy our immediate desires and interests, but by a learning founded on the full sweep of our culture's and our world's canons of importance, are we made safe from gullibility and obscurantism.

Middling Deans

"Political correctness" is a donkey's tail of vilification recently pinned on the cultural Left. But it belongs on the rump of the cultural Right as well, for, to quote a useful definition, the politically correct are those who operate in terms of "a prefabricated sense of values, a predetermined set of assumptions about what is good for people and what is bad for them" (Caserio). The educational leaders at our cathedrals of learning—presidents and chancellors, academic deans and provosts, department heads and committee chairs—become unwilling participants in these pin-the-tail games whenever the issues have to do with faculty rights or curricular requirements. And since most campus issues always have to do with both these things, it is no wonder those in positions of educational leadership sometimes think of themselves as apprenticing for a job with the NLRB or with a Palestine-Israel negotiating team. What can we do, if anything, we potential or actual educational leaders, to help attain some modicum of peace, order, and tranquility on our campuses among these contentious star-crossed folk whose excess of prefabricated assumptions and prejudged convictions threaten the cathedral?

To require of students that they learn anything not of their own choosing or of faculty that they teach anything mandated by some authority higher than their own professional judgment is to advocate some kind of evaluative distinction, to create a canon concerning what is to hold a privileged place in the curriculum—to determine that this discipline is more important than that one, this course the more worthwhile, these texts or concepts or methodologies the more crucial. But those judgments, that canon with its requirements, can be questioned, not just the what of it but even the that, the very fact of having a canon at all.

Were these disputes merely matters of rhetoric, of shout and threat, ploy and counterploy, the power plays of one special interest group against another, then my advice to deans and their ilk would be simple enough. Machiavelli has said it all—be cunning as the fox when you lack effective power; act boldly as the lion when for some brief moment the tide of opportunity flows with you. It would seem that presidents and provosts whose well-thumbed copies of *The Prince* are bedtime reading will be the ones who live to die in their beds of old age rather than dying too young on some curricular battlefield, knifed in the back by their faculty or their trustees or both.

I don't think, however, that the canonical wars have to do merely with force of arms. As I have been arguing, they have to do with beliefs about the way the world is, with claims about the nature of reality. Thank goodness, for deans and provosts were trained to be scholars not soldiers, educators not politicians. When the political correctness facades are pulled away, there is a real issue at issue in the dispute between those who would require all students to study certain traditionally important materials and those who reject such privilegings as arbitrary. In these times it is time for the cathedral deans to become pragmatists. Not pragmatists in the crass Machiavellian sense, but pragmatists of the stripe of William James.

The work of academic leaders should be to attempt to effect for their campus the marriage of traditional beliefs and practices with the novelty of present experiences that James talked about, to prepare young people and often adults to become citizens able and willing to attempt to effect that marriage for our country. It is our civic duty as Americans to know and appreciate the systems of belief—the mythic cosmologies, the scientific laws, the commonsense attitudes—that in times past have served to give coherence and purpose to our life together. It is also our responsibility as citizens to be acquainted with and appreciate the motley of particulars—individuals whatever their kinds or styles or stations in life, ideas whatever their seeming worth, practices whatever their scope or legitimacy—that are encircled by the horizons of that coherence and purpose.

And if this be so, our work as educators and as advocates of a well-functioning American educational system is to develop citizens possessing three sorts of competence. Properly educated citizens must be at home in the canons that compose the formal and material reality of their heritage, its values and valued treasures. They must equally be at home with the varied individual accomplishments and aspirations that compose the material and imaginative reality of their actual present life. And they must be able to devise constantly canonical frameworks, grammars of interpretation, that marry those ancient canons and novel particulars in a renovated canon that integrates as fully and complexly as possible all its participant elements.

This marriage process, as it is carried on over time, results in a dynamic nicely caught in James's metaphor of grease spots. The intruding inappropriate glob of grease falls onto the cloth of tradition, spotting it. "The novelty soaks in; it stains the ancient mass; but it is also tinged by what absorbs it" (78). The new fact stains the ancient truths, forcing them to adjust their framings in some small but irreversible way in order to take account of it. But the new fact is changed as well by the encompassing system of beliefs into which it is now set. Always ready with yet another metaphor, James shifts in midsentence to his notion of a stew: "It happens relatively seldom that the new fact is added *raw*. More usually it is embedded cooked, as one might say, or stewed down in the sauce of the old" (78). The flavor and substance of the stew are altered because of the new ingredient. The ingredient is altered as well, however, cooked down by the stewing until it has become an integral aspect of the whole.

This last metaphor would seem to make campus leaders into cooks, responsible for the curricular goulash we hope will be tasted by our students and will provide them a proper nourishment. But it would be more accurate, and more faithful to James's point, to see academic leaders as stirring masters. Not cooks, because no president or provost has the authority or wisdom to determine what the traditional ingredients in this stew will be. Nor does any faculty member have such authority. It is our educational traditions that provide us the cooked ingredients, the leftovers from prior feasts, the hand-me-down recipes that have been tried and proven to provide truly tasteful, nourishing resources for our citizenry. Nor do faculty or administrators have the outsiders' persistence, the marginalized person's outrage, the willingness to take risks that comes from having nothing to lose, that is needed to be the creators of the raw novelties that challenge tradition, to be the inventors of untried and unproven recipes that alter our tastes and feed the undernourished aspects of who we are.

Academic leaders bake no pedagogical bread, let it be acknowledged, nor make any educational stews. But it can be said that without them no bread is baked, no stews prepared. For the art of stirring has its virtues too: the craft of keeping the curricular concoction together lest it separate into the bland and the bitter, into traditions simmered until they are only pious platitudes and into novelties too indigestible to be of benefit. In addition to the Right and Left of learning, there is a place for a third locale: the middling, muddling, mixing, mediating center without which things fall apart and educational institutions no longer educate.

Pragmatic realism, metaphysically understood, requires this triple sense of objectivity: novel human doings in need of guidance, long-enduring systems of belief that provide the schemata of interpretation by which that guiding can be done, and opportunistic skill in sculpting act and theory, fact and canon, into a coherent, fruitful basis for intelligent action. A genuine educational canon, pragmatically stirred, should be able to marry the cultural Left and the cultural Right. Jamesian deans and cathedral deacons should minister to these protagonists, showing them that their current dispute has entrapped them each in an ideological isolation of partial truths. Campus leaders who read James instead of Machiavelli should invite canonists and anti-canonists to kiss and make up, to exchange rings in celebration of a vow to join together as one flesh in the adventure toward a better educational environment, toward a better American culture and a better world, an adventure that requires them both.

Bothering to Try

The obvious question is: why bother? Is the aim of all this mediating, this attempt to marry viewpoints uninterested in reconciliation, simply in order to attain a modicum of peace, to still the angry voices, to stand down the armies? That's certainly reason enough, but Francis Oakley provides us with a more substantial justification, based on what he calls a "central educational intuition":

> No education which truly aspires to be a preparation for living can afford to ignore the fundamental continuities that exist between the cultivation of specific areas of specialized knowledge, expertise or skill (without which we could scarcely endure) and that more fundamental and wide-ranging attempt to penetrate by our reason the very structures of the natural world, to evoke the dimensions and significance of the beautiful, to reach towards an understanding of what it is to be human, of one's position in the universe, and of one's relations with one's fellows, moral no less than material. Towards that attempt we seem impelled by the very fiber of our being. In its total absence, while doubtless we survive, we do so as something surely less than human. (1992a: 171)

Oakley sounds a bit like an unrepentant foundationalist here, with his talk of "the very structures" of nature, the normative tone of his "understanding of what it is to be human," and his claim that unless we strive for these values we will be "surely less than human." But Oakley is making a pragmatist-process claim, not a foundationalist one, even if it might be somewhat obscured by his traditionalist vocabulary. He celebrates the "attempt" to penetrate, to evoke, to reach. What is key for him, however, is not even the attempting, much less succeeding, but rather our impulse "towards the attempt." What makes us human is not the quality of our goals or of our striving, but the quality of our attempt to strive toward those goals. Toward this "toward" we are "impelled by the very fiber of our being."

Hence, Oakley finds his theory of human being in Aristotle, who defined humans as "the animal that desires to know":

> Or, as the sociologists of knowledge would now put it, human beings are animals that appear impelled by the very urgencies of their constitution and from the very wellsprings of their creativity to infuse the universe with meaning and direction, to comprehend their own existential situation, and to frame for themselves moral goals. In

the face, then, of waves of change that break upon the very bastions of meaning that men and women have erected in their anxious quest to make themselves at home in a mysterious and frequently hostile world, one must question the adequacy of educational approaches that are willing to sacrifice to short-term vocational advantage the age-old struggle for some breadth of intellectual perspective and the attainment of interpretative depth. For there can be no real coping without some richness of understanding. There can be, that is, no *ultimately* practical preparation for living if it leaves one bereft of the wherewithal to comprehend one's situation from a vantage point less partial and a perspective less impoverished than that afforded by the task-oriented, means-end, functional rationality at which we so excel. (170)

Oakely is arguing that what works educationally—what constitutes an "ultimately practical preparation for living"—is not the tools for accomplishing this or that particular task, the "functional rationality" that gives us the ability to chose the best means for achieving a particular end. That "specialized knowledge, expertise or skill" is necessary—without it "we could scarcely endure"—but it is hardly sufficient. It needs always to be located within a context that gives it "meaning and direction." We need to know where we are and to fathom the significance of that fact—we need to achieve "interpretive depth"—if we are to be able in the light of that perspective to frame for ourselves worthwhile "moral goals" sufficient to guide and critique our specialized pursuits. What works, therefore, is the marriage of a heritage of meaning, of orienting values, with the "waves of change that break upon the very bastions of [that] meaning." Our desire to know, says Oakley, to "infuse the universe" with meaning, is what makes us "at home in a mysterious and frequently hostile universe." The task of education ought above all else to open us to this need and equip us for pursuing its open-ended, ultimately unattainable, fulfillment.

The Aristotelian perfections cherished, as we saw in chapter 1, by the familiar taken-for-granted attitudes toward education that are now in disarray, have been retained but transformed in this notion of education as preparation for a life that is always a toward. Students remain the material cause of education, except that who they are, as individuals and as a student body, is recognized to be a question requiring constant reexamination. The formal causes are the principles of disciplines that the process of learning requires, but they are ones that constantly show themselves to be inherently inadequate to their task. The final causes of education are ideals of developing selfhood, serving the needs of society, and achieving workable knowledge, but these ideals are not timeless essences but rather functions of their historical context. And the efficient cause is the desire of students to realize those ideals in some concrete, individual manner, although this desire is dynamic and dialectical rather than fixed. Without canonical order, this causal matrix for education collapses into nonsense. But an order of things need not transcend human artifice to be of enduring significance.

An educational canon is a perch, a place to which a community of learning comes. It sums up a struggle to bring something stable out of the noise and bustle of a prior contentiousness about what is worth studying, by whom, in what way, and for what purpose. This struggle cannot go on indefinitely, for a community needs to work from some common assumptions regarding what of its heritage and present experiences are worth passing on to the successor generations. The summing up must somehow be done, for there are schools to build, professors to hire, curricula to plan. Whatever the consensus, be it rough hewn or carefully crafted, be it a tissue of compromises or a coherent program, it must come to be what it is. The task then is to implement what has been agreed upon, to work out from it in making the various concrete choices that are the ongoing functional realities of that community's educational process.

So the perch afforded by an educational canon allows a community to orient itself within the world, to take stock of its purposes, its ways of doing things, to get a grip on what it thinks important. This perch may be sufficiently solid so that for a long time nothing will be needed except to adjust our stance in order to improve our initial grip or to get a clearer view of what lies ahead. But eventually the perch will no longer suffice, and it will be time to take flight again into some new cacophony of academic disputation, seeking a new vantage point from which to order things.

There are no timeless canonical branches on the educational tree where a college or university might perch impervious to challenge and to change. Nor is it possible to sustain oneself in endless flight. I have proposed a middle way between dogmatic essences and pyrrhonic relativism, between an absolute canon and none at all. A community conversing earnestly about educational issues is one that is all the time fashioning unifying standards of importance out of its constitutive diversity. But these standards are always inadequate to their task, in part because of the inadequacy of the humans that fashion them but also in part because perspectives are unavoidably partial. So we live by them, and call them into question, and make new ones by which to live again, although now somewhat differently.

What Dennis O'Brien says about a system of ethics applies to a educational canon as well. A workable canon is always "at the historical state of the art." What counts as canonical is constantly needing to be reformed, so that we can think of a canon as "the development of a series of valued historical actualities with each new step fitted into the series" (4). Thus, an educational canon is "open-textured." It is like "an extended family in which there is always some 'family resemblance'" among its various historical manifestations. We cannot do without a canon, but neither can we allow it to be made into an idol. Therefore it is "quite legitimate"—I would say crucial—"to argue about what should be in the canon, for there are always marginal works, and former classics can be outclassed by historical development" (5).

Gloria Anzaldúa gives us a helpful metaphor to reexpress O'Brien's point in a multicultural rather than multitemporal context: the notion of a "borderland" (the quotes that follow are from Banks). A border is the "narrow strip along a steep edge," separating inside from outside, the familiar from the alien, "the safe from the unsafe," friends from enemies, "us from them"— the canonical from the uncanonical. A borderland is in the area nearby a border, where different borders are in proximity, a no-man's-land "in which people of many different cultures can interact, relate, and engage in civic talk and action." A borderland is what prevents borders from becoming fixed demarcations, because it is always putting their precision into question. By opening out a space for canonical interaction, for "civic talk" among the proponents or this or that canon and those who oppose it or hold to another canon or to none at all, it allows new boundaries to emerge, even new kinds of boundary. A borderland is a "vague and undetermined place created by the residue of an unnatural boundary. It is in a constant state of transition" toward some different unnatural boundary.

Always the perches are leaning toward new flights, and the flights are always toward new perches. Always the new child is fitted into the series of family members, how she looks going a long way toward resembling her parents and their parents, but also going off toward some important nonresemblances. Always the older border stretches toward its borderland and that borderland stretches toward new borders. Always and again, and ever again: toward. The process of giving reality to a dynamic and dialectical educational canon is in harmony with the procession of our own shared human reality. And thereby our voices are integrated into a cosmic musical canon, the comings to be and perishings of which compose the complex harmonic process that is the workable world's reality.

Chapter 9

Education for a Democracy

Science and Democracy

John Dewey was an enthusiast for the scientific method, an apologist for democracy, and an advocate of educational reform. He thought that the three—science, democracy, and education—if properly linked could unleash powers of human creativity that would promote "the general social welfare and the full development of human beings as individuals" (1946: 58). As Bruce Kimball puts it, Dewey thought "that science fosters democracy and that democracy encourages science" (1995: 80), and that education was how they could best be linked together.

The opposing views of the cultural Right and cultural Left are united in at least this one way: they are both at odds with Dewey's position. Traditional canonists are wary of democracy, anti-canonists of science. The hierarchical character of a canon is explicitly elitist: those who have mastered the canon, whether it be a content or a procedure, possess the qualities of mind or of character needed in order to be effective in the pursuit of truth or the social good. The general populace lacks the requisite education, the trained judgment, necessary for doing scientific research or running a government. Those who oppose a traditional canon do so in part because of this elitism, since they find it to be at odds with the egalitarian values a democracy institutionalizes. Everyone deserves an equal say in the governing of a people, and so although experts are necessary their role should be clearly subordinate to the will of the general populace, whether expressed at the ballot box or through public opinion polls, in town meetings or by referenda. Science can be tolerated in a democracy only if closely regulated by citizen oversight groups.

I have been arguing that the quarrel between canonists and anti-canonists, elitists and egalitarians, can be resolved through the notion of a pragmatic canon. The aim of this chapter is to explore the rationale behind Dewey's version of this claim. Dewey helps us see why education—if understood as the means by which citizens can learn how to appreciate, utilize, and contribute to their culture's pragmatic canon—is what makes both good science and good government possible.

Dewey was impressed by the ways an experimental approach to problem solving had transformed the natural sciences. Accepting ideas as true only if they could be validated by publicly confirmed empirical evidence, scientists had gained an understanding of nature sufficient to harness it as a resource for improving the human condition. Dewey proposed that this method be extended to the social sciences as well, where the benefits would be even more far-reaching. The American nation would be the better were its policies formulated, implemented, and assessed scientifically. Democracy was in need of what he called "habits of intelligent action": the rigorous and systematic application of the experimental method to "the problems of men" (1946: 4). In this sense, Dewey is through and through a procedural canonist, a firm believer in the capacity of the scientific method not only to improve the human condition by the material benefits of the technologies its understanding of nature makes possible but also, when applied to societal issues, to improve the human condition by fashioning social structures that liberate people from dehumanizing and inequitable forms of work and leisure.

An educational system equal to this challenge was crucial, Dewey argued, because the methods of science obviously needed to be learned in order to be applied. And the earlier in life these methods are acquired, the better. Experimental thinking needs to be a habit of mind, a disposition to approach problems in a certain way. Once young people—and improperly educated adults returning to school for further education—have become practiced in the art of intelligent action, they will be consistent in its use. Rightly educated, people will insist on addressing social problems in the same way they addressed the problem of predicting and controlling the forces of nature.

So it is easy enough to see why Dewey could argue that scientific method is an important instrument for social good, and that American democracy would be preserved, indeed strengthened, if what worked to produce our technological benefits were made use of systematically to improve the quality of our community arrangements. It is less clear why he should insist, as he does, that the scientific method and democracy are essential to each other. Granted, if our society happens to be a democracy, and if a scientific approach to its problems will improve the quality of life for its citizens, then obviously the art of intelligent action is good for a democracy. But if our society had another form of governance, even if it were a monarchy or a dictatorship, surely an experimental approach to problem solving would be beneficial for it as well. Scientific method delivers the goods. It's a powerful tool for removing the impediments in the way of realizing our goals, whatever those goals might be and whatever the form of government under which we pursue them. Hence, Dewey is often accused of being blind to the undermining of individual liberties that can result when the virtues of science are uncritically adulated. He is said to be unaware of the sinister pathway that begins by privileging scientific method, leads to advocating the social engineering of change, and ends in thinking governments should determine the goals thereby engineered.

But of course Dewey rejected any such arbitrary separation of means from ends. Intelligence is an instrument for constructing and validating individual and collective ends, just as much as it is an instrument for designing and testing the means for achieving those ends. With respect to societal ends, Dewey argued that an intelligent inquiry into the character of human interactions shows that "the keystone of democracy as a way of life may be expressed, it seems to me, as the necessity for the participation of every mature human being in formation of the values that regulate the living of men together" (58). The essence of democracy, apart from any particular institutional mechanisms, is the idea that societal ends should be based on "asking other people what they would like, what they need, what their ideas are" (35). So an experimental approach to societal issues will value democracy more than any other known form of political organization because it is based on the premise that the members of a society are alone competent to determine what outcomes that method should be designed to attain.

Dewey's claim, however, is not simply that democracy will benefit, as do the sciences, from a proper method of inquiry—as though democracy and the scientific method were two separate habits of intelligent action. He insists that the method used by science *requires* democracy, and vice versa. The skills of intelligent problem solving are dependent on dispositions that democracies nurture and tyrannies inhibit. Conversely, without a scientifically educated citizenry, democracy is crippled and conditions fostered that encourage the emergence of authoritarian regimes. Science and democracy are each a necessary condition for the other.

What sense can be made of such a seemingly implausible linkage? I want in the remainder of this chapter to explore the claim that science and democracy are inextricably linked, and then to identify some of the ways a pluralistic society such as ours can avoid the sort of social fragmentation that is the enemy of democracy. Dewey may have been naive in his assessment of the goods science can deliver, but he saw wisely that genuine intelligence and genuine liberty—the goals of canonical knowledge and anti-canonical individuality—are inseparable ideals, that each is the foundation of the other, and that only through an education of the kind we have called pragmatic can these yoked ideals actually be achieved.

Scientific Scripts

Let me begin with science, and with its canonical center, the scientific method. The key to this method is being able to think up good hypotheses. Hypotheses become important when situations become problematic. Usually, however, there is nothing at all problematic about the situations in which we find ourselves. We go about our affairs operating pretty much by habit: we do what we need to do without thinking about it. I get up in the morning, shower, eat breakfast, brush my teeth, take a walk, do a day's work, eat supper, do something relaxing, go to bed, and fall asleep. As long as all this is fairly routine, my accustomed habits suffice. It's as though I were following a script, or rather a set of scripts. No need to think; just look up the proper response and do what it says.

Scripts—of which DNA molecules, habits, and computer programs are species—are sequences of instructions which if followed achieve a prescribed outcome. A recipe in a cookbook is a script; so is advice from Miss Manners; and so is the job description for a new opening at the local bank. A script is not very useful if it can be used only once, however—if it has no iterative power. The whole point of a habit is that it works over and over again. A good script is therefore general, in the sense that its instructions can be followed more than once. If I follow the script, I'll get a certain result; follow it again and I'll get a similar result. Vague approximation with respect to procedures and outcomes, rather than strict replication, is usually for the better because it means I can replay the script under slightly different situations and still produce acceptable results.

What makes a script good, therefore, is that it refers not to the specifics of a situation but to the pattern that situation exhibits. The instructions can be followed once and then a second time and eventually a hundredth time, because they are about features of the situation that are not unique to it. They refer to a kind of situation: to a certain structure of relationships rather than to the relata that exhibit them. The recipe calls for three cups of white flour, but it is indifferent to the brand of flour I might use, much less to the specific package I happen to pull off the shelf. The proper way to use a knife and fork is advised in language that pays no mind to what the table setting is, nor whose table, nor on what occasion. My teeth-cleaning habit adjusts for differences in toothbrush, toothpaste, water temperature, and time of day because the script refers to kinds of equipment and ranges of behavior rather than to anything particular. The more specific a script's instructions, the less likely it will be reusable and the more likely its instructions will go awry. If I don't know what to do when a new red toothbrush replaces my old blue one, I've been relying on a poorly developed because overly specified habit.

So it's good to be generic: to focus on the patterns, structures, typifications, models, or frameworks featured by concrete situations—Goffman's schemata of interpretation. Because things come with generic features, our ways of dealing with them can be generalized into typical responses such as habits, rituals, conventions, protocols, programs, assignments. Otherwise everything would be radically unique and nothing at all could be anticipated, nothing made sense of, nothing planned for in advance. But a script can only be as general as the features of the pattern to which it refers, and even the most general script is not likely to anticipate every possible situation in which it is set running. And so, often or occasionally or eventually, the script breaks down.

I take it for granted that the woman approaching me with outstretched arm and smiling face wishes to shake my hand and to secure my approval. I will respond to this gesture by grasping her hand palm to palm, thumbs overlapping, and giving it a slight pumping motion. This ritual form of touching does not require my attention, which frees me to focus on more pressing concerns. Who is she? What does she want? How can I extricate myself from this exchange quickly but graciously? The handshake will itself become problematic, however, if the woman's grip is too tight or too loose, if her palm is sweaty, if she uses the leverage of our clasped hands to pull me closer than my sense of social distance finds acceptable, if the hand she proffers is her left. This awkwardness will be distracting because the breakdown of habit means I will need to think about the interactions of our bodies as well as puzzling out the question of her intent.

Even very sophisticated procedures are dominated by scripted habits. Indeed, their very sophistication requires that a considerable range of activity be routinized so that the complex problems needing to be addressed can be given concentrated attention. A stuck lever on the computer keyboard is irritating because it forces me to think about what my fingers are doing when what I want is for them, as though by magic, to translate into phosphor arrangements on the screen my desire that certain words and sentences should represent some meaning I am trying to articulate. In preparing to run my experiment, I do not want to have to wonder if the reagent bottles are accurately labeled, the scales properly calibrated, and my assistant cognizant of what he is to do and when. But if the results of my experiment are unexpected, my thoughts will need to turn back to examine closely what I had been taking for granted—including, if necessary, a rethinking of the ideas presupposed in the design of my experiment.

With DNA or other biologically determined programs, the failure of the script means the termination of the trait, or of the organism that would have resulted were the script to have run to completion. If a revised script is needed, it will not arise in direct consequence of the problematic situation but for unrelated reasons such as random mutation. But with habits, computer programs, and any other set of instructions fashioned by human ingenuity, the necessary alterations can be made as a direct response to the problem, and might even permit a timely restoration of progress toward the outcome initially sought. What was made by thought can be repaired or altered by thought, so that the problem at issue in a problematic situation is whether or not the new thinking called for will be good enough to get the job done.

A problematic situation is one without a script—or, rather, without a script that works. A new script is called for, and if I am to write it, if I am to develop a new procedural habit, I will need to reassess my assumptions about the structure supposedly characterizing the situation that has become problematic. This situation is a problem for me because I was apparently mistaken about the pattern of relationships that hold among its constituents. The framework within which things are taking place would seem to be different than I had thought it to be. The script won't work because the world probably isn't shaped like I had imagined it was.

The problem might not be the pattern as such, however. Perhaps I was too up close, reading my situation too narrowly, looking at a local corner of the pattern which if seen fully would make it clear how my script needs to be reworked. I've been trying to talk to this elephant by whispering up its trunk; as soon as I broaden my context, it will be clear what I should do. Alternatively, I may need to come in more closely. The pattern may need to be refined, its details explicated more fully. Or, just the converse, the pattern may be so busily detailed that its primary features are being obscured. In all these kinds of cases, what I need is a more appropriate representation of the familiar pattern, which the old scripts can then be adjusted to reflect.

For example, when the astronomer Urbain Leverrier discovered that Uranus was not following an elliptical orbit, he found himself with an inadequate script for predicting and confirming the planet's future locations. The pattern embodied in Newtonian celestial mechanics formed the basis for a procedure of observations that, once Uranus had been discovered and its presence well established, could be routinized. That routine was no longer adequate: it instructed the telescope to look for Uranus at places where in fact it was not located. Leverrier first rechecked the observational data and did whatever was needed to fine-tune the numbers those data supported, but the phenomena were still not appearing where they were scripted to appear. So he widened the scope of the Newtonian pattern to include the presence of material bodies not previously presumed, then calculated the mass and location of a body sufficient to account for the discrepancies in Uranus's orbit. Telescopes turned to this location immediately confirmed the presence of a planet. Once

Neptune was added to the astronomical situation, Newton's laws were reconfirmed as its governing framework, and Uranus's orbital determinations could once again be routinized. The old script had not taken enough factors into account; the pattern on which it was based was too narrow. Its scope adjusted, the script once more worked well and Leverrier could turn his attention to other matters.

Sometimes, though, the problem is with the pattern itself and not simply with its range or detail. No matter what the breadth or depth of the pattern, it may still be unable to make sense of the given situation. It may simply fail to fit the facts it purports to represent. Leverrier used the same strategy he had applied to Uranus when he discovered deviations in the orbit of Mercury. His analysis predicted a planetary body located between Mercury and Venus. This time, however, there were no observations able to confirm Leverrier's prediction, and his hypothesis that the missing planet, which he called Vulcan, was made of material that absorbed rather than reflected light was too ad hoc to survive scrutiny. The Newtonian pattern, no matter how carefully and broadly applied, was not able to account for the facts.

When this sort of thing happens, what is needed is a new pattern. One might be ready at hand, for societies are repositories of tried-and-true ideas and of ideas, old or new, that are unused or underused. When my righthanded response to the woman's extended left hand results in an awkward failure to complete our handshake, I am not stranded without recourse. I should recognize that the woman's right hand is injured, temporarily or permanently, and once I've reconstituted the situation along those lines I know that I can either reorient by hand and negotiate a different kind of grip or quickly extend my left hand to her instead. The proper scripts are available, and once I've recognized that the situation is not ordered in the way presumed by the typical right-hand/right-hand form of greeting, I can pull a different script from my social repertoire and put it into play. If I am unaccustomed to these scripts, however, it may take some practice before they are rituals of interaction that I can perform unthinkingly. The script may need to be run with step-by-step conscious attention a few times before it becomes habit.

But every so often no available pattern will prove suitable: the situation will turn out to be genuinely puzzling. As when arthritis cripples my hands and I can no longer brush my teeth, or the smiling woman suddenly slaps me with her outstretched hand, or no new planet shows up where Newton's laws predict it must. Now what? A whole new way of seeing is needed, one that organizes the situation quite differently, heightening the importance of previously neglected factors, realigning the routes of primary connection, connecting what before was unconnected, separating what had once been thought inseparable. For instance, Einstein's general theory of relativity proved to be a pattern capable of accounting for the same data as Newton's but able at the same time to encompass anomalies such as the perturbations in Mercury's orbit that had confounded Leverrier.

I'm engaged in a creative act when I invent some new framework for organizing the elements of a given situation, thereby reconceiving it as a different kind of situation than it had been previously taken to be. I'm no less creative if I adapt an old pattern, nor should anyone slight my originality if I'm clever enough to know that an overlooked but culturally available preformed pattern fits the situation at hand perfectly. The plumber was certainly right when he charged me $105 for a thirty second house call: $5 to adjust the set screw a quarter turn, $100 for knowing that this was why the bathroom fixture wasn't working properly. Our task is not easy when we are challenged to come up with a framework that re-presents a situation in a way that permits us to write a new script based on it, a script that will guide us fruitfully toward the fulfillment of our ends. Whether my move is to find that the right pattern is already in the cultural toolbox, or to adapt an existing pattern to my new purpose, or to make one up from scratch, I need to be informed, imaginative, and bold all at once.

So in science, forming good hypotheses, inventing or invoking novel patterns for describing a problem, is key. Good data concerning the facts are important, for without their clarity and accuracy I might not even realize that there's a problem, that the script I'm following is out of touch with things and that a new pattern needs to be hypothesized. Good data are equally important for testing the predictive accuracy of my hypothesis, to confirm or refute its claims for how things must be functioning if they indeed are patterned as the hypothesis proposes. But the most difficult and the most important part of science is formulating good hypotheses.

Unlike the other aspects of experimental problem solving, there are no scripts—no algorithms, no automatic decision procedures—for determining the best substitute for an inadequate situational pattern. How nice it would be were there a sort of super-script available that I could trust to lead me unerringly to the new pattern for which I'm looking. But it is precisely the absence of this higher-order script that makes problematic situations problematic. Scriptless, I have no choice but to think—to invent a new way of seeing how things relate. I am scientific in my thinking if I develop a disposition to formulate plausible claims about the patterns that best relate the available data for a situation, and that also predict accurately additional data about it and about other situations. I am scientific in my approach to problems when I deal with them by using my intelligence to cast a new cloak of relationships over a situation where the old cloak has become too frayed to provide adequate coverage, then by carefully ascertaining that it really fits, and by repeating this same process over and over again. Repeating it without end, for cloaks are made of fragile threads and are always wearing out, and the situations they were designed to clothe are always changing, and our sense of what counts as good cloth or adequate coverage is always changing too.

Democratic Scripts

Let me now shift the discussion from science to democracy. What happens when the art of intelligent action is made the method by which a society approaches its problems? I want to begin, however, not by analyzing a specific problem but by considering the most general of the frameworks within which people live, those providing the patterns of relationship that undergird our social scripts about how to live a meaningful life. Let me call such a framework a cultural perspective: a structure for the whole landscape of my experience up to the horizons beyond which my understanding and actions cannot reach. My cultural perspective defines my world; it is the skeleton that gives shape and integrity to my life.

When people speak of my character, they are referring to my characteristic ways of thinking and behaving, my style: the scripts I have a disposition to utilize. To say that I have character, that I am a person of character, is to make a moral judgment about me, to praise me as someone whose actions are informed by principle, who responds in varying contexts by reference to the same underlying sense of how the world is ordered and what this means for how I should think and what I should do. Because I was born and raised in the United States, it is American culture that has provided me with my sense of who I am and how I ought to behave. In being true to what I think is right and proper, I reflect its underlying patterns—its traditions, its social practices. I am most fully myself when I'm reading from the American cultural script.

We are not all clones of one another, however. Cultures come in versions. I was taught to be boy and man in a middle-class Midwestern community of north European immigrants whose homes featured pictures of Jesus, Lincoln, and FDR. Each of these natural and historical aspects of who I am reflects a version of the American cultural perspective, a standpoint from which it is appropriated. The sort of American I am is shaped—to mention the currently popular fourfold mantra—by my race, ethnicity, gender, and class. It is also shaped—to name a few other versions—by my religious beliefs, ethical commitments, political affiliation, residential location, sexual preference, and type of employment. These versional influences are also affected by such things as my genetic makeup, birth order, and immune system history, as well as by my parents' caring practices, my teachers' pedagogical styles, the quality of the public library's holdings, and the effectiveness of the local sports programs. My individual point of view, the person I uniquely am, is a weighted intersection, and finally a distinctive integration, of these versions of my culture.

We Americans are not replicas of one another, thanks to these variations in our culture and in our experiences of them. We all bear a family resemblance to one another, nonetheless, because these versions are, after all, versions: variations on a more fundamental cultural theme.

Of all these cultural versions, my ethnicity is probably the most important because its origin lies outside the reach of the dominant culture. I am an American, but if my ethnic heritage is Ghanian or Italian, Chinese or Scottish, Cuban or Cherokee, then my way of being an American has its root in a non-American perspective. Cultural perspectives are ultimate points of view. Yet even though I am therefore most fundamentally an American in how I view things, that viewpoint contains a second ultimate viewpoint in the form of the cultural perspective from which my ethnic perspective derives. That ancestral culture has lost its ultimacy under the metamorphic pressures exerted by the primary culture. Yet even though deultimatized, it still manages because of its once-ultimate features to exert massive pressure on the shaping of my character.

The difference between the American perspective and the perspective afforded by an ethnic heritage can be relatively minor and hence the process of ethnic subordination and integration easily accomplished. This is the case when the ethnicity has historically been a dominant presence in American culture, as is the case for most European immigrants, especially those like myself of Anglo-Saxon or Celtic backgrounds. Where the cultural heritage needs to undergo considerable metamorphosis in order to be fused with American culture, however, and especially where that ancestral culture has powerful resources for resisting change, the integration may be only partial and unstable.

In the American cauldron, therefore, the melting points for the cultural heritages vary, as well as the time needed for the melting to take place. Moreover, the immigrants coming to this nation, whether before its founding or just within recent months, had lived or are still living the cultures they brought with them, living those cultures in as many versions as there are versions of the American culture with which they then had to cope or now are coping. The melting pot always contains chunks and bits of unmelted and partly melted ethnicities. Recall William James's metaphor that what we take as truth is like a stew, the new both being transformed by the old and in turn transforming it. His metaphor is equally apt as a description of American culture. We are more a stew than we are the puree implied by the notion of a melting pot.

We would be mistaken were we, wanting to deny the puree, to imagine America as like a mosaic or a quilt, multicultural in the sense of being a patchwork of self-contained ethnic groupings. For the whole makes a difference to its constituent elements; the melting in fact occurs. However much it might be transformed by the counterpressures of the ethnicities it transforms, the ethnic perspectives end up as versions of the American Way and not alternatives to it. Sometimes it is very difficult to see the American perspective we share, given the salience of the differences among our ethnic versions of that perspective. Yet, for instance, African Americans are more American than African. Their search for roots, their discovery of Africanness, their recovery of an Islamic faith or their participation in Kwanza celebrations, is as American as apple pie. Sometimes, in contrast, the ethnic heritage of people may be so subordinate and so explicitly repudiated that it is as if they had no non-American past shaping their American present. But that flight from their heritage is also a slice from that same apple pie. Ethnic canonists in the United States tend to forget that their intellectual canon is a version of a wider nonethnic American canon—that it is a distinctive and legitimate way of reading it, but a version of it nonetheless.

It is an educational truism that studying abroad, learning to see the world from a cultural perspective not my own, is the best way to become aware that how I see things is from a perspective also. To recognize the framework of my culture as a framework is to discover two important truths at once: that my way of seeing things is limited, and that it is a matter of historical happenstance. I don't need to study abroad to learn this, however, because what is true for cultures is true for their versions as well. By living amid, working with, or even just reading about an American ethnic group other than my own, I become aware that my ethnic version of America is indeed just a version. I realize that other ethnicities open up horizons not otherwise available to me, and that my own horizon need never have come to be and one day will be no longer.

Don't forget, however, that these comments about how different ethnicities foster a sense of plurality, and hence a sense of the finitude of our own ethnic location, are only illustrative. Our discovery of alternatives to the kinds of cultural versions other than ethnic which we incarnate can, and should, have the same consequence: our recognition that Americans need not share our gender, religious faith, political ideology, sexual orientation, or regional accent in order to be as American as we are.

We discover in these experiences something of what Dewey calls the "plasticity of human nature" (1946: 191), the amazing capacity we have for creating worlds, and versions of worlds, and versions of those versions, again and over again endlessly. This is not to embrace the "blank slate" theory of human nature, against which Steven Pinker fulminates, however, for our biological heritage sets firm parameters to that plasticity and our history as a civilization-making species has added further conventional but deeply contoured constraints. It would seem, for instance, that we humans have a disposition—I am tempted to say an instinct—for handling any encounter with difference by rejecting it. I'm perfectly capable of not seeing a different world as different, like wealthy people who can drive through the slums and not notice the economic squalor. Or I can isolate myself from difference, which is what those rich folks must have done if it was necessary for them to drive to the slum in order not to see it. Or I can devalue that other world, viewing it with contempt, a contempt that at its extreme can justify my choosing to eliminate the difference by destroying those who embody it, those who see and feel and live in a way so decidedly not my own.

Why I should want to deal with difference by negating it is obvious enough. If I am oblivious to any experience not framed by my culture's framework of meanings, then I will think my ways natural and whatever varies from them unnatural. The familiar scripts and the intellectual canon undergirding them will be taken as transcripts of reality, tethers tying my beliefs and practices to the solid ground upon which all things rest. I will find religious faiths and their rituals ungodly if they differ from my own, because I am so sure mine are undergirded by a godly promise about their significance. If I take my culture not as a perspective but as an objective characterization of things, then another's point of view is either inadequate, a limited version of my own, or simply wrong. And it is very comforting to know that this is so.

What's unsettling about a different world is that it puts my own in doubt. I can no longer presume my taken-for-granted truths and virtues and hopes. The canon of these presumptions no longer provides self-evident regulative answers to my questions about how things are, what I should do, and why. The encounter with other worlds and even other versions of my own world tears up my book of scripts. Wrenched from my habits and thrown into a problematic situation, I have two choices. I can start to think, and eventually I may come up with a reasonable solution that might or might not work, a new script or even a renovated canon by means of which I can establish a new repertoire of suitable habits. Or I can solve the intrusive problem quickly and assuredly by convincing myself that it is not really a problem, by refusing to acknowledge the reality, importance, or relevance of its prior conditions, its immediate impact, or its eventual consequences. The bane of content canonists is the ease with which they are tempted by their absolutist claims to venture out onto the slippery slope that carries them all too soon into dogmatic self-insulating closure.

The method of intelligence Dewey asks that we practice is thus no easy matter. It's an unnatural act, in the sense that our natural inclination is to prefer our habits. Indeed, the only reason to think is in order to put an end to the unsettling need to think. The difficulty with experimental intelligence is that it asks us to run upstream against the strong current of our desire for a world we can count on. This is especially so when the world is the one that frames our beliefs about the most important things in life. The procedural canon Dewey advocates has undermined wide swatches of the content canon of our beliefs about physical nature. It has been hard enough to think that what common sense tells us is true is actually not true, that the earth isn't flat,

Education for a Democracy

that rocks are mainly empty space, that organismic kinds evolve by mechanisms devoid of purpose, and that sometimes it isn't safe to drink good fresh milk. But when Dewey asks that the scientific method be extended from studying stones and stars to examining how we might best change our interactions with one another in order to achieve a better common good, he asks the seemingly impossible. He puts in question a content canon that undergirds our most fundamental beliefs. To begin thinking that we are under no absolute obligation to love our neighbors, that our soul might not be immortal, or that our destiny as a people might not be manifest: such thoughts are outrageous, a fundamental threat to who we know for sure we are. They are, quite literally, beyond belief.

Everything having to do with altering our perspective is difficult, after all. It requires considerable imaginative skill to discern a new way to organize my experience of some problematic situation. It requires as much skill to recognize the relevance of an already existing pattern, which with some modification can be put to this new use. The wider the scope of the problem or the more complex its details, the more difficult the task of adapting old and inventing new perspectives, renovating long-trusted canons, rewriting our everyday scripts. And when the problems are about human communities, and when change in the framework involves tampering with our cultural perspective and hence with our selves, the difficulties are gargantuan.

However, Dewey is arguing, unless we become good at the reframings required for problem solving at community, regional, national, and international levels, social change will simply continue to be the consequence of the current canonical scripts. Our choices will be made unthinkingly, which means our actions will be framed in accord with passion, prejudice, and caprice rather than intelligent judgment. Plato has Socrates argue, at the end of the *Meno,* that those able to grasp intuitively the cultural canons by which to guide social change are blessed by a god-given genius, for which education is irrelevant. Hence, it is a matter of luck if a community has good leaders or not. Socrates, with a sigh, can only dream of a time when there might be leaders with the humility and self-knowledge necessary for rising above intuition, for learning rationally and systematically the canonical truths and goods they need to know. Plato looks for his Guardians among those who can know the unchanging Forms upon which all changing things depend. Dewey amends Plato only by insisting that these forms are inventions rather than discoveries, and that those intellectual canons are and must be always changing if they are to organize the flux of things sufficiently to make possible genuine resolutions through democratic processes of the real problems of actual living human beings.

So something must be done to change our habits. We must become willing to believe what we once thought unbelievable; we must be willing to make actual what we once thought not even possible. That is, we need to change our point of view concerning the origin and nature of social issues and concerning how they should be addressed. For our democratic ways to remain viable, we need to create a new canon for evaluating our intellectual canons, so that we can devise new problem-solving scripts and hence deploy new and more worthy habits of social interaction.

Playing with Scripts

Here's where education comes in. We need to be taught how to invent forms for fitting incompatible things together, for making sense from nonsense, for bringing chaos into order. We need to be taught how to find forms that might be relevant to this task and how to adapt them to new uses. Since these are societal forms, canonical frameworks for shaping democratically acceptable social policies from the disparate agendas of various interest groups, our work will include, and crucially, making new forms of cultural meaning. The task of education, says Dewey, is to develop people with the "enduring dispositions and attitudes" (1946: 165) needed to think this way: people whose habit for dealing with social issues is to look for the resources harbored in the cultural versions available but too often neglected by a community, and to put these to creative use as primary tools for problem solving.

New tools can be wonderful, but their novelty makes them awkward to use. If I'm unfamiliar with a tool, even a simple one, I may not hold it correctly or I may try too hard or my timing may be off. There's a learning curve to tools, and so I frequently find myself growing impatient with them. Often I give the instrument a try, find that it isn't as good as I'd thought it would be, and so put it aside and simply make do with the old tools. There's many a VCR under the TV blinking its "12:00" proof that the owners never did figure out how to program it. Many a woodworking tool hanging on a pegboard above the workbench is an unused testament to a weekend carpenter's failed dexterity. If new tools and gadgets put us off because we cannot easily adapt to their ways, it should be no surprise that we are all the more put off by unfamiliar social ways, by oddly used words, strange presumptions, offbeat customs, and outlandish attitudes.

The way to overcome this reluctance to change is by learning how to play (see Allan 1997: ch. 5, "The Playfulness of a College"). The virtue of play is that it mimics life, but without life's risks. The game is for an afternoon, the rules and the goals are clear, the disagreements unambiguous, and the results definitive. But the losers don't forfeit their lives or prospects or material goods, and although the happiness is brief so is the pain. There is no better way for me to learn the skills I will need for some serious purpose than to practice them in a nonserious situation that has a similar form. I can practice my engineering skills by doing crossword puzzles. I can learn to adjust my goals in the light of others' purposes by playing chess or basketball. Poker teaches me how to distinguish others' real from their apparent intentions. Pilots practice takeoffs and landings in a flight simulator before ever starting down an actual runway, and soldiers engage in war games. Politicians rehearse their options by running through alternative scenarios, and simulation games have become a classroom staple in social science courses. It's no empty claim that eighteenth- and nineteenth-century Britain wrought the leaders for its empire on the rugby fields at Eton.

Playing with other worlds is a way for me to inhabit them without having to give up my own. War, pestilence, and flood alienate people from their familiar cultural worlds and force them to find refuge in another world. Brutal facts create the necessity to inhabit a novel worldview, and the refugee succeeds or fails at this, to whatever extent, for all the usual reasons. The rewards in the life-and-death real world for managing to make a shift from a former world and its canonical presuppositions to a new one are significant, but so is the price of failure. Far better for me that the other world should first be experienced playfully—visited in imagination or as a temporary resident, without my having to give up permanently my familiar perspectives. As I become more skilled in seeing things differently, more versed in working from within another version of my cultural perspective or in acquiring a way of thinking and acting sharply at odds with my usual practices, I will increase my ability to move among worlds intelligently. I will be able to enlarge my repertoire of frameworks available for the serious tasks of real-world problem solving.

How might a college or university school its students in a variety of alternative cultural perspectives? How might it bring them to be familiar with the various versions of their point of view already available for them in the person of their own fellow students? How might students become not only skilled in this or that other style of thinking and feeling and doing, but skilled in learning new styles wherever and whenever they might be encountered? How can professors evoke from their students a disposition to acquire and make use of the rich resources of cultural difference?

Certainly the answer is not that faculty should edify students by imparting to them whatever information about other cultures and other ethnicities they or their students might find interesting or important. Telling me the bare facts about an alien perspective is a funereal exercise, an inculcation of what Whitehead calls "inert ideas" (1916: 1) . All the instructor does is walk me through a mausoleum of dead conclusions and consequences, preserved in marble or formaldehyde. This way of teaching differences is what Dewey calls "aesthetic esotericism": the tourist who oohs and aahs over the oddities produced by other cultures but cannot quite imagine that anyone ever actually lived that way, ever used those things or believed those ideas. Our country is filled with people who know that Plato had a doctrine of abstract universal Forms that he claimed were more real than the solid rocks that bruise our flesh or the lovers whom we embrace. But few of these people have ever imaged that a normal human being could actually believe something like that, much less that they themselves might come to believe it.

A well-worn image for how a pluralistic democracy should work is two people with different worldviews—different religious faiths or metaphysical beliefs—who nonetheless agree to work together to repaint the village lampposts green (Frankel: ch. 5). I need not see things the way another person does for us to cooperate. In fact, our ability to live together in the same community is because we can agree to disagree on certain things, even and especially on ultimate things, while cooperating on more mundane, practical matters. Our neighbors, so this story implies, have quaint customs which we can enjoy at weekend art shows and community festivals. These ways of life have no relevance, however, when it comes to grappling with the practical everyday problems for which we need to find a common solution—such as making sure the lampposts are painted green. Yet tolerating differences in fundamental versions of a shared cultural perspective by regarding those difference as without important practical consequence is just another form of aesthetic esotericism.

At its very best, says Dewey, appropriating the dead products of other cultures results in a "passive toleration" (1946: 42) of difference, acknowledging these strange forms of life as human possibilities but denigrating them. As he notes, we Americans can be tolerant of others in this narrow sense, but that's quite compatible with our continuing to be anti-Semitic, racially prejudiced, and suspicious of immigrants. Indeed, my study of cultures as interesting artifacts may only serve to strengthen my prejudice that there is one natural way for humans to live: my way, my white middle-class mainstream way, the American way. I come away from these supposedly broadening experiences thinking that what I have learned about other peoples, places, and ideas reveals some of the surprising ways in which the right way can be distorted by those who lack the requisite breeding, knowledge, or motivation to be truly civilized. How ironic, that in the name of globalizing the curriculum so many of our colleges and universities merely reinforce their students' parochialism by requiring them to take at least one course in an esoteric topic. We need not be ignorant to be bigots.

I come much closer to the kind of cultural appropriation Dewey calls for when I learn to appreciate how other viewpoints can be of use to me. After I have learned the utility of difference, after I have come to respect the problem-solving power of frames of reference other than my own, I may finally be ready to cooperate with others without requiring them to agree with me. In being open to ideas that work but that are based on presuppositions I do not share, I acknowledge the incompleteness of my own point of view.

Sometimes the situation calls for tools I'm not handy at using or that I didn't even realize existed, so it's wise to have lots of different skills and perspectives represented in the group of persons in my classroom, among whom I live, with whom I work. We can pool our resources and together get done what we could not accomplish separately. Out of our plurality, comes power.

My appreciation of difference in this case is opportunistic, however, and approached from the outside. I only know my classmate's or neighbor's perspective as an expertise: a black box. I don't know how it works, and I don't really care. I have reason to believe that it can produce the desired results, and for me that's all that counts. But the problem is knowing when we need an expert, and which expert we need. So I have to become an expert in selecting among the available experts. I have to know how to make the right choice of an expert at the right time. There is something self-contradictory, however, about being expected to know when and if it's time to use a perspective I've never occupied. Yet if only experts can tell when they are needed, then I am likely to use them only in the ways predefined by the perspectives that justify their expertise. There is likely to be little room for the creative imagination and the inventive daring needed for effective problem solving.

The more I am at home in a variety of perspectives, Dewey argues, able to "engage in some kind of imaginative translation" (1946: 194) of each into the others—taking, for instance, Paula Rothenberg's empathetic approach to the study of difference—the more likely I am to recognize the relevance any one of them might have for a given situation. The more I am practiced in shifting from one to another point of view, the more likely I am to try one out just to see how it works when set running in a new environment, just to see what happens if I tweak its possibilities. The more my thinking is multi-perspectival, the more alert I will likely be to the limitations of my own perspective and the more likely I will be interested in upgrading it: by varying its theme or modulating its key or tempo, by remolding it or melting it down or melding it with something else, by borrowing this or that from another frame to patch my own, by extending a familiar pattern beyond where it has ever gone before.

We are none of us gods, however. We will always be much better at some versions than at others. Our empathy has its bounds. There will always be more perspectives in heaven or earth than those with which we are familiar, no matter how encompassing our philosophy. Nor can some perspectives easily be set aside or modified. He will never lose his Spanish accent; her abuse as a child will forever scar her trust of men; they took me out of the Iowa cornfields but they were never able to take the Iowa out of me. Nonetheless, as the range and variety of our experiences expand, we become better at seeing problems with the fresh eyes of an informed imagination. As my world expands, it is more likely that I will recognize a problem as not my problem but ours, that I will see its resolution not in terms of a restoration of the canonical world that has heretofore supported the onflow of my own habits, but instead in terms that integrate my world with those of others, such that the habits our world supports are for all of us renovations of what we once thought quite sufficient.

For example, if my ethics class is interested in the problem of social justice, I might decide to approach the issue in my usual abstract fashion. However, my set of lectures on Kant's categorical imperative and Bentham's utilitarian calculus may come across to the students as so much information to be learned by rote and at best appreciated as wonderful examples of sustained esoteric prose. It would be better were I to begin with a real problem, one that bites into the lives of my students, one they think it important that they resolve. My students will each see the problem differently, of course, and one of our tasks will be to make those differing viewpoints obvious to one another, to explore the framework beliefs and histories from which they each draw, and to analyze together the ridges of our agreement as well as the furrows of our disagreement.

At this point, it might make sense to turn to Kant and Bentham, but not as though their ideas were answer-artifacts in a museum display case. Even if the display of philosophers were enlarged by adding the answers of other ethicists, including those excluded from the Western educational canon for various hegemonic reasons, it would still contain only dead artifacts. If, however, my students know the problem as a genuine one—know it as their own problem—then the philosophers whom we invite into our discussion will come to it as new voices, vibrant and alive, bearing new points of view for us to examine in the same analytic and empathetic way we have been examining one another's points of view. Kant, for instance, might prove to be a fresh unsettling presence were we to study him thoroughly enough to become able, even if still awkwardly, to move around within his world of ideal wills unbiased by passion and of the canon of moral obligations those wills respect categorically. Some of us might be surprised to discover that Kant had been saying in his own way almost exactly what we were trying to say. One or two of us might even suspect that our similarity to the Königsberg recluse was more a matter of cultural genealogy than happenstance.

And after sufficient facts had been ascertained and enough viewpoints fully explored, my students and I might begin to invent an interpretive framework for our problem, a way of organizing what we know so that it yields the glimmer of a possible solution. We would need to secure everyone's agreement on its reasonableness, and it would be likely that what seemed at first to be a sturdily built solution will run into some immovable fact and break apart. Quite a long time might ensue before our class had a solution they would have good reason to believe might work, or at least one they could agree had been worth the try.

This is why democracy and scientific method fit hand in glove. A democracy is inherently pluralistic because it tolerates differing cultural versions rather than insisting that one version be dominate and all others be suppressed or made subordinate. The essence of democracy, says Dewey, is the realization that no one perspective is adequate enough to organize the world meaningfully for everyone, that no one person or group of people is wise enough to rule others without their consent. So government must function by methods of "mutual consultation and voluntary agreement" rather than "fixed subordination" (1946: 58), by appealing to reasons and interests rather than intimidation or force of arms.

Policy makers, from my county zoning commission to the U.S. Congress, need to be skilled at seeing the issues as others see them. They need to understand adequately, and so take reasonable account of, the views of those whose consent they are expected to secure. They need to be adept at the creative reconciliation of the inevitable conflicts among those viewpoints if they are to make the workable decisions expected of them. Policy making is an uncomfortable role. No wonder that people charged with this responsibility all too typically settle for solutions that exclude differences rather than reconciling them, or find themselves unable to arrive at solutions imaginative enough, informed enough, or bold enough to resolve the problem. Too often, as a result, the decision made is one that unfairly benefits those who share the policy maker's point of view, or the decision in trying to please everyone benefits no one.

In a democracy, we need to be governed at all levels by people with precisely the skills, and the disposition for utilizing them, that Dewey advocates. Democracy, he says, is a way of life and not reducible to this or that mechanism for effecting its ends. It is not the secret ballot or proportional representation or regular elections that is key, but a habit of the heart: the disposition to think about problems multi-versionally. The prerequisite for this disposition is a familiarity, bred of reiterated experience, with the vast multiplicity of our culture's versions and with the people for whom those versions are ways of life, for whom these are worlds of serious belief and arenas of significant practical action. A democracy provides the multivariant soil needed for nurturing citizens adept at the art of intelligent practice. Citizens, willing and able to act intelligently in this pluralistic sense, become the instruments by which a democracy can actually learn to govern with the consent of the governed.

So democracy and science are each other's necessary conditions. Without democracy, people will lack a sufficient repertoire of variant canonical beliefs and practices that are rooted in the different available versions of their shared worldview, versions they know firsthand or near-hand in all the splendor of each one's rainbowed variety, as only long years of experiencing them makes possible. Possessing a relatively meager repertoire of canonical scripts, they will be hard-pressed to respond as creatively as they should to the difficult problems they mutually confront as citizens. Without the method of intelligent inquiry as the way by which the citizens of a democracy address these problems, without a repertoire of script-making techniques, manners of selecting, remodeling, and reconciling what their collection of traditional scripts provides, they will be equally hard-pressed. Their differences will increasingly separate them, factionalize and fracture their common life, replace the open-ended canon they had shared with a collection of closed canons. Amid the resulting chaos, the smooth voice of monochrome despotic saviors promising narrow but guaranteed modes of peace and security will sound ever more attractive. This two-sided danger, a democracy bereft of the method of intelligence or a science bereft of ends based on needs determined and addressed by all citizens cooperatively, is why Dewey puts so much emphasis on devising an approach to education able to provide the American nation with people whose character has been formed by the habits of experimental inquiry practiced in a context of pluralistic democracy.

Easier said than done, but that goes without saying. The method of intelligence is no divinity, some sort of absolute and constant canon by which to master the rabble of democracy's ever-changing wants and desires. Like any pragmatic canon, it comes in versions and so needs constantly to be adapted afresh to the ways in which actual historical cultures and their conflicting versions create the problems needing resolution. The difficulty is not whether intelligence is required of us, but how to craft its relevance in any given context. The difficulty lies in actually managing to apply the method, being good at using it and good at knowing when it should be used, tailoring it and deciding when it needs tailoring, and being resolutely committed to its appropriate and proper use.

The knowledge required for what Dewey calls "the experimental production of social change" (1946: 157) is not easily acquired because it demands that we be at home in more worldviews than one—but other worlds are strange, complex, subtle, and threatening. Nor is the skill in applying this knowledge to the real problems of men and women in their various communities easily acquired, because it involves playing imaginatively with the most important things in life—deeply felt beliefs, well-tested practices, the bases of our most treasured memories and most fervent hopes—and doing so fully recognizing that as a result of this playfulness the things most precious to us will never be the same again. Nor is the commitment to this sort of problem solving easily made, because it means venturing beyond the solid ground of the familiar with no assurance of success. Yet it is just this knowledge, this imagination, and this commitment that intelligence requires. As Dewey makes quite clear, a pluralistic democracy is hard work. There are no shortcuts in the scientific quest for warranted truths capable of serving the democratic quest for a common good.

Chapter 10

Religious Education

Romance

In a 1908 essay, "Religion and Our Schools," Dewey assails a proposal that religion be taught as part of the public school curriculum. Proponents see it as a way to instill in students the moral character prerequisite to good citizenship, but Dewey thinks "education in religion" is an oxymoron, the didactic promulgation of parochial irrationalisms. American education is already plagued by a tradition of "dogmatic, catechetical and memoriter methods" of instruction (172). Its problems would only be exacerbated by including instruction in that most dogmatic of all subject matters.

Dewey is equally hostile, however, to those secularists who argue that character and citizenship are best inculcated by teaching students to revere science and democracy rather than God and the Church. They invest science with "the same spiritual import as supernaturalism" and think that the social conditions for democracy are the same as for feudalism, imagining that they are enlightened moderns because of a few "slight changes of phraseology," giving marginally "new shades of meaning" to old symbols. "Such beliefs testify to that torpor of imagination which is the uniform effect of dogmatic belief" (167). Genuine science is a method of inquiry open to critique and requiring empirical verification, not a set of dogmatic conclusions, and genuine democracy is a mode of association based on equal access and shared responsibility, not on hierarchical authority.

What Americans need is a new "intellectual attitude," a new "interpretation of the world" that carries with it a new approach to social interaction and hence a new sense of what constitutes the moral life. It needs a new intellectual canon. We ought "to labor persistently and patiently," says Dewey, "for the clarification and development of the positive creed of life implicit in democracy and in science, and to work for the transformation of all practical instrumentalities of education till they are in harmony with these ideas" (168).

We cannot teach superstitious people to think rationally nor unjust people to act justly unless there is "an accompanying thorough reorganization of social life and of science" (171). Unless we reconceive religion in a way compatible with the methods of science and the ideals of democracy, it will only be an obstacle to the liberation of persons from ignorance, prejudice, and suffering. Religion if rightly understood, however, if taken as "a natural expression of human experience," as the "natural piety" persons should cultivate toward their potential for achieving fulfillment through "a broader and more catholic principle of human intercourse and association," can be "the fine flower of the modern spirit's achievement" (176, 177).

Dewey argues that, if teachers foster the values implicit in scientific inquiry and democratic association, students will develop this natural piety, committing themselves to the ideal of human betterment as a concretely realizable possibility. They will understand that they are natural creatures able to improve their lives by taking seriously their "implication" with other natural entities "in a common career and destiny" (176). Religion, interpreted in this way, should be integral to an educational system that aims to help people become skilled in the uses of experimental intelligence for the enhancement of human goods.

Alfred North Whitehead asserts at the conclusion of a 1916 essay on "The Aims of Education" that "the essence of education is that it be religious," for instruction is educational only insofar as it "inculcates duty and reverence." Reverence arises from the perception that "the present holds within itself the complete sum of existence, backwards and forwards, that whole amplitude of time, which is eternity." Our sense of duty is then the recognition that "our potential control over the course of events" is what constitutes that present (14).

Earlier in the essay, Whitehead contrasts "inert ideas" with "understanding." Ideas are inert, a student thereby suffering "mental dryrot," if they "are merely received into the mind without being utilized, or tested, or thrown into fresh combination" (1). Understanding, however, is the active appropriation and integration of ideas, ideas "illumined" by "the spark of vitality" because seen as "useful" (2). Understanding is "of an insistent present." It involves "knowledge of the past" not as an end in itself but with respect to its constraints and possibilities, its usefulness as a way "to equip us for the present" (3). Teachers encourage a reverence for life when they help students understand their world, their cultural heritage, in terms of its concrete relevance to the attainment of what is good. The present is where values are made and unmade, where we honor past achievements by putting them to work in the fashioning of new ones. Nowhere else but now can there be good.

To understand that this is so, that the present and the sacred are the same, that the present "is holy ground; for it is the past, and it is the future" (3), is for us to have attained a religious sensibility.

Realizing this, we therefore also recognize that what we know or could have known has bearing on what we can do, and how well we utilize what we know will determine the quality and character of what in fact is done—or not done. We are responsible for the good we could have accomplished. "Where attainable knowledge could have changed the issue, ignorance has the guilt of vice" (14). Education inculcates duty insofar as it brings students to this awareness of the role that they can, and therefore that they should, play in the shaping of present value.

Whitehead calls the practice of attempting to fulfill our duty "the sense for style": an "admiration for the direct attainment of a foreseen end, simply and without waste" (12). The point of action is to attain a goal, whatever it be, and to that extent any means is justified that harnesses the power necessary to produce the desired results. But a poor choice of means can have unintended consequences, give rise to unfortunate "side issues," create "undesirable inflammations." With style, says Whitehead, "you attain your end and nothing but your end" (12). We restrain the power we have harnessed so that our actions become "calculable," our means suited to our ends, tailored to the task for which they were designed. Power, by being thus restrained, is not curtailed but augmented. "With style your power is increased, for your mind is not distracted with irrelevancies, and you are more likely to attain your object." Foresight, the fruit of style, "is the last gift of gods to men" (13).

Thus, a proper education for Whitehead is one that teaches students their duty by making them aware that they have the power to alter the present for the better, by helping them understand what the resources are relevant to their task, and by encouraging them to find a stylish way to its accomplishment. Because it is the keystone to achieving what is best in the most elegant available manner, "style is the ultimate morality of mind" (12). Developing in students this sense of duty toward the present, toward the holy ground where whatever good there might be must be made, is the moral imperative that good teaching should communicate, and it is in this sense that the essence of education can be said to be religious.

So both Dewey and Whitehead argue that genuine education is religious education, that the aim of the teacher should be to develop a student's religious sensibilities. But they understand religion as natural piety, a faith in the potential humans have to create together the conditions for living mutually fulfilling lives. And hence the education they both advocate is practical, having to do with how students can be taught the skills by which that potential can be cashed out, that fulfillment realized. Dewey and Whitehead reject an approach to education that takes the accomplishments of the past as accesses to timeless truth, an approach advocated by both content and procedural canonists. However, they also reject an anti-canonical approach that dismisses such accomplishments as irrelevant or pernicious. These contrary approaches are both forms of dogmatism and are idolatrous because they take the highest human values to be either transcendent or private. Instead, Dewey and Whitehead advocate a pragmatic canon, one that is postmodern rather than modern but constructive rather than deconstructive, for it embodies values understood as both objective and contingent, made by the efforts of fallible humans working cooperatively to improve their world—working as best they can within the limitations and opportunities provided by the natural resources, both cultural and physical, available to them.

This characterization of Dewey's views paints an expected portrait, except possibly for the surprisingly early evocation on his part of the themes famously articulated a quarter century later in *A Common Faith*. The portrait painted of Whitehead is not so familiar, however, since the importance in *Process and Reality* of God, as source of novelty and preserver of good, has given a transcendental cast to what are usually considered the key features of his philosophy. Yet in these brief and comparatively early essays, both Dewey and Whitehead are strikingly nontheistic in their orientation. They both argue that the good is contingent and creaturely, and that its creation is a collaborative this-worldly task. They think that education, kindling a love for learning that is motivated by a natural piety toward furthering the common good, is the only way by which new generations can learn to use well what their predecessors have wrought so as to enhance rather than degrade the quality of their lives.

The question immediately becomes how we should take these two essays. Are they merely occasional pieces, ephemeral bouquets of passing interest, or do they mirror accurately and adequately each man's fully developed philosophical system? I shall argue that they are the latter, that they are miniatures—medallions—of the full-blown theories of education each advocates and that those theories are integral to their views of person, value, and nature—to their metaphysical ontologies. If so, then Dewey's pragmatism and Whitehead's organicism are birds of the same feather, both philosophies of process. And we should take seriously their dual warning that ignoring a process interpretation of religion, and hence of the proper relation of religion to the aims and methods of education, can have disastrous results for democracy and for human fulfillment.

Dewey, always indefatigably optimistic, warns of the dangers of an uneducated citizenry in order to call us to the tasks required for their overcoming:

> We need ... to accept the responsibilities of living in an age marked by the greatest intellectual readjustment history records. There is undoubted loss of joy, of consolation, of

some types of strength, and of some sources of inspiration in the change. ... Yet nothing is gained by deliberate effort to return to ideas which have become incredible, and to symbols which have been emptied of their content of obvious meaning. (168)

Whitehead sounds less sanguine in his roll call of "the broken lives, the defeated hopes, the national failures" that are a result of the current "frivolous inertia" among his fellow citizens with regard to improving how the nation's youth are educated:

It is difficult to restrain within oneself a savage rage. In the conditions of modern life the rule is absolute, the race which does not value trained intelligence is doomed. Not all your heroism, not all your social charm, not all your wit, not all your victories on land or at sea, can move back the finger of fate. To-day we maintain ourselves. To-morrow science will have moved forward yet one more step, and there will be no appeal from the judgment which will then be pronounced on the uneducated. (14)

Precision

In attempting to compare the views of Dewey and Whitehead with regard to education, we immediately run up against a problem of centrality. Dewey's philosophy is fundamentally an ethics, a set of claims concerning the optimal conditions for achieving our aims and for determining what they should be. Truth is a function of practices that satisfy those conditions, practices best exemplified in natural science research and formalized by Dewey as the method of experimental intelligence. A theory of educational practices must be the core of any adequate philosophy because schooling is at the core of any society, the institutional manner by which people attempt to assure the continuance from generation to generation of the conditions for achieving good.

For Whitehead, however, education is far removed from the concerns that drive his metaphysical reflections. The only references to education in his major systematic works are brief asides, a single paragraph in *Process and Reality*, for instance, extolling the importance of cultivating a student's imagination (338). Education was a topic he wrote about frequently, but always in the form of addresses given on specific occasions for a general audience. Educational theorists quote Whitehead constantly because these essays are filled with stimulating insights pithily expressed, but he made no effort to connect those insights to his metaphysics, to show the relevance of his very abstract scheme to the concrete experiences of learning and the proper forms of schooling. He proposes no explicit theory of ethics and hence provides no explicit grounds for making normative judgments about educational practices and the role they should play in the attainment of individual and societal goods.

An obvious strategy for permitting a comparison between Dewey and Whitehead is to elicit either a metaphysical framework from Dewey's thought or an educational theory from Whitehead's. But a formidable obstacle immediately blocks either route. As we know from our brief discussion of it in chapter 6, there are two kinds of process in Whitehead's system, but they are not straightforwardly connected. At the "microcosmic" level, process is the becoming of what occurs, the making of space-time quanta. At the "macrocosmic" level, process is how certain features of these quanta come to be replicated in the features of their successors. Thus, there are no direct connections among the enduring macro features. A space-time quantum—an "actual occasion," to use Whitehead's terminology—achieves a particular character, and this momentarily achieved character influences what then comes to characterize its successor. One quantum constrains another; the result is a similarity between them that reflects that constraint. Because our senses are unable to distinguish the individual quanta, however, we experience space-time as an extensive continuum. We take sequences of discrete micro processes as a single macro totality, disregarding their coming to be and attending only to the determinate features they fashion, treating episodic similarities as enduring identities. "There is a becoming of continuity, but no continuity of becoming" (1929b: 35).

Almost everything that human beings think important are enduring objects of some sort, regions of the macrocosmic extensive continuum. To describe the coming to be and perishing of enduring macro objects in terms of the coming to be and perishing of their constituent micro quanta is awkward, however, just as it is difficult in the natural sciences to describe molar events, such as teaching a student how to read, by referring only to molecular events such as light waves interacting with the retina. It can be done, and perhaps even done nonreductively, but what is important—the learning process going on—is drowned in the details.

We seem to be impaled on the horns of a frustrating dilemma: either abandon our insistence on using macrocosmic terms when developing theories about educational processes, or abandon Whitehead as a resource for systematizing those theories within a metaphysical framework. The way between the horns is to recall what we have been arguing in chapters 6 through 8. Whitehead's assertions about micro quanta are not descriptions of itty bitty event-things, because abstract theories are not descriptions at all—they are schemata of interpretation (in Erving Goffman's sense). If so, then we can take Whitehead's metaphysical schema and interpret it in other ways than he did. We can use Whitehead's theory about the coming to be and perishing of microcosmic entities as a framework for interpreting how human beings come to make, preserve, and allow to perish macrocosmic cultural artifacts such as educational institutions and educational canons.

Dewey would like our approach because, as any pragmatism should, we are rejecting the copy theory of truth. We are taking any theory as a working hypothesis, a way of construing experience that can be judged as warranted or not by its fruitfulness—in this case, by its ability to marry Dewey's ideas with Whitehead's. The methods and the content of dialectical pragmatism are thus in harmony: the metaphysical theory we propose, and the intellectual and educational canons it identifies, are justified not by their capacity to mirror a reality taken as independent of them, but rather by their capacity to improve that reality so that it better supports our warranted ends.

So I will treat Whitehead's metaphysical scheme as a framework of abstract concepts, and then give it a new interpretation in which its categories apply not to actual occasions but directly to enduring objects. I will take a pattern normally understood as applying to one sphere, that of micro events, and I will apply it to a second sphere, the everyday world of macro events. One schema in two versions. Metaphors function in exactly this way. They exploit the isomorphic features of reality in order to link one of its regions or levels or aspects to another. The aim of the linkage may be to reveal neglected features of the one by means of familiar features of the other. Or the aim may be to highlight the link itself, to propose that regions which until now had seemed quite disparate should henceforth be taken as similar in form and maybe therefore as identical in origin or orientation or destiny, or as causally connected.

To create this linkage, I need to introduce the notion of a "root model." I will use "root" in the same sense that Stephen Pepper uses it in *World Hypotheses*. With respect to a philosophical system, a "root metaphor" is the "original area" of "commonsense fact" upon which the system is based, in terms of which "structural characteristics" and "basic concepts of explanation and description" are developed for interpreting "all other areas of fact" (91). My root models are these structural characteristics that Pepper says formalize a root metaphor. As Dewey insists, however, these structural characteristics must be understood as dynamic not static, as having a "genetic-functional" and not merely a "morphological" shape (1937: 151–53).

My hypothesis is that Dewey and Whitehead can be usefully understood as working from the same root model. I propose taking Whitehead's theory of actual occasions as the root model for his philosophy, a model applicable primarily to microprocesses of becoming, but also applicable to macroprocesses, in particular to the thoughts and actions of human beings. I propose taking the root model for Dewey's philosophy to be his theory of inquiry, the primary application of which is to human actions when proceeding in accord with the norms of scientific method, with a secondary application to human interactions and social institutions. So actual occasions and experimental inquiries can be interpreted as having the same, or at least a very similar, fundamental shape. They each stipulate the same dynamic form for "doing," identify its functional conditions. They are models of the same species—providing kindred accounts of the structural character of human agency (see Allan 1990: ch. 1). If so, we have a warrant, a good reason, for claiming that Dewey's and Whitehead's views are similar with respect to that form of human activity we call educating.

I will take Dewey's model of experimental inquiry from its most careful articulation, that found in *Logic: The Theory of Inquiry*. And similarly, I will use *Process and Reality* as my source for Whitehead's model of the becoming of actual occasions. The process each model traces can be said to have four phases or facets, reminiscent of Aristotle's four causes—the material, final, formal, and efficient conditions by reference to which he said a thing, in this case an action, can be understood to be what it is. Let me use these notions to help structure my account of how Dewey's and Whitehead's models are congruent.

The first of Aristotle's four conditions of anything existing is that it have a material cause. Dewey refers to these material factors as the "indeterminate situation" from which inquiry arises. Whitehead refers to them as the "initial data" that constitute an emerging actual occasion's origin.

For Dewey, "the antecedent conditions of inquiry" are the natural forces—inorganic and organic, human and nonhuman—that encompass a person, that compose what is for her an "indeterminate situation" (1938: 109). This situation may in the past have been a resource satisfying her needs and desires, but it is dynamic—"disturbed, troubled, ambiguous, confused, full of conflicting tendencies, obscure" (109)—and so indeterminate "with respect to its issue," to its "significance," to the "import and portend" of her interactions with it (110). This unsettling indeterminacy of the very things one is dependent upon is the material condition for inquiry.

Whitehead's material condition for the becoming of quantum events is similar. The emergence of an actual occasion begins with "the mere reception of the actual world as a multiplicity of private centers of feeling, implicated in a nexus of mutual presupposition" (1929b: 212). This reception is through a process of "abstraction," however. It is not at all a "mere reception" but rather one shaped by its potentiality for relevance. The initial data are "felt under a 'perspective' which (for each initial datum) is the objective datum of the feeling" (231). The objective data, the resources out of which the actual occasion will become, need to be taken account of. But it is unclear how; they are indeterminate with respect to their issue.

The second Aristotelian condition for a thing's existing is that it have a final cause. A final cause is an orientation toward a result, where that result has not yet been specified but only recognized as important. According to Dewey, this orientation is what transforms an indefinite situation into a "problematic situation." For Whitehead, it is the emergence of an actual occasion's "initial aim."

When, in Dewey's account, a person's needs and desires cease being satisfied—when the significance of what is going on seems to threaten the continued success of her interactions—the situation becomes "problematic." This shift marks the "evocation of inquiry," for "to see that a situation requires inquiry is the initial step in inquiry" (1938: 111). A contrast has emerged between the person's situation as it is and as she wants it to be, and this want orients her within that situation toward its alteration. Her goal is to eliminate this contrast. The possibility of doing so functions as a final condition—an outcome aspiration—that governs her behavior. The factual and conceptual constituents of the situation will be henceforth "entertained" or "dismissed" because of assessments of their "relevancy and irrelevancy" to this goal—to her effort to resolve the contrast, to return her situation to a nonproblematic status (112).

In Whitehead's system, the equivalent to the human organism's continual need to satisfy its desires, to have an end toward which it strives, is its "subjective aim." The creative advance of the cosmos means that the perishing of the multiplicity of the determinate entities composing present actuality will give rise to successors that are each "other than the entities given in disjunction" (1929b: 21). Thus, the actual occasion must have an aim, an orientation toward some definite outcome, such that right from the first its character is not just that of a process but that of a process of becoming some sort of determinate entity. If there is to be a solution to the problem of unifying a multiplicity of initial data, the perspective from which those data are appropriated must be one that includes their potential for integration into something determinate. They are "compatible for synthesis" because an aim at synthesis governs the actual occasion from its inception: "The one subject is the final end which conditions each component feeling" (223).

Such an outcome, however, is vague with respect both to its character and to how it might be actualized. So a third condition is required for something to exist: it must have a formal cause. A "hypothesis" is formulated, in Dewey's theory, as a way to resolve what is problematic in one's situation, to provide a method capable of effecting a satisfactory determinate outcome. Whitehead's notion of a "proposition" plays this same role: suggesting a way to overcome whatever might hinder the actual occasion from coming to completion, from becoming a concrete determinate time-space quantum.

The person in Dewey's model of inquiry formulates a plan, a course of action that she thinks will solve her problem. Any such plan has two aspects: "facts" and "suggestions." "The facts in the case" are the "settled" constituents of the problematic situation, the observable "conditions that must be reckoned with or taken account of in any relevant solution that is proposed" (1938: 113). A "suggestion" is a vague possibility—the beginnings of an "idea," or "meaning," or "hypothesis"—for how the observed facts might be linked together into a more complicated fact, "examined with reference to its functional fitness; its capacity as a means of resolving the given (problematic) situation" (114). The person's plan of action thus involves taking her situation not in terms of its immediately given features but with respect to a structure those features are taken as illustrating. The structure she comes up with, her idea for how things relevant to her problem might be seen to hang together meaningfully, is the formal condition for achieving the ends she desires. It links what is actually given to possible alternatives by means of a general form, a schema or script that points to how the given can be reformed, that indicates how it can be reordered so as to provide what she wants of it.

For Whitehead also, the final condition is initially vague. The aim of the actual occasion is at "some" outcome, and so is always a "lure for feeling" (1929b: 85), an always-functioning evocation of possible ways of ordering its content so as to effect a resolution of whatever indeterminateness still remains. But what the actual occasion's aim might be changes as the "subjective forms" that are the formal conditions for achieving that aim alter. A subjective form is a pattern, and when it functions as a structure of how it might be possible for available data, both physical and conceptual, to be harmonized, it is a "proposition"—"a manner of germaneness of a certain set of (possibilities) to a certain set of actual entities" (188). Propositional feelings reorder the data with respect to their mutual relevance. They suggest how a multiplicity of inherited data can be treated either as one datum or as contrasts, as coherent and consistent despite, or rather because of, their differences. "The process of concrescence is a progressive integration of feelings controlled by their subjective forms" (232). These integrations increase the degree of determinateness characterizing the process of becoming, clarifying and constraining the ways of reconciliation still available and hence the likely result.

So the root models used by Dewey and by Whitehead both specify material, final, and formal conditions for the processes they model. They likewise each have a fourth condition, the equivalent to Aristotle's efficient cause. For Dewey it is "reasoning," for Whitehead "creativity"—sources of the dynamic energy that uses available formal patterns of relationship to reorganize the materials of a situation in a way that will give rise to a satisfying result.

"Reasoning" for Dewey is the process of connecting meanings to other meanings, formulating a "proposition" that "indicates operations which can be performed to test its applicability" (1938: 115). The facts and ideas taken as relevant to the problem are made "operational," linked up "in the definite ways that are required to produce a definite end" (117). A pathway toward a solution is devised, and appropriate "existential operations" then "bring about the re-ordering of environing conditions required to produce a settled and unified situation" (121). But it is not that the reasoning comes first, followed by the existential operations, for as the environing conditions alter so also the facts and ideas taken as relevant alter. The facts are always "trial facts" (117), the ideas always tentative propositions, the character of the problematic situation and hence its resolution always at issue. Elsewhere, Dewey calls this whole transformational process "thinking": "that mode of serial responsive behavior to a problematic situation in which transition to the relatively settled and clear is effected" (1929: 181). Thinking is the efficient condition for success, the process of practical reasoning by which the person's hypothesis is concretized. Thinking is the trajectory of her interactions with her situation, as guided by her ideas, as she effects the changes to which she aspires.

In Whitehead's ontology, the efficient condition of this transformation, this making from a multiplicity of atomic accomplishments a new accomplishment, is "creativity." For each process of becoming the creative advance is canalized, sheer cosmic energy ordered by the determining functions of data, aim, and form into a concrete actuality. Past actual occasions are not efficient causes, even though Whitehead often refers to them as such. They provide all the resources that are available to a newly emerging actual occasion, and so they condition what it manages to become, but they do not account for why there is a result. This "vector character" to the cosmos is beyond explanation because presupposed by every explanation, every attainment, and every obligation. It is "in the nature of things" that through the power of creativity "the many, which are the universe disjunctively, becomes"—again and yet ever again—"the one actual occasion, which is the universe conjunctively" (1929b: 244).

And so in sum—the root model for experimental inquiry and the root model for the becoming of an actual occasion both involve a given material situation, a orientation toward its being made more satisfactory, a corrective reforming possibility, and the effecting by its means of a new situation. This fourfold of conditions, endlessly iterated, constitutes a general model of human action explicit in Dewey's theory of inquiry and implicit in Whitehead's metaphysical scheme. Dewey's summative definition is that "inquiry is the controlled or directed transformation of an indeterminate situation into one that is so determinate in its constituent distinctions and relations as to convert the elements of the original situation into a unified whole" (1938: 108). This definition could just as well be describing the phases of becoming that explicate Whitehead's notion of an actual occasion. Both models, one of inquiry and one of quantum events, articulate the same dynamic conditions for a process of any sort—in particular, for that kind of process we call a human action.

Generalization

The cash value of this long excursus into the root models structuring the thought of Dewey and Whitehead is that we can now understand better why both philosophers should think religion so important educationally. I have argued that their root models are functionally identical, and that therefore the theory of inquiry and the theory of becoming are two versions of the same schema of interpretation. Dewey's and Whitehead's approaches to educational issues are similar because they are based on the same interpretive framework. Their views are mutually illuminating, not by accident but for fundamental systemic reasons.

The root models when interpreted with respect to human beings characterize their activities as always concretely situated. Religion has to do with ultimate ends and ideals, with canonical meanings that fundamentally orient our lives, and so it functions as a final cause, a goal that sets an outcome condition on our actions. If education is a societal institution the aim of which is to develop adults able to act effectively, to resolve individual and communal problems, to improve their situation so that it better supports their potential for self-fulfillment and better provides for the common good, then it must have a religious dimension.

Natural piety, for Dewey, is the vague orienting confidence that in any given situation there are realizable possibilities for human betterment. It is the belief that the problems we face are addressable through human effort, that our making a positive difference is a reasonable guiding principle for belief and action. Seeking to meliorate the human condition is in this sense a moral imperative that we need to feel and accept in order to become good persons.

For Whitehead, reverence for the present is the confidence that our physical surroundings and cultural heritage are relevant for actions able to reshape the present so that it might better fulfill human needs. It is the realization that we have a duty to take up this challenge as best we can. Developing the skill to use ideas effectively needs to become an aspiration essential to our sense of who we are, to our character.

Thus, the importance both philosophers accord religion is not a rhetorical gesture but exactly what follows from understanding the world as a natural process in which humans are situated organisms. Our actions are always contextual, arising over against that context as an urge toward possibilities for achievement the context does not provide or does not guarantee. To be pious or reverent is to take such possibilities seriously, to be committed to the difficult task of finding a way to make them into worthwhile ends and workable means. Religion is about ideals—intellectual canons, normative methods and contents—that should be at work in the world, enhancing the quality and character of what gets done, meliorating the human condition. Religion is a factor in things being accomplished in a manner that is properly intelligent or civilized.

The method of scientific inquiry, according to Dewey, is thus the most important skill students need to learn because it echoes their nature normatively. *Homo sapiens* has evolved as an organism with the capacity to interact intelligently with its environment. Thinking is the Darwinian tool by which humans can optimize the conditions for their survival and flourishing. The capacity to think may be genetic but its effective exercise is learned, and students can only learn to inquire intelligently if they are situated in inquiry-oriented learning environments. For inquiry is a practice not a fact, a set of skills to exercise not a body of information to possess.

Good teaching, therefore, means not lecturing on the nature and function of inquiry but surrounding students with contexts worth inquiring about. The teacher should find or invent a situation students find problematic, encourage them to explore ways the problem might be resolved, then critique with them the results of their effort. By reiterating this pattern of experiment and critique, students will develop their ability to discern what ends are best in a given situation and what means most appropriate. They will learn to think and act in terms of a pragmatic canon—first as apprentices to the use of it that is their cultural heritage, eventually as masters adapting that inheritance to the changing needs of their changing situation. "Every subject and lesson," says Dewey, should be "taught in connection with its bearing upon creation and growth of the kind of power of observation, inquiry, reflection and testing that are the heart of scientific intelligence" (1946: 168). That is, subjects "should be treated in their social bearings and consequences—consequences in the way, on one side, of problems and on the other side of opportunities" (182).

It is not enough for us to learn how to be good problem solvers, to become expert technicians. We need also the confidence that our efforts are functionally worthwhile, that the hypothesizing and the effecting are not their own justification but that they further the good of human beings. We need the meliorative confidence that a fully functioning person is a genuine possibility and that it is in the nature of being human to aspire to realize such a possibility. "The religious attitude," says Dewey, involves both "a sense of the possibilities of existence" and "a devotion to the cause of those possibilities" (1929: 242). So the task of education is to nurture the development of good people by helping them learn to appreciate their natural capacity for doing good and to exercise it intelligently.

A democracy needs intelligent citizens; it is only as good as its people are good. For in the making of public policies it is not enough that those affected by a law are genuinely involved in its determination. Such a law and its implementation will be for the common good only if the citizens involved in its formation are able to distinguish between their desires and their needs, and only if they understand their own well-being to involve that of others. The context for human action is always a social context, involving a shared heritage of accomplishments institutionalized in an intellectual canon of attitudes, customs, rituals, ethical beliefs, and systems of law. Aspirations for social change or for resisting change arise in response to the perceived limitations and the fragility of that heritage. Public and private efforts to secure those aspirations lead to conflicting goals, strategies, and tactics, to conditions of instability in which both established and proposed values are put at risk.

These conditions call for citizens who are able to advocate their individual interests without reducing them to factional dogmas, who are able to keep them interlaced with the general interest of a community and its long-term viability, seeking compromise where possible while avoiding the recurrent exclusion of any particular minority or the continuing dominance by any particular majority. Likening it to "the method of effecting change by means of empirical inquiry and test," Dewey argues that "the very heart of political democracy is adjudication of social differences by discussion and exchange of views" (1946: 157).

Citizens in a democracy have a religious vision insofar as they seek reconciliation and healing, not merely by ad hoc responses to immediate problems but also by crafting a pragmatic canon that will reconstruct the normative conditions for how their society functions. They are religious if they aspire to fashion a good society, one in which citizens use their differences and disagreements as a resource for cooperatively making a way of life that enhances the quality of the goods each can and does enjoy. A good society is one that functions intelligently and so makes it possible for its members to live good lives. Just as much as good citizens are prerequisite to the making of a good society, so also they are only as good as the pragmatic canons of their societies make it possible for them to be.

Whitehead's version of the human action model, because its root is cosmological rather than ethical, helps us notice features that Dewey's version tends to neglect. For instance, and I think most importantly, a meliorist faith should not be utopianist. Actual occasions, and hence actual persons whose actions have the same functional form, will always find their situation problematic. Successful applications of the method of experimental inquiry may improve things, but meliorations of this sort do not entail any eventual utopian outcome. The resolution of a problem, even the refashioning of a canon, is never more than a temporary solution, because it is impossible to include all that has been experienced and nonetheless fashion it into a maximally intense unity. Breadth must be sacrificed to gain intensity, and intensity to preserve breadth. The best bread baked for a situation is always half a loaf, no matter how promising or how meager its ingredients.

Whitehead's thought is susceptible to an unintended utopianist interpretation, however. He introduces as a "derivative notion" to his scheme of metaphysical categories a primordial actual entity, God. One of God's functions is to provide each actual occasion with an initial aim, the originative orienting final condition of its becoming (1929b: 108). Whitehead explicitly insists that this aim is relative to the particular givenness the new occasion supersedes: the aim is "at the best for that *impasse*," which in certain situations can be so meager a finality as to make God seem "ruthless," "remorseless," the "goddess of mischief" (244). And an occasion is always free to forsake that aim for another. But it is an easy enough mistake to extend God's provision of the best possibility for a situation to include the coordination of all such parochial bests into a best possibility for the whole. Were this the case, God's orienting lures would always have an ultimate totalized good in view, bending the world progressively toward its realization.

Whitehead needs no God, however, to account for the originative orientation of each particular actual occasion. And here Dewey's version of the root model helps to correct a misuse of Whitehead's, by indicating that the past is resource enough. Dewey shows how situations can be experienced as insufficient, and how energy can be oriented toward their improvement, without having recourse to anything other than the features of that situation. No *deus ex machina* (nor even a *deus animans*) is required to explain the capacity of temporal things to idealize their given world and so be lured toward a better one.

In the absence of God and all similar transcendent powers, with their potential for visions and lures of unlimited scope, we are less in danger of imagining erroneously that a temporally ultimate and all-encompassing best world is possible. For if all aims are ineluctably situational then all outcomes are unavoidably limited. No matter how successful they may be deemed when seen from one perspective, there are necessarily other perspectives that will show them as less successful or even as failures. Indeed, the endemic inadequacy of every achieved good is why the cosmos is essentially dynamic, its actuality always surpassing itself toward new actuality.

Whitehead expresses this counter-utopian point at the macro level by distinguishing in *The Function of Reason* between appetition and entropy, and with respect to the discipline of appetition between speculative and practical reason. In *Adventures of Ideas,* he makes his point by a series of contrasts: Barbarians and Christians, Steam and Democracy, Instinct and Intelligence, Theory and Method, Beauty and Truth.

The first of each pair are the forces of novelty: conscious or senseless agencies that expand the scope of what counts as experience, as interpretable fact, as the given. They are, or they are urges toward, adequacy—toward the world experienced in all its discordant, confusing, often senseless, multiplexity. The contrasting members of each pair are forces of order, effecting some sort of unity from things, making the relative chaos into an intelligible world, a meaningful and well-wrought harmony of components. This harmony can be achieved only if the components and the modes of their relationships are clarified, but doing so means limiting how they are defined and functionally determined. Adequate scope of detail must be sacrificed in order to obtain intensity of integration.

On the one hand, the problem with speculation, with the creative power of originality, is that it cannot distinguish between the important and the trivial; novelty becomes a narcotic that makes the speculator insensitive to the practicalities involved in achieving and sustaining genuine values. On the other hand, the problem with systematization, with expertise, is that its success blinds it to what those achievements have had to exclude, separating the experts—ironically—from the practicalities requisite for successful adaptation as the conditions for genuine value change. As I argued at the close of the previous chapter also, neither speculation nor systematization, neither originality nor expertise, by itself suffices. Whitehead warns against both the "dogmatic fallacy" and "the fallacy of discarding method" (1933: 223), extolling in their stead "the almost incredible secret" that speculative thinking can be "itself subject to orderly method," that it can be divested of "its anarchic character without destroying its function of reaching beyond set bounds" (1929a: 66).

This interplay of speculative and practical reason is, of course, scientific inquiry in the reformed sense Dewey advocates, a style of thinking he finds as appropriate to metaphysics and the social sciences as to the natural sciences. So Whitehead echoes Dewey's emphasis on the centrality of inquiry, and his pedagogical observations thus emphasize students in active situations using ideas with imaginative freedom and then testing those uses rigorously. The result of any inquiry, however, is necessarily—is in principle—inadequate, because the method required to attain the result has framed the situation selectively. In excluding what was irrelevant to the task at hand, inquiry lets slip away what might be crucial for the next situation. Students, learning how to think experimentally, need to learn the limits as well as enjoy the fruits of their success.

Whitehead's three "stages of mental growth," famously outlined in an essay on "The Rhythms of Education" and already discussed in chapter 7, need to be interpreted in this light. Romance and Precision are incommensurable activities, the one valuing adequacy, the other coherence. Romance is an originative grasp after the importance of a thing, "the excitement consequent on the transition from the bare facts to the realisations of the import of their unexplored relationships." Precision, in contrast, subordinates "width of relationship" to "exactness of formulation," to the accuracy of expert analysis (1922: 18)—so that the import of a thing, the full width of its possible connections to other things, fades into the background.

Two incommensurables—unfocused raucous inclusiveness and focused frameworks of ordered relevance, anti-canonist and canonist, thesis and antithesis. Generalization, the final stage of mental growth, is thus "Hegel's synthesis. It is a return to romanticism with added advantage of classified ideas and relevant technique" (19). The synthesis is not a procrustean Precision imposed on the Romance, nor a protean Romance shrugging off such impositions. Synthesis is the integration of Romance and Precision: the breadth of a thing's possibilities deepened by their ways of relatedness receiving evaluative interpretation, the resulting insight into the precise nature of the thing enlarged by being taken as the focal center of a context. It is the process of renovation, the making and remaking of a pragmatic canon.

To understand by means of Generalization "is always to exclude a background of intellectual incoherence" while at the same time "confronting [that] intellectual system with the importance of its omissions" (1933: 47). Generalization is thus inherently unstable because it both achieves its goal and recognizes the goal's insufficiency. Hence, "education should consist in a continual repetition of such cycles" and "we should banish the idea of a mythical, far-off end of education" (1922: 19). The melioristic vision belongs to Romance: a faith in the importance of ideals because they are realizable as ends and are useful as ways for achieving those ends. Precision is how tools are sharpened that give those ideals a cutting edge. But when the tools are put to use in Generalization, clearly defined ends wrought by clearly stipulated methods, the limiting focus this honing requires can be saved from dogmatism only if kept always in the context of the initiating religious vision—so that Generalization's effectiveness is always understood as incomplete.

Hence, for Whitehead, social intelligence in a democracy is Sisyphian, endlessly addressing the problematic in the hope of achieving a workable solution, but never expecting, nor even yearning for, a final solution. The Art of reconciling Truth and Beauty is an Adventure the successes of which are unavoidably partial and failure endemic. The values we have achieved are always at risk, those we seek always just beyond our grasp. Peace not Utopia is the religious vision: that even failure and loss can have a use, can be redeemed by becoming relevant data for subsequent efforts:

The meaning of Peace is most clearly understood by considering it in its relation to the tragic issues which are essential in the nature of things. Peace is the understanding of tragedy, and at the same time its preservation. ... Amid the passing of so much beauty, so much heroism, so much daring, Peace ... keeps vivid the sensitiveness to the tragedy; and it sees the tragedy as a living agent persuading the world to aim at fineness beyond the faded level of surrounding fact. Each tragedy is the disclosure of an ideal:—What might have been, and was not: What can be. The tragedy was not in vain. (1933: 286)

The greatest educational challenge for anyone committed to a constructive postmodern understanding of the Dewey–Whitehead variety is how to teach students a method of inquiry, a strategy for achievement, that is imbued with religious vision but avoids utopianism of either a progressivist or foundationalist variety. The allure of Utopia detracts from the problems of men and women by denying that ideals are only regulative principles by which to assess the intelligence of our efforts to redeem in some momentary way an ever-perishing present. Utopianism makes ideals into constitutive principles that draw our interest and energy away from holy ground toward the chimeral idolatry of an imperishable reality objectively immortal beyond our world or still to come as its apotheosis.

The counter-utopian religious pragmatism advocated by Dewey and Whitehead is the better way, but also the more difficult. For it promises "undoubted loss of joy, of consolation, of some types of strength," and so disvalues our "heroism," our "social charm," and all our "victories on land or at sea" (Whitehead 1916: 14). We ought to heed their pragmatic advice not despite but because of this difficulty. We ought to make of education a place where natural piety and reverence for life's possibilities lure students to acquire the stylish intelligence required of fully functioning citizens in a genuinely democratic society. If we fail to do so, our common lot is not likely even to be meliorating but rather, as with all obscurantisms, to be a slow or not so slow descent into situations that are ever more narrowing in the opportunities they provide for human fulfillment.

Chapter 11

Education for Our Common Good

Modes and Phases

Whitehead, in a 1917 talk on "technical education," claims that the future of our civilization hinges on teaching "handcraft" to students, teaching them to work with their hands. He deplores what he calls the "brain lethargy" of our leaders in both the private and public sphere: in business and industry, government, education. Having no manual dexterity except the ability to write legibly and speak clearly, perhaps supplemented by the ability to kick a soccer ball or play a decent game of tennis, they lack the capacity for creative thought crucial to a society's well-being. Those who read too much, says Whitehead, are almost always "timid conventional thinkers" (51).

So what are we to make of this? What does learning to work with our hands have to do with receiving a proper education, learning how to be a responsible adult in a functioning democracy, gaining the practical expertise and moral vision needed to be a productive citizen willing and able to contribute to the common good? In this high-tech globalized information age, what relevance is there to Whitehead's insistence that we should emulate that medieval European monastic approach to manual labor he calls "the Benedictine ideal"? A hint of the answer to these questions is his summary of what the Benedictines believed. They were convinced, he says, that "work should be transfused with intellectual and moral vision and thereby turned into joy, triumphing over [work's] weariness and its pain" (44).

When Whitehead advocates the importance of handcraft, he is talking about activities that result in a material product, about the skills by which physical things are made. The fine arts, of course, involve handcraft. They too require manual dexterity and result in a tangible product: carving a woodblock and pulling a print from it, stretching a sized canvas and brushing oil paints onto it, glazing clay turned on a wheel and firing it in a brick kiln. But Whitehead's focus is upon the practical arts: the skills of a weaver, carpenter, bricklayer, or farmer. He is talking about the importance of practical labor, activity in which our body is a necessary instrument for achieving a useful outcome, in which our muscle and bone, our strength and subtlety, are needed in order to persuade a reluctant physical medium to take on a desired form in order to serve a needed function.

Whitehead's celebration of handcraft is not the result of some romantic nostalgia for the good old days of his boyhood in a small village of northeast Kent when farmers plowed their fields behind a team of horses while their wives spun thread from a distaff and their children dipped candles or gathered firewood from a nearby copse. He is insisting that first-hand make-a-difference concrete involvement in a productive activity is crucial to a person's development as a human being, and that the development of such persons is crucial to civilized existence. Education, says Whitehead, must be rooted in and for the sake of a life fully engaged with its surrounding world, a world felt and understood non-passively. "First-hand knowledge is the ultimate basis of intellectual life" (51).

It will be useful to pause here a moment in order to locate handcraft within the complex topography of Whitehead's theory of education. Whitehead calls learning a handcraft "technical education." It is technical because it involves acquiring the ability to utilize a technology. Wherever some physical object in the world, whether found and modified or constructed from scratch, is made use of as an instrument for transforming that world, we have a technology. We are technically educated when we have learned how to use tools in order to realize our practical ends, taking advantage of the constraints imposed by the causal efficacy of a material inheritance to transform that inheritance into an occasion of enjoyment.

Whitehead contrasts the technical arts with the liberal arts. The one manipulates physical objects; the other manipulates symbols. A "liberal education," the study of languages and texts, teaches us aesthetic and moral appreciation for the achievements of human culture. It develops our sensitivity to values that give meaning and significance to our lives but that endure only as long as our culture sustains them. We gain this sense of what is supremely worthwhile by becoming acquainted with the great books and works of art created by our ancestors, but also by learning about the customs, laws, and institutions they have fashioned, knowing the story of their triumphs and tragedies generation after generation. The cultivation of disinterested appreciation is an important contribution to the development of ourselves as civilized persons.

Thus, a liberal education in Whitehead's sense is the kind advocated by content canonists. What students should come to appreciate is Matthew

Arnold's "the best which has been thought and said." I have been arguing, however, that the values to which we are to sensitize ourselves, the supremely worthwhile great books and works of art to which an arts and sciences education should introduce us, are enduringly but not timelessly significant. A pragmatic canon for liberal education, I have claimed, sensitizes us to the value of cultural achievements that have been pushed to the margins of acceptability as well as nurturing our appreciation for those entrenched at the center. Only if it is open to criticism and counterargument, to the constant competition of what has not been judged the best, can the center truly be said to have stood the test of time.

Eva Brann has rightly insisted that because of their "indefinitely rich interpretability," their "originative" power, the great books have both an individual and, when read in temporal succession, a collective "quarrelsomeness" to them that "assures a balance of views" (1999: 164–65). But this quarrelsomeness should be extended to include the way in which neglected, ignored, and disdained works—or simply those that are new—can serve to hone the established canon. Disinterested appreciation of the canonical should not entail a lack of interest in what is not canonical. The appreciation acquired through a liberal education should be active, not static or passive: an engagement not only with a valued heritage and with the standards by which it has been so highly valued, but also with standards for critiquing and transforming what is valued and therefore with works that embody such critiques and suggest transforming possibilities. If we enlarge Whitehead's notion of liberal education in this pragmatic way, we strengthen the validity of his characterization of it as important because it teaches students to appreciate the achievements of culture for their intrinsic value.

Whitehead distinguishes both technical and liberal education from "scientific education," which is about knowledge. Scientific inquiry involves empirical observation, and in this sense teaches us a firsthand involvement with things, but the aim of science is to understand not to transform. Its goal is to formulate the general ideas that concrete experience illustrates. Science involves the skills of pattern recognition and formulation; its highest expression is mathematics. The procedural canonists take scientific method as paradigmatic, some such as Dewey or E. O. Wilson wanting to extend that method to all areas of human endeavor, others wanting to parallel it with other methods designed explicitly to be paradigmatic for those other areas. Here also the notion of a pragmatic canon gives us a way to enlarge and thereby enhance the importance of science—by interpreting its methods as correctable, as needing constantly to be improved, altered, or replaced in the light of shifting material and cultural conditions.

Let me now complicate this brief sketch of Whitehead's three modes of education—liberal, scientific, and technical—by mapping them onto the three phases of education explored in chapters 7 and 10: romance, precision, and generalization. Think of the modes of education as three dimensions of each phase. So, for example, we can deepen our sense of what romance is all about by asking what is involved when the romance is in a liberal mode, as distinct from when the mode is scientific or when it is technical. Conversely, think of the three phases of education as temporal articulations of each mode. So, for instance, we can sharpen our sense of what is involved in scientific education by noting what its initial phase of romance is like, and how that education changes when the phase shifts to scientific precision and then to scientific generalization. These mixings of modes and phases might be arranged so that learning would be seen as taking place in nine steps. Such a schema of interpretation might be a helpful heuristic device for suggesting ways by which to organize a course or a curriculum so that it is helpfully developmental.

As Whitehead insists—and how could someone who called his metaphysics a "philosophy of organism" think otherwise?—each mode of education is completed by the other two, just as each phase requires the other phases. So all modes and all phases of education are internally related, according to Whitehead, all in some way ingredient in each. The romance phase of liberal education should include a student's awareness, no matter how inchoately, of the phases yet to come and the modes abutting it, just as the technical mode of generalization should be infused with memories of earlier phases and related modes. And so on, ramified throughout a ninefold typology of the facets of learning, facets iterated in endless complication in the various real world contexts where educational experiences take place. No wonder teaching is such a difficult profession, and why merely talking about teaching, as I am doing, seems a fool's errand.

With this sketch of a typology of the learning process as background, I will focus for the remainder of the chapter on the technical mode, illustrated by the handcraft of weaving. And although I will discuss both romance and precision, I will be doing so in order to get to generalization. For it is in the form of learning where handcraft technology comes to generalization that we can begin to see why, without an education in the ways of the Benedictine ideal, humans will be unable to sustain viable forms of democratic community and will find themselves unavoidably sliding into cultural decadence.

Fabric Weaving

The complexity of the concrete for human beings begins with an appreciation of themselves as bodies in a natural environment, but it extends immediately to include themselves as bodies in a cultural environment, bodies that respond in characteristic learned ways to a semiotically integrated interpretation of both these environments. Weaving, for instance, has a cultural meaning. The weaver's skills are an expertise, a practice for achieving a certain sort of end, a way of going about the transformation of raw materials into finished products, a craft for making possible goods into actual goods. This way of making fabrics has a long history. The reasons for proceeding as one does are not that this way is necessarily more efficient but that it is the way these things have always been done. Weaving is a traditional expertise.

A weaver learns these requisite skills by emulating them, by copying the standard incarnated in his master's actions and heeding the master's iterated critiques of his apprenticeship. These practices come clothed in an aura of myth and story, ritual and tradition, concerning their origins and importance, their intrinsic worth and their relevance to the common good. The weaver has a social status by virtue of these beliefs and practices, a dignity, a location within a world of enduring meanings. His excellence as a weaver is judged not just by the quality of the woven fabrics he has produced but also by the degree to which his way of producing them has been true to the cultural expectations for how skilled weavers behave. Weaving is both a practical and a moral undertaking.

The romance of the weaver's craft is about our experiencing the concreteness of these meanings. Since they are cultural meanings, having to do with the conditions of our civil association as well as with the conditions of a particular kind of livelihood, they are relevant not only to weavers but also to the rest of us who share a common culture with them. For us, the enduring worth of this handcrafting activity, its importance as an expression of our people and their traditions, is incarnated before our eyes in the weavers who are our next-door neighbors and around whose looms we played as children. Or rather, such was the case before the Industrial Revolution plucked the weavers out of the neighborhood and set them to work in factories tending power looms. The romance of weaving would have been a dimension of our everyday experience had we lived, as Whitehead did while a youth, in a small nineteenth-century village beside the narrow English sea. But where the familiar boundaries of this concreteness have been erased, where weaving and the other handcrafts are no longer skills at which we all are amateurs and at which a few among our neighbors become expert, how can the romance phase of technical education remain genuinely concrete?

It is not enough to take our students to visit a museum where handcrafted clothing is on display, nor to ask them to bring their family heirlooms to class—displaying for show-and-tell the frayed shawls and dusty tablecloths once woven by their parents or grandparents. Such experiences abstract from the processes by which the clothing was created. Their concreteness is only a matter of their being appreciated. Our students can enjoy these creations both for the value achieved and for the skill and effort required by that achievement, but their experience is nonetheless passive, their relation to the weaving essentially that of spectators.

This passivity is a feature of all three kinds of romance. We appreciate for their intrinsic worth the polished lyric poem in blank verse, the elegant simplicity of the mathematical formula expressing a scientific law, the carefully articulated scholarly thesis accompanied by adequate supporting evidence and arguments, the new concert hall with ample seating and adjustable acoustic controls, the well-tailored suit in a grey flannel wrinkle-proof fabric. But these products appear as though manna from heaven or Athena from the head of Zeus, their value simply given, inexplicably but delightfully available for our enjoyment. To take the concreteness of aesthetic observation as fully concrete is to take the partial as the whole and so to commit what Whitehead calls the "fallacy of misplaced concreteness." "Education must pass beyond the passive reception of the ideas of others" (47), avoiding ideas that are inert because experienced only as finished products, treated as separate and independent of the process of their being made.

The romance appropriate to a technical education, therefore, should get beyond merely an appreciation of results to an appreciation as well of the processes that lead to those results. With respect to products of the weaver's art, our students can appreciate the beauty of the woven cloth, its striking design, its interesting choice of material, the complicated techniques employed in its making, and they can write detailed accounts of the weaver's art or celebrate it in poetic hexameter. But only by weaving the cloth themselves will they experience how their bodies and their tools find in fiber and structure a way through a morass of potential mistakes and misdirections to a result worth appreciating and worth understanding. Direct appreciation of the weaving activity, of the technical process itself, is an engaged kind of appreciation, kinesthetic rather than visual: the immediate appreciation of a lived experience by reliving it, by interacting with the world in a way that requires the assistance of available technologies to be fruitful.

The thrill and wonder of romance in all three of its modal expressions should be about means as well as ends, about the weaving not just the woven, about the getting there as much as about the arriving. The romance should be first of all by direct acquaintance and then only in supplementary ways by secondhand description. The insistence that the primary aim of both a liberal education and a scientific education is to inculcate "disinterested intellectual appreciation," the one of the works of culture, the other of the workings of nature, "is a psychological error," Whitehead argues. "Action and our implication in the transition of events amid the inevitable bond of cause to effect are fundamental" (47). His point is not that, in addition to their classroom training in aesthetic and theoretic intellectual appreciation, students should be involved in physical activities of one sort or another. Whitehead is insisting, rather, that appreciation of any sort, divorced from the actions by which something appreciable was fashioned, is secondhand. It is limited to results and so misses the concrete processes without which there would be no results to appreciate.

We take something for granted whenever we fail to appreciate the effort that had gone into its creation. We dismiss the damask tablecloth as backwoods folkcraft until we try to replicate it on our own loom. We think the dance step easy enough until we try to dance it ourselves. The philosopher's argument strikes us as compelling until we are asked to restate it in our own words. The need for new legislation seems self-evident until we are charged with the task of drafting a bill that has some reasonable chance of being passed. The scientific paper proposing a new theory based on fresh experimental data looks convincing until we try to replicate the experiments in our own laboratory. These firsthand experiences of the making deepen our appreciation of what is made.

The firsthand experiences of the making also increase our appreciation of the making. The excitement of an ideal, the anticipation of its being realized, the tingle of a venture now begun, the joy of a shared enterprise or of a solitary responsibility, the satisfaction in having mastered the needed skills, the adrenalin rush of unexpected complications faced, the thrill of the light first glimpsed at the end of the tunnel or the dread that there might be no such light, the shouts of victory or the tears of defeat, the letdown afterward—how different our experience of an outcome is when we have been involved in the effort of getting there. "The second-handedness of the learned world is the secret of its mediocrity," says Whitehead. "It is tame because it has never been scared by facts" (5). It has never wondered how a specific result could have been attained or might have been prevented, has never been amazed at why these things exist rather than nothing at all.

Romance is only the beginning of learning; precision is also required. In order to achieve an outcome of value, we must transform the treasure of romance from a polyglot hoard of interesting experiences, comfortable habits, attractive possibilities, and vague hopes into a single unifying experience. To do so, the original abundance, the concrete richness of our inheritance and our aspirations, must be simplified. Aspects of it must be neglected, whole regions eliminated or relativized, distorted, reworked, transmuted beyond recognition, so that what is left will fit into a reconciling framework of interpretation and practice. We must murder to dissect, and we must dissect in order to create, even if all that is created is no more than a replication of what we murdered.

The application of precision to the creation of woven artifacts is the quest for an adequate model of the finished product and of the techniques for making it. Familiarity with the empirical data is crucial to this process: an appreciation of wool or cotton or flax, of looms and shuttles, of actual woven pieces of clothing and actual weaving skills. The aim of the precision, however, is to look away from these concrete things to the abstractions they exhibit—the design of color and texture patterns in the fabric, the step-by-step procedures for producing it, blueprints for the tools needed in order to carry out those procedures—and then to generalize them as much as possible.

The ideal result would be a generic form of which the traditional forms are versions, just as the actual design in an actual bolt of cloth, the actual assembled components of the loom, and the actual weaving activities done by actual weavers are versions of the traditional forms. Expressed as a twenty-first-century technology, the ideal result would be a computer program for generating an endless variety of design patterns and procedures, including any and all of those that happen to have been instantiated historically. As Noam Chomsky's generative grammar sought to do for languages, so similarly the goal of applying the precision of scientific abstraction to weaving would be to formulate a generative weaving program that captures the underlying necessary structure of the weavers' art.

Precision has an aesthetic of its own, of course, when its abstractions are taken as ends in themselves, as immediate objects for enjoyment. There is a romance to the formal patterns of relationship and to the abstractive enterprise as such, a good example of which is the speculative reason Whitehead associates with Plato—"enthroned above the practical tasks of the world," it "seeks with disinterested curiosity an understanding of the world" (1919a: 37–38). But precision is always fundamentally utilitarian. We rarely simplify or generalize or organize for no reason except the joy of doing so, but rather in order to achieve a purpose. Our reasoning is usually practical. Plato might find contemplation of the Good the highest human end, but Ulysses has a more practical end in mind—"to render purpose effective" through "the piecemeal discovery and clarification" of problem-solving methodologies (37). And so we find Ulysses is always headed off somewhere across the wine-dark sea in pursuit of some advantage he expects to effect for himself and others. Precision is the instrument by which we frame plans for how best to undertake an odyssey that aims at making things better, not just imagining them better. It is Dewey's experimental intelligence engaged in the formulation of working hypotheses, of scripts for achieving needed results, recipes for baking bread, roadmaps or seacharts for getting to some desired destination. "It is essential that the generality of the method be continually brought to light and contrasted with the speciality of the particular application" (1917: 52).

Consequently, for our students to become technologically proficient they must learn the precision that is proficiency's necessary condition. They must learn the forms important to weaving, which they can do only by weaving cloth of their own. They need to put the forms to work in order to learn them, to find out what the precision of a weaving technique means in practice and why without precision nothing as complex as a length of cloth could ever be woven. To become competent weavers, both expert and originative masters of its craft, students need to transform these techniques into a dexterity in their fingers and into well-honed judgments concerning the right moment to adjust typical procedures in order to take account of unfolding actual variations and flaws. They need to gain confidence in manipulating intricately interdependent variables so as to effect an envisioned outcome. The abstract generalizations learned in the precision phase of a technical mode of education are tools of production, the forms which when ascribed to things make it possible to transform those things into the new objects and new relationships we think more likely than the old to fulfill our desires.

Romance and precision are always for the sake of the generalization they permit, so it is crucial that the aims of education be the realization of important outcomes. The importance cannot be faked; it must be sensed as important because it really is. The Great Books studied in the liberal mode of education must in fact be great books, rooting deeply into the core meanings to be found in human experience and ranging widely across the varieties of the ways those roots have developed. The Great Ways learned in a scientific mode of education, along with the theories to which they give rise, must be able to explain actual things in their actual locations: fish in the sea, stars in the sky, institutions functioning in societal and natural environments. And likewise, the handcrafts learned, the training in cloth weaving, must be undertakings that address actual human needs. The generalization sought by means of the skills learned in a technical mode of education should be the fulfillment of practical needs: clothing to cover someone's nakedness, merchandise to trade for shoes or food. But practical needs are not limited to their material utility. Technical products should also meet aesthetic and scientific needs: the clothing made for its beauty and in celebration of the traditional skills and dignity of weavers who have shown themselves masters of their craft.

Weaving the World's Goods

The ultimate technical generalization of which we dream is that of a common human good, the good of the Peaceable Kingdom concretely realized, the coming of a world community in which our natural, personal, and cultural differences are both honored and reconciled. This generalization usually strikes us not simply as a dream but as an idle dream, mere wishful thinking, because it is so obviously constrained by the meager resources for its realization. Neither in our history as a culture or a species, nor in our concrete experience, nor in our abstract reflections about the limits of what is possible or even of what is merely conceivable, are there grounds for believing this is a dream that could in fact be actualized. We don't live in or even near a common human good. We live in ghettoes determined by class and ethnicity. We tear down the precious long-standing achievements of our culture's past to make room for our concerns of the moment. We fragment knowledge into specialties that we then lack competence to understand or assess. As a result, we fail to appreciate the world's abundance, not even realizing that it exists, imagining that the limitations of our parochial locations are the horizon of the only world that counts. Beyond our familiar narrow seas lie monsters, so we are content to stay at home, to go our own way and not worry about any good more common than our own or that of our neighborhood.

The notion of a good all humans, indeed all creatures, might have in common is a shimmering fantasy, a dream of a perfect community, of an ideal place that somehow ceases being nowhere and is achieved someplace specific—a place no longer merely utopic but henceforth decidedly entopic. For this fantasy to become a reality, for a common good to grow beyond familiar but narrow unities, for neighborhood goods and national goods to become planetary goods, its technological implications must be explored. Handcrafting the Peaceable Kingdom will call for our becoming technically educated about a global community and its conditions, an education that takes us through all three of the phases characteristic of any genuinely educative process.

We will need, in the first place, a technical romance that is global in scope, the constituent elements of which are redolent with their immediate importance. That concreteness needs to be of many sorts. For instance, the treasures of the world's cultures should be studied, their depths and subtleties fully appreciated, the incredible diversity of the expressions of the human spirit, both now and over the span of human history, celebrated for the intrinsic values they manifest. The noncultural world should also be studied, its flora and fauna, its rocks and oceans, in their current configurations and with respect to the geologic and biologic pathways of their evolution. On the basis of these concrete appreciations of what our planet and our species have been and are now, we will then be able to speculate about world governments, religious reconciliation, ecological mindfulness, unified theories of nature, and integrating metaphysical systems. These speculations must be as concrete in their own way as the concreteness of the facts upon which they are based, for they will be idle and empty meanderings unless vividly presented. They may be fantasies, but they need to have practical import, serving as lures that evoke our emotional engagement with their importance and our careful consideration of their plausibility. As another way of being imaginatively concrete, we should acquaint ourselves firsthand and intimately with actual technologies, both traditional and industrial, that might be adaptable as tools for producing and distributing resources—material, political, cultural—that might possibly be able to satisfy the needs of a global village.

These gossamer imaginings, blossoming in the fertile soil of solid practical fact, if experienced so directly, so personally, so intimately, and hence so powerfully that their worth commands our loyalty and their loss seems an intolerable even if nonetheless real possibility, will not thereafter so easily be set aside in favor of the old familiar unities. The challenge of education for the twenty-first century is finding a way to kindle this fierce flame of romantic feelings, without it becoming a conflagration that overwhelms our students and ourselves. An aroused appetite for new ideas, like an undisciplined appetite of any sort, can engender a kind of blind exuberance that quickly proves itself unable to rise to its expectations. In the despair and confusion of collapsing ideals, we become vulnerable to the worst of all the likely eventualities: that our narrow self-satisfied parochialism might be transformed into a yet more narrow but far more intense parochialism, that of the aggrieved fanatic.

The technical ideal of a global community that we seek to actualize will require, in the second place, a precision able to grow beyond the accustomed frameworks of understanding and action that we would bring to the world's concreteness. It does no good to globalize the content of our experiences and imaginings if our way of interpreting them is still parochial. The science we teach needs to get beyond the imparting of enormous bundles of information and the standard formulae for their manipulation. It needs to be familiar with its own history, able to find in the various methods of inquiry invented by humans over the ages a constant resource for self-criticism, able even in the inexorable trajectory of its increased specialization to remain influenced by the other specializations. We need to show our students how to exercise their rational imaginations, to be adept at casting nets of interpretation onto unlikely waters where they might yield an abundant haul of new insights and theories and even paradigms. We need these same students also to see the practical implications of their abstractive play, to have a good eye for novel procedures that can get things done, that can solve problems and mediate disputes efficiently but also holistically—that are respectful of previous tradition, present diversity, and future long-term consequences.

Our reasoning powers are exercised whenever we test the established limits of our canons of understanding and action, hypothesizing new schemata of interpretation that we think might be better suited for dealing with a changing world. These frames and models are worthless, however, until disciplined by our practical concerns, by our insisting that they prove their worth by actually solving the problems they were designed to solve, that their promissary note be shown to have a cash value. Precision within the mode of any sort of technical undertaking is thus a matter of replacing vague notions with ones that are clear and distinct, subjecting them to logical standards of coherence and consistency, developing predictable consequences entailed by their claims, fashioning replicable experiments involving observations or instrument readings or personal experiences that will confirm or fail to confirm those predictions.

Since the notions constituting our sense of a common human good are exceedingly vague, dreams and stories and musings that have only a tenuous connection with actual historical achievements, the role of technological precision is crucial. "The supreme verification of the speculative fight," says Whitehead, "is that it issues in the establishment of a practical technique for well-attested ends" (1929a: 80). This technique is not, as it is in a scientific experiment, a matter of devising laboratory protocols, however. "In human history, a practical technique embodies itself in established institutions—professional associations, scientific associations, business associations, universities, churches, governments" (81). The precision needed is one able to design institutions that if established will function to transform our current parochial institutions into ones with a global impact and a reconciling aim.

If, as the phase of technical romance suggests, the first task of twenty-first-century education should be to stir young people to imagine strategies of reconciliation that do not too easily sacrifice breadth or depth or both, the second task, as the phase of technical precision suggests, should be to foster in those same young people the habits of imaginative systematization by which they can rise creatively to the challenge of the possible world they have imagined. The alternative to inventing new ways of cooperative endeavor is a discouraging surrender to the various forms of disharmony that have been heretofore the plague of human interactions. Or even worse, the inability to reconcile our differences adequately is likely to lead to situations where disharmony is papered over and we are content with empty shibboleths about unities real but not apparent, unities supposedly predestined or apocalyptic or lying at deeper putative levels of reality, ideals for which we ourselves therefore need not ever work.

Having insisted on how important it is to have robust phases of romance and precision in a technological approach to our common human good, I come now, in the third place, to generalization. All the aesthetic appreciation and scientific theorizing we require cannot be simply for their own sake but must be for the technical improvements they make possible. So the key to life in a global village, and the key to an education that prepares our students for such a life, is the ability to take a fully appreciated but disharmonious inheritance of parochial ideas and practices, to interpret it in terms of its potential for exemplifying expected or unexpected harmonies, and then to transform that polyglot inheritance into an actual world-encompassing unity. Generalization is this transforming process.

Whitehead emphasizes handcraft because of the three modes of education the technical is the one most akin to generalization. The technical mode and the generalization phase share an emphasis on the centrality of the art by which new realities are woven from the old. The weaver's skill is both an example of what technical education makes possible and a metaphor for all the possible ways by which to weave the world's goods. Without romance, the weaving will be unmotivated, its design obscure, the commitment to its creation vapid, devoid of moral energy. Without precision, the weaving will be haphazard, amateurish, its design poorly executed, the difficulties impeding success debilitating. But without the weaving activity itself, neither enlivening aspiration nor efficient expertise can be sustained, because without the making they serve they soon will lose their sense.

The weaving of a common human good is a labor that has many versions. Those of us whose proclivity is toward the liberal mode of education can work at the making of the Peaceable Kingdom by reading carefully the texts that compose our intellectual canon, seeing if we can discern their implications for what a common human good entails, while at the same time opening ourselves to the canonical materials from other cultural traditions, alert to their implications for what that good might mean or imply, accepting the resulting discord as an opportunity. For, as Whitehead notes, "the basis of every discord is some common experience discordantly realized" (1929a: 86). In the clash of canonical truths we should be stimulated to undertake a new adventure, to explore—in the shape of a notion about global community—another version of Whitehead's idea about the primacy in our cosmos of an upward urge from the good toward the better and the best.

If we are more scientifically inclined, we can invest our energies in the construction of working hypotheses for how best to spell out the implications of the notion of a common good for personal identity, political community, and ecological harmony. What ethical insights would result, for instance, were we to take seriously the fact that all things are fundamentally interdependent? If the Benthamite moral principle of seeking the greatest happiness for the greatest number were understood as encompassing all life forms and as referring to optimal adaptive success—then the environmental cost of fulfilling our human desires would become a relevant constraint on their character and extent. If the Kantian moral principle of a Kingdom of Ends were understood as meaning that the freedom of any creature to exercise its natural capacities should be not only respected but also actively furthered—then social justice would become a matter not of rights but of responsibilities, of compassion and solidarity as well as of fairness and equity. And if the claims of pragmatism and process thought, that all such moral principles are historical achievements rather than timeless givens, were taken to mean that the good is always contextual, disputable, and fragile—then we would realize that we all have a stake in working together, first to preserve our natural and cultural heritage of accomplished goods, then to transform that heritage by using it as a resource for fashioning the novel accomplishments required by the globalized horizon of our sense of what is morally possible.

However, the most difficult work for us to undertake lies outside the confines of this or any book. It is the task of doing the world justice, each of us contributing to the handcrafting of an improvement in the actual conditions for the creation of value available to all creatures great and small. For the common good is there for us to construct, no matter how everyday and seemingly trivial the context. Our family life needs to be rooted in the same values that we think justify us speaking of the family of nations and calling other animals our brothers and sisters. An adequate education for ourselves and our children calls for us not only to demand but to help create fresh approaches to teaching and learning, to the evaluation of both, and to the ways in which schooling is understood, neighborhoods defined, educational facilities funded, and teachers paid. The conditions for our being good citizens in a functional democracy, the appropriate ways for us to express our loyalty and patriotism, begin with the habits of mind and heart that we develop as we interact with friends and strangers, those like us in looks or manner or attitude and those who differ from us. The generalization phase in the technology by which we weave our common good is a matter of getting the details right, making sure that in this particular pass of the shuttle the correctly chosen woof thread will alternate regularly among the warp threads, confident that if this simple task is done well, then even if it is all anyone of us or any group of us can do, it will suffice. For in no other way can a fabric be woven except one row at a time.

Generalization—liberal and scientific generalization, to be sure, but technical generalization above all—is where the work gets done, where the compromises have to be made, the differences mediated, the glowing ideals tailored to the stark realities. Between the azure sky of unrealized but desirable possibilities and the solid bedrock of physical necessity, both demanding our loyalty, lies the practical world, the fertile earth of usable technologies, the middle realm where new worlds are always needing to be wrought.

The Benedictine Ideal

My aim in this chapter has been to argue for the importance of a vibrant appreciation of our natural and cultural heritage and for the importance of a well-honed rational imagination, and therefore also for the crucial importance of the work involved in reconciling them. I have sought to celebrate the supreme value of the day-after-day multidimensional meliorative struggle with a problematic world, a labor to which Whitehead and the pragmatists call us. It is a difficult labor because it can rely on no absolutes. The technological effort to get things done that are for the better is a labor in which both the past on which it relies and the future for which it hopes are at risk, the achieved value of the one always in danger of being lost, the other's alluring possibilities in danger of never being attained.

With so much at stake, with our lives, our fortunes, and our sacred honor hanging in the balance, Whitehead argues that our ideal, that for the sake of which we are willing to risk all that we have and are, should be the ideal of the medieval Benedictine monks. That ideal "remains the sole hope of toiling humanity," of us all who suffer "the curse that has been laid on humanity" that "by the sweat of its brow shall it live" (1917: 44). Hence, it is the task of technological education to be sure human beings everywhere have learned the handcraft skills by which the practical things of life are made, "so to mould the nation [and the world] that daily it may pass to its labours in the spirit of the monks of old" (44).

What is this ideal that should inform the most serious of all enterprises, our common effort to live and to live well? It is to create "a commonwealth in which work is play and play is life," in which work is "turned into a joy triumphing over its weariness and its pain" (44). And so with the Benedictines we are brought back to one of our themes in chapter 9: the importance of play. Now, however, with a twist, for Whitehead is arguing not only that play is important in the education that is our preparation for work, but also that it is important for work itself.

Without enjoyment, work is drudgery—a task valued only for its results, for the goods produced or for those provided by the wages earned. We will find joy in what we do only if we understand its significance, only if we see our labor as realizing some worthy ideal. The exercise of our skills is pleasurable because we find it meaningful, a form of self-expression that is at the same time a value benefiting our community, serving ends greater than our own. Workers of all sorts—employees and employers, imaginative theorists and shrewd practitioners, sweet-tongued poets and callous-fingered lath turners—therefore need to be educated in all three modes of learning: liberal, scientific, and technical. When so educated, they will find joy in what they do because they are able to appreciate ideals and to fashion them, to assess alternative hypotheses and to devise them, to solve problems independently and in collaboration with others.

The Benedictines "rejoiced in their labours because they conceived themselves as thereby made fellow-workers with Christ" (44). Different meanings, more suited to our secular age, may be the ones that infuse our own labors. But a meaning as fundamental for us as the Benedictines' Christ was for them is requisite if our work is to be fulfilling—if it is to be exhilarating, pleasurable, a joyous expression of our selves, a form of play that gives us lives we think worthwhile.

Whitehead holds up the Benedictines as our role models, because "alike for masters and for men a technical or technological education, which is to have any chance of satisfying the practical needs of the nation [and world], must be conceived in a liberal spirit as a real intellectual enlightenment in regard to principles applied and services rendered" (45). People need the firsthand knowledge that comes only through actually making things, by handcrafting objects able to satisfy our needs. Such technological effort is genuine and effective, however, only if infused by ideals that justify the worth of those needs and the appropriateness of the means by which they can be attained. The Benedictines saw work in this way—they "saved for mankind the vanishing civilization of the ancient world by linking together knowledge, labor, and moral energy" (58).

Here, in the early years of a new century and millennium, we need an approach to education wherein students will learn a new version of the Benedictine approach. We need an education that will help make it possible for our vanishing parochial civilizations, with their local traditions and narrow-sea ideals, to be redeemed by becoming the resources for their transformation into a world civilization, our disparate cultural goods the warp and woof by which we are able to weave at long last a common planetary good.

Chapter 12

Cathedral Ruins

Emancipation or Obligation

Bill Readings argues that the University "has lost its historical raison d'être" (19). It is a creature of the modern Western nation-state, its medieval antecedents reshaped to serve as instruments for "the production of sovereign subjects"(154), for the fashioning of good citizens able to contribute effectively to the nation's well-being. This purpose, says Readings, is no longer viable. The cathedral of learning has become a ruin: its foundations have crumbled so completely that their repair or replacement is no longer possible. Nor even desirable.

We explored in the early chapters of this book a triad of competing notions about what constitutes an educational canon—canons of content, of procedure, and of egalitarian openness. In doing so, we have already encountered Readings's critique of the historical forms of higher education, forms I associated with these three sorts of canon, forms he calls the Universities of Culture, of Reason, and of Excellence. I went on to argue that relativist canons can best be understood as versions of these three. My aim in this chapter is to consider Readings's alternative to these failed forms, his alternative to attempting vainly to shore up a cathedral in ruins, and to relate his suggestions to the notion of a pragmatic educational canon I have been developing since chapter 6.

The problem with all three approaches to education and to the canons they articulate, according to Readings, is that they are based on an "ideology of autonomy" (154). They make the University a "site of emancipation," a place where students learn to become independent, to think for themselves, to make their own choices. Education is seen as the process by which we are able to free ourselves from accustomed traditions, blind prejudice, and the influence of others. We learn to control our passions, to act rationally and deliberately in accord with the moral and intellectual standards that define a fully functioning adult human being. We imagine the ideal person to be self-contained, self-sufficient—autonomous.

Education as emancipation means nurturing persons who aspire to what Readings calls a "utopia of self-transparency, of a society immediately present to itself," one "in which all members communicate unrestrictedly with all of the others all of the time and without misunderstanding or delay" (190). Communities and their canonical value systems should result from "the autonomous decision of individuals to communicate with each other as subjects of a state" (181). Only by being free and adult can they enter into a rational discussion about the possibilities for mutual advancement, leading to the formation of a social covenant they will find reasonable and so can embrace knowingly, with eyes wide open. Aristotle's *polis,* populated by people of excellence; Kant's kingdom of ends; Habermas's society of communicative rationality—all are communities sustained by and sustaining individuals who are able to understand the implications of their choices and who on that basis have agreed to cooperate. Individual autonomy is a prerequisite for genuine community.

If the emancipatory University is a microcosm of the civic macrocosm, exemplifying the ideals of citizenship it seeks to inculcate, then its faculty should be clear-headed autonomous thinkers and doers, and its students, taking them as role models, should be on their way to attaining that same condition, on their way to becoming compleat persons. Professors are those who have achieved the ideal, or rather some reasonable approximation thereto. They are the ones who are cultured, the experts. The pedagogical task of the faculty is to turn their students into replicas of themselves by exposing them to the Great Books and Great Ways that are the essential content of that culture and the methodological conditions for that expertise. Anti-canonists only depart from this model by locating in students important aspects of culture and expertise, aspects the professors may well lack—thereby giving students some authority for determining what counts as the essential contents or methods to be learned, so that the aims of the courses they take need to be negotiated rather than simply inculcated.

For Readings, this vision of autonomous selves means that "to have knowledge is to gain a self-sufficient monologic voice" (156–57). The task of teaching is to help students speak in their own voice, to appropriate their general cultural heritage, and to achieve a specific expertise. Their knowledge should involve fully understood interpretations, principles, conclusions, methods, theories, and data, a body of knowledge they can express in their own words, and to which they can contribute, their new voices added to the old. Yet because these achievements are each monologues, each autonomous voice having its own distinctive say, the family or classroom or neighborhood or parliament is not understood as an arena for the exchange of ideas, for genuine "dialogue." It merely serves as an occasion for "divided monologues" (154), people negotiating their differences as though so many bargainers in a market place, entering into or living up to the terms of a contract.

Readings proposes, in contrast, that we think of communities, educational and civic, as marked by interdependencies that are inescapable givens for who we are, connections not to be overcome but cherished, not outgrown but grown into. Universities should be understood as "sites of *obligation*," he argues, as "loci of ethical practices" (154). For knowledge involves not "the abandonment of a network of ethical obligations" but its cultivation (156). Acting ethically is a matter of living our obligations, not fleeing them. It has to do with opacity rather than transparency. We are ethical when we open ourselves to others and to relationships that are not contractual, not carefully delimited with respect to our rights and obligations. We are ethical when we nurture interdependencies that have no definable conditions nor any specified termination dates. Our relationships—as professors, students, and fellow citizens—call for conversations in place of monologues as the mode by which we should share what we know or seek.

If ethical relationships can never be brought to completion, if emancipation from their bonds is not the reason for going to school, then in an important sense education has no goal—because knowing what the correct answers are and developing the proper techniques for acquiring, assessing, and applying them is not what transpires when learning takes place. Knowledge is not a matter of learning an answer but of exploring an unanswerable question, or rather of exploring a question for which no answer or set of answers is sufficient. Learning is an open-ended and open-textured process, resting on no unassailable foundation, oriented toward no predetermined end, guided by no self-evident truths or fixed principles.

Readings indulges in the obscurantism of recent French philosophizing by calling this sort of interminable fluidity "the name of Thought." The aim of education, he argues, is not at attaining Truth, at acquiring a final, definitive knowledge of first principles or essences, even when that goal is understood to be beyond the capacity of any individual or any cultural tradition to achieve—even when, as Kant would say, it is taken as a regulative but not a constitutive ideal. Readings wants us to understand teaching and learning as features of an inquiry that does not presuppose its ends or means, in which everything is questionable. He says, therefore, that the "referent of teaching," the goal of genuine pedagogical activity, is "empty." "The name of Thought precisely is a name in that it *has no intrinsic meaning*" (159). Educators should acknowledge that they have no definitive truths to teach, no certain answers to their students' questions. They cannot justify their assertions by appealing to the authority of Thought, to some body of established truth, because it is not Thought they know but only the name of Thought. "Since a name has no signification, only a designatory function, it cannot have a truth-content. The meaning-effects of a name are structurally incapable of final determination, are always open to discussion" (160).

Plato anticipates Readings. Meno, prodded by the unremitting sting of Socrates' questions into realizing that he does not know what it means to be virtuous, and learning that Socrates is every bit as perplexed as he by the question, wonders how they will ever find out what virtue means if they have no idea what it is or where to look for it. "How can you aim to search for something you do not know at all? If you should meet with it, how will you know that this is the thing that you did not know?" (*Meno* 80d). Socrates responds that learning is a "process" the pursuit of which requires that we be "brave," not "fainthearted," that we be "energetic and keen on the search" (81d–e). He offers the notion of "recollection" as a way to structure that pursuit, but then indicates the speculative character of such a notion and concludes: "I do not insist that my argument is right in all other respects, but I would contend at all costs both in word and deed as far as I could that we will be better men, braver and less idle, if we believe that one must search for the things one does not know, rather than if we believe that it is not possible to find out what we do not know and that we must not look for it" (86c)— and also rather than if we believe that we have already found it out, if we believe, as Meno had initially believed, that we do not need to look for virtue because we possess either it or a guaranteed method for attaining it.

Recognizing that all perspectives are limited and so necessarily incomplete, that any truth claim will always be in need of critique and reformulation, we teachers and students, we masters and apprentices, should nonetheless seek whatever truths we can as best we can. "To listen to Thought," says Readings, "to think beside each other and beside ourselves, is to explore an open network of obligations that keeps the question of meaning open as a locus of debate" (165). He calls this educative style "pragmatism," by which he means a mode of inquiry that is "without *alibis*, without 'elsewheres,' " without any appeal to "a truth whose name might be invoked to save us from responsibility for our actions"—including even the alibi of claiming that what we do is justified because we are being pragmatic (168).

When Readings says that the University is in ruins he thus means that its foundations are in ruins, that there are no rock-solid fixed principles able to support our claims about what we know and how we know it. He rejects not only attempts to shore up or rebuild the old foundations but also proposals for fashioning some new sort of foundation. Any such approach is emancipatory, oriented toward and justified by an ideal of autonomy: the autonomy of knowledge and the autonomy of the University as both the caretaker of that knowledge and the tutor of citizens able to achieve the personal autonomy it claims to provide. The alternative Readings proposes is that we do without foundations altogether, that we think of education as having no emancipatory goal. Quite the opposite: the function of education should be to aid us in recognizing and deepening the ways in which we are bound up with others in a network of non-emancipatory dependencies. What we share is our ignorance, our struggle to understand our selves and our world—and, with what we think we understand, to improve in some measure our individual and our collective lives. Readings asks us to dwell amid the ruins of the cathedral of emancipatory learning, bound together in a seeking that seeks not to escape from our moral responsibilities but to take them seriously.

Emancipation before Obligation

Richard Rorty thinks our academic cathedrals can be saved from ruin by our refusing to accept Readings's forced choice for education between the ideal of emancipation and the duties of obligation, between becoming an autonomous individual and accepting the responsibilities of our interdependence with others. He associates each polar option with a political tendency in American culture, then argues that each by itself is inadequate. Educational and hence cultural integrity can be achieved if the two are seen as complementary sequential features of a whole.

For conservatives on the political and cultural Right, argues Rorty, the purpose of education is the development of our rational capacities because reason is the one sure instrument for getting at the intrinsic nature of things, for attaining the truth about its essential features, including the truth of our own nature as human beings. "Deep within our souls there is a spark that the right sort of education can fan into flame. Once the soul is afire with love of truth, freedom will follow—for freedom consists in realizing one's *true* self; that is, in the actualization of one's capacity to be rational. So the right concludes, only the truth can make us free" (1999: 114). This approach is Platonic: by awakening to truth we are awakened to our freedom as selves.

The political and cultural Left, according to Rorty, inverts this Platonism. Reason is an instrument of "acculturation engineered by the powers that be," so the task of education is liberation from the constraints this reason has imposed on us. We need to be freed to make our own selves. "If you take care of freedom—especially political and economic freedom—truth will take care of itself. For truth is what will be believed once the alienating and repressive forces of society are removed" (115). By awakening to our freedom as selves we are awakened to truth.

Those on the cultural Right are worried about natural self-expression, which they see as the unbridled passion of raw appetite or sinful selfishness. They think we can be emancipated from our passions by learning how to control them through the exercise of rational constraint, thereby becoming civilized mature adults. For those on the cultural Left, the problem lies in social convention and prejudice, in the ways civilized life distorts natural self-expression. They think we need to be emancipated from these unthinking traditional ways in order to become self-determined mature adults. Both Right and Left appeal to emancipation, freedom from something negative, and to autonomy, the freedom to be truly oneself—but they have differing senses of what those key concepts mean. "Both accept the identification of truth and freedom with the essentially human. The difference between them is simply over the question: Is the present socioeconomic set-up in accordance, more or less, with nature? Is it, on the whole, a realization of human potentialities, or rather a way of frustrating those potentialities?" (115).

Insofar as these contrasting interpretations are taken as an either/or, the result can only be an endless warfare between two half-truths. Their reconciliation is possible, however, Rorty argues, once we give up the notion of an essential human nature. We should take seriously claims about both the importance of societal values and the centrality of the individual. Both are legitimate, but we should think neither is a claim about something essential. A societal convention is not by definition a prejudice, nor is a passionate departure from convention by definition a sin. We need the nurture a society provides, its repertoire of useful scripts, its emancipatory training of our natural capacities. But we also need to stand over against society, tailoring its values to our own style, creating our own versions of its moral practices, writing our own scripts. Autonomy should not be understood as independence from a network of obligations but as the skill to function effectively and appropriately within such a network. Freedom is not independence from society and from others; it is having opportunity to explore forms of interdependence different than those inherited from our past.

Political democracies, Rorty contends, have embedded this reconciling strategy in their educational institutions through "a fairly simply, fairly satisfactory compromise. The right has pretty much kept control of primary and secondary education and the left has gradually got control of non-vocational higher education" (116). The task of primary and secondary education is to acculturate students, to teach them "the moral and political common sense of the society as it is," to "inculcate most of what is generally believed." Those who then go on to college, who enroll in an undergraduate arts and sciences program of study, are taught to be critical of these commonsensical beliefs, to be aware of the limitations of what has been long established and to think about different and maybe better alternatives. Once they are attending college, and hence thoroughly acculturated into the American way of life, it is important for students to become "a little more conscious of the cruelty built into our institutions, of the need for reform, of the need to be sceptical about the current consensus" (116).

Rorty the deconstructive postmodernist therefore finds himself agreeing with the foundationalist E. D. Hirsch Jr. He thinks that Hirsch is "dead right," making the same sort of reformist critique Dewey makes, when he argues in *Cultural Literacy* "that we Americans no longer give our children a secondary education that enables them to function as citizens of a democracy" (Rorty 1999: 118). Hirsch defines cultural literacy as "the network of information that all competent readers possess," the basic facts and concepts that provide the crucial but "unstated context" to what we read in newspapers, magazines, or popular books, that we hear on radio or see on television and in the movies (Hirsch: 2). We can't function competently as citizens in a democracy unless we understand what's going on, what the politicians are proposing and their critics debunking, what the changes in cultural fashion are and how seriously to take them, what purports to be fair, seemly, or plausible, and what unjust, obscene, or false. Schools, Hirsch says, should "teach the ways of one's own community" to each new generation of students (18) by providing them with at least the bare minimum requirements for citizenship: a grasp of, and an appreciation for, the "shared schemata" of beliefs members of the community take as obvious and important, that are the source for the "unspoken systems of association" that have become "second nature" to them (68). For Hirsch, in other words, we are culturally literate if we inhabit that culture's worldview, if we are at home in its way of construing things, if we know how to use its basic scripts, if we see things as our neighbors see them and can find in that shared way of seeing the basis for our commonality and hence for our shared pursuit of common ends.

Hirsch's claim that schooling should concentrate on teaching cultural literacy rests on four key distinctions. First, inculcating the basic information our culture presupposes that its citizens know only constitutes the "extensive curriculum": it is preparatory for the "intensive curriculum" that should then be built upon its minimalist foundation. We should be undertaking close readings of Shakespeare's plays and sonnets, but we need to bring to those readings some basic information about European history, the Bible, folk mythologies, and the character of human desire, pride, nobility, and deceit. Second, the literacy Hirsch would have the schools inculcate is not about the "public discourse" in which our conflicting aims and modes of action are pursued, defended, and adjudicated (102). It has to do with the backdrop for this discourse, "the concrete politics, customs, technologies, legends that define current attitudes, actions, institutions" (103).

Third, the basics of culture Hirsch wants the schools to inculcate is that of our "national culture," which he carefully distinguishes from the "narrow tribal cultures"—genealogical, ethnic, religious—and the "transcendent world culture" to which we also belong (18). And fourth, what composes the basic cultural content needing to be taught is open-ended rather than settled, enduring but not timeless, utilitarian instead of intrinsic. The cultural content will change as the times change, as our culture alters, as our needs and interests render some traditional information obsolete and rediscover the relevance of other previously neglected information.

Hirsch's problem, of course, was that he delineated the scope of the cultural basics in which contemporary Americans should be literate in the form of a list. *Cultural Literacy* lays out a roster of some five thousand items: dates (1066, 1492), places (Adirondack Mountains, Acropolis), people (Adam and Eve, John Adams), terms (abolitionism, abominable snowman), institutions (Atomic Energy Commission, American Legion), and cliches (actions speak louder than words, am I my brother's keeper?)—to list only the first two items in each of his list's sublists. These are a pile of disconnected items, torn from their contexts and arranged by that great exemplar of the arbitrary, the alphabet. They are meant as pointers, suggesting the great works of literature and art, the important historical agents and events, that we must study carefully if we are ever to find them intelligible. It is easy enough, however, to concentrate on the pointer rather than on that to which it points, then either to reject Hirsch as having trivialized the notion of cultural literacy or to trivialize it ourselves by accepting his list as what needs to be learned.

If we are careful to avoid these pitfalls, Hirsch's point is Dewey's and is in accord with Rorty's: the first task of education is to provide young people with a knowledge of and appreciation for the beliefs that constitute the least common denominator of their cultural heritage. The second task may be—and, indeed, must be—to critique that heritage, to develop the capacity to engage it creatively, to transform it by seeking to give vitality to its unrealized ideals. But there can be no viable second task without the first task having been accomplished. As Rorty puts it, "socialization has to come before individuation, and education for freedom cannot begin before some constraints have been imposed" (1999: 118). First emancipation through cultural appreciation, then the obligations of critique and reform.

Hannah Arendt agrees. Her critique of American education is that it pushes the freedom stage of learning down into primary and secondary education, thereby undercutting the crucial place of socialization in a child's development. "The essence of education is natality, the fact that human beings are *born* into the world" (174). What Arendt means by "the world" is civil society, Hirsh's realm of "public discourse," the public arena of human interactions where political decisions are negotiated, material goods produced and exchanged, cultural artifacts fashioned and enjoyed, laws promulgated, gods worshiped. Children are born into that world but are unprepared to function within it. The task of education is to prepare them to do so. This process of educating a child, developing his or her capacities for worldliness, needs to occur away from the world's influence, Arendt argues. "Because the child must be protected against the world, his traditional place is in the family, whose adult members daily return back from the outside world and withdraw into the security of private life within four walls" (186). Children, like all kinds of vegetative life, need privacy and security when they are young: "However strong its natural tendency to thrust itself into the light, it nevertheless needs the security of darkness to grow at all" (186).

Schools provide a transition stage between the privacy of the family and the public world of the wider society. Students are first introduced to the public world through their teachers, whose authority rests on their role as the world's representatives. They are authorities not because of their learnedness, their academic degrees and specialized expertise, but because they represent the cultural tradition to which students are to be introduced. "Vis-à-vis the child it is as though [the teacher] were a representative of all adult inhabitants, pointing out the details and saying to the child: This is our world" (189). The public sphere is the arena for criticism and innovation; the private sphere, including the traditional institution of the schools, is the arena for appreciation and conservation.

Arendt argues that it is a mistake to import these private values into the public sphere. "In politics this conservative attitude—which accepts the world as it is, striving only to preserve the status quo—can lead to destruction, because the world, in gross and in detail, is irrevocably delivered up to the ruin of time unless human beings are determined to intervene, to alter, to create what is new" (192). If students are only taught to appreciate their heritage, they will enter the public sphere prepared only as conservationists. So what needs to be conserved in the educational process is not only the cultural tradition but also the children's newness, the creative originality that their youthful energy and lack of public experience provide. Precisely because children are not yet engaged in the public pursuit of important ends, they need not be held accountable to the world's standards. They are allowed to be playful about what their tradition offers rather than having to take it seriously precisely because they, and the consequences of their irresponsible play, are walled off from the world. Schooling conserves both the wondrous achievements of the hoary past and the delicate possibilities by which it might be delivered from the ruin of time.

Rorty's way of making Arendt's point is to identify nonvocational postsecondary education as the developmental stage where students should be awakened to the fact "that they can reshape themselves—that they can rework the self-image foisted on them by their past, the self-image that makes them competent citizens, into a new self-image, one that they themselves have helped to create" (1999: 118). Moreover, what applies to the self applies to society as well: students should awake to the possibility that the established understandings and practices of their community can be reshaped, a new cultural self-image devised and implemented. Higher education should be "a matter of inciting doubt and stimulating imagination, thereby challenging the prevailing consensus" (118). This awakening to their obligations as citizens can occur, says Rorty, by providing students with a "narrative of freedom," a "narrative of national hope" in addition to the narrative of national accomplishment told by their primary and secondary schooling (122).

The possibilities for societal and individual improvement inherent in freedom and hope are not arbitrary inventions. They are already implicit in the account of past accomplishments, for whatever people have achieved is ever only an approximation to what they had hoped to achieve. Those still unrealized possibilities haunt the past as ideals for future realization. Arendt lauds the way in which young people during the Roman Republic were taught to revere their ancestors, to take the past as authoritative. She quotes Polybius when he says that to educate is simply "to let you see that you are altogether worthy of your ancestors" (194). The goal is not to imitate our ancestors, however, but rather to imitate their idealization of themselves, to imitate their attempt to think and act nobly, to live up to what they took to be the ideals inherent in their heritage as Romans. The cultural past is to be conserved not merely because our predecessors accomplished great things but because they give us hope, because they promise us that we too have the originative capacity, and so can create the opportunity, to accomplish great things as well.

What Rorty celebrates in the thought of pragmatists like Dewey is their conviction that a key feature of American democracy is our embrace of such a narrative of hope. They thought that the socialization American students receive in the process of their schooling consists, at its best,

in acquiring an image of themselves as heirs to a tradition of increasing liberty and rising hope,... as proud and loyal citizens of a country that, slowly and painfully, threw off a foreign yoke, freed its slaves, enfranchised its women, restrained its robber barons and licensed its trade unions, liberalized its religious practices, broadened its religious and moral tolerance, and built colleges in which 50 per cent of its population could enrol—a country that numbered Jefferson, Thoreau, Susan B. Anthony, Eugene Debs, Woodrow Wilson, Walter Reuther, Franklin Delano Roosevelt, Rosa Parks, and James Baldwin among its citizens. (1999: 121–22)

The key to democratic education, says Rorty, is not truth but hope: "the ability to believe that the future will be unspecifiably different from, and unspecifiably freer than, the past" (120).

Arendt concurs:

> To preserve the world against the mortality of its creators and inhabitants it must be constantly set right anew. The problem is simply to educate in such a way that a setting-right remains actually possible, even though it can, of course, never be assured. Our hope always hangs on the new which every generation brings; but precisely because we can base our hope only on this, we destroy everything if we so try to control the new that we, the old, can dictate how it will look. Exactly for the sake of what is new and revolutionary in every child, education must be conservative; it must preserve this newness and introduce it as a new thing into an old world, which, however revolutionary its actions may be, is always, from the standpoint of the next generation, superannuated and close to destruction. (192–93)

Emancipation and Obligation

So Rorty and Arendt propose that we reconcile the conserving and liberating functions of education by sequencing them. Initially, we should take an appreciative approach to teaching students their cultural heritage. Then, when the students grow sufficiently mature in their understanding of that heritage, we should shift to an evaluative mode. We first must understand what we would change.

What do we do, however, when a community has been so radically transformed that to conserve its old traditions is to undermine its promise? If a cultural tradition has been parochial, its national narrative narrowly tribal, how can it be used uncritically even in early schooling by a multi-tribal cosmopolitan nation? In contemporary America, teaching the Puritan story of the founding of God's New Israel and its parallel secular account of the founding of a Republic of yeoman farmers, then teaching about the Manifest Destiny of the Anglo-Saxon peoples, is to focus on one tribal heritage at the expense of all the others. Scottish, Irish, and Scandinavian immigrants might easily enough rework their ancestral stories until they are compatible with this essentially English narrative, but those from Mediterranean Europe and the Middle East will have a harder time of it. Those from countries of the former Spanish and Portuguese New World empires will have more difficulty still, and descendants of East and South Asian families are likely to find few points of connection with the English narrative. Those whose ancestors came to America on English slave ships will find no connection at all. The primary critique of the educational canon traditionally taught in American schools is precisely its embarrassingly parochial nature. It excludes too much to be treated as the appropriate instrument by which children of all backgrounds are socialized into American culture.

Dewey's suggestion is that we focus on procedure rather than content, that we make "free and open encounters" among the conflicting traditions found in a pluralistic democracy the key to education (Rorty 1999: 119). But open encounters are moments of critique, occasions for the clash and celebration of differences. What can pluralistic openness mean during the acculturation phase of education? How can encounters among differing tribal traditions flourish in the primary and secondary education schools without turning classrooms into arenas for dispute, for challenge and negotiation, for working out modes of mutual tolerance or even reconciliation? Yet if early education is to take on these critical roles, it can do so only by giving up its appreciative function. The egalitarian values of the public arena, so crucial to the democratic negotiation of difference, will shoulder aside the unquestioned authority of the old that is so crucial to a child's acculturation. The loss of that authority will soon be followed by loss of the old itself, and thus the point of critique will have been undermined, the resources overlooked by which criticism can be reconstructive rather than merely destructive. Moreover, by becoming emancipated from the authority of the old, "the child has not been freed but has been subjected to a much more terrifying and truly tyrannical authority, the tyranny of the majority" (Arendt: 181)—the tyranny of a conformity negotiated by the current members of the community on the basis solely of their current preferences.

Dewey escapes this seeming dilemma by rejecting the sequencing Rorty and Arendt advocate. It is a mistake, he says, to think "the business of childhood is to grow into the independence of adulthood," and hence to think that "the process of education as the main business of life ends when the young have arrived at emancipation from social dependence" (1920: 184). Sequencing our lives into appreciative and critical phases is to succumb to the emancipation narrative Bill Readings was attacking. It presumes that education has completed its task as soon as students have attained two things: first, an understanding of their cultural achievements, and then the tools with which to sustain and improve them. If school is where children learn to be adults, as Rorty and Arendt are saying, then our schooling should cease when we have attained the qualities needed to function effectively as responsible citizens.

This notion of adult autonomy as the goal of education is just one more instance of the "fixed ends" Dewey was always railing against. Arendt may have held such a view, but Rorty should know better. As Dewey and as pragmatists and process philosophers of every ilk argue, goods are never fixed. They are always particular and contextual, always arising as possibilities for improving whatever might be the case:

Moral goods and ends exist only when something has to be done. The fact that something has to be done proves that there are deficiencies, evils in the existent situation.

This ill is just the specific ill that it is. It never is an exact duplicate of anything else. Consequently the good of the situation has to be discovered, projected and attained on the basis of the exact defect and trouble to be rectified. (Dewey 1920: 169).

Understanding is always the precondition for reform, an improvement always a creative response to the perceived inadequacies of what is understood. So our lives from childhood to old age, says Dewey, are constantly an interplay of conserving appreciation and transforming critique. We are always in need of being educated—self-educated, educated by others, educated collaboratively—because we are always in situations that can be improved once we know their limits and appreciate their potential.

We are never autonomous, never fully grown: from the moral obligations that fill our lives there can be no emancipation. Our education is lifelong, Dewey continues, because our growth with respect to goods of every sort is endlessly open-ended. Our goal in life should not be thought of as "a terminus or limit to be reached. It is the active process of transforming the existent situation. Not perfection as a final goal, but the every-enduring process of perfecting, maturing, refining is the aim in living" (177). Dewey would call individuals or groups educated not on the basis of something they might have achieved, such as becoming culturally sophisticated, nor on the basis of certain skills they might have developed, such as becoming an adept critic of one or another cultural shortcoming. Instead, he would call them educated on the basis of their growth in cultural sophistication and critical adeptness, their growth as persons and as members of societal institutions. For Dewey, morality is a matter of trying to improve the actual in the light of the possibly better.

Dewey draws the egalitarian consequence from this understanding of good: "Anything that in a given situation is an end and good at all is of equal worth, rank and dignity with every other good of any other situation, and deserves the same intelligent attention" (176). There are no fixed hierarchies of good and no predetermined authorities for what constitutes its content. There are only the situations in which we find ourselves, our appreciation of what they are and what they could be, and our ability to transform them for what we take to be the better. Since the growth thus sought, effectively or otherwise, involves the same processes that we have seen are involved in educating someone, it should be no surprise that Dewey identifies growth and education:

Getting from the present the degree and kind of growth that is in it is education. This is a constant function, independent of age. The best thing that can be said about any special process of education, like that of the formal school period, is that it renders its subject capable of further education: more sensitive to conditions of growth and more able to take advantage of them. Acquisition of skill, possession of knowledge, attainment of culture are not ends: they are marks of growth and means to its continuing. (184–85).

For Dewey, the "moral meaning" of democracy is that it is a form of government in which "the test of all institutions of adult life" should be "the contribution they make to the all-around growth of every member of society," to the development of "the capacities of human individuals without respect to race, sex, class or economic status" (186). A society is not to be judged to be good on the basis of how well it satisfies the wants, desires, needs, and interests of its citizens. Its worth, rather, is a function of its success in "*creating individuals*"—where to be an individual is to have "wrought out" a character marked by "initiative, inventiveness, varied resourcefulness, assumption of responsibility in choice of belief and conduct" (194). For Dewey, in other words, individuality is a value-laden notion, a moral accomplishment, an excellence. But what is achieved is a manner of action not a state or condition. Individuals initiate and invent, cleverly and responsibly. They develop liberal, scientific, and technical skills for improving the quality of their lives and, most importantly, skills for improving those skills. Growth is open-ended and so individuality, understood as a moral excellence, is dynamic, a result always in process of being transformed.

We can grow more individual only through our association with other individuals, Dewey argues. The goods we seek are "enhanced by being mutually communicated and participated in," so our growth as individuals entails association with others (205). Since Dewey is pluralistically egalitarian in the goods he thinks promote growth, he advocates a society in which "all kinds and varieties of associations" are encouraged, voluntary organizations "for the cultivation of every conceivable interest that men have in common" (203). The role of government is like that of an orchestra conductor: "to foster and coordinate the activities of voluntary groupings" but not to determine the goals those groupings were formed to achieve (204). The function of a democracy is to enforce societal conditions that encourage the creation of groups organized for the mutual enhancement of their members' capacities and the successful accomplishment of their shared purposes.

"Freedom for an individual means growth," says Dewey, so a free society—a genuine democracy—is one that nurtures this freedom, this "release of capacity from whatever hems it in." Reciprocally, a society is "strong, forceful, stable against accident only if its members can function to the limit of their capacity" (207–208). By creating conditions that support the continual education of its citizens, support their progressive liberation from whatever inhibits their development as fully functioning persons, a society creates citizens who are able to deal constructively with its problems, effecting its growth as a fully functioning human commonwealth.

Bill Readings, awkwardly, uses Jean-Luc Nancy's notion of a "community of dissensus"—more aptly, a "community at loose ends"—to make Dewey's point. Nancy envisions an ideal society as one that is essentially incomplete, composed of persons who are "singularities," related to one another in a "network of obligations that the individual cannot master" (Readings 185). Readings wants us to keep this network going, preventing any members of our community from thinking they can become autonomous captains of their own destinies, preventing society from presuming itself to be that captain. Where Readings and Nancy celebrate the contingent temporary associations of free individuals in order to emphasize the negative consequences of a community defined by some shared consensus about fixed social ends, Dewey celebrates these associations because of their positive aspects, because of the growth in individuality they promote. For all three, education brings freedom not because it liberates us from our dependency on others, living or dead, but because it helps us realize that we can grow as individuals, can become effective singularities, only insofar as we freely acknowledge and work to strengthen our mutual interdependence.

"We are left, "says Readings, "with an obligation to explore our obligations without believing that we can come to the end of them" (190), to promote "heterogeneity" by refusing some sort of ultimate consensus as a societal good, aiming instead for only "provisional forms of agreement and action" (187). We are left, says Dewey, with the pluralism by which democracies thrive, with individuals associated in "groupings for promoting the diversity of goods" they severally seek, each group adding "its own contribution of value to life," to the interdependent life of a society in which each person's achievements have their "own unique and ultimate worth" (1920: 204).

Chapter 13

Constructive Pragmatics

The Narrative Core

So we have work to do, here amid the crumbling cathedrals where we have chosen to live. The times are tough, the aims of higher education are in disarray, the ruins of so much that we have achieved and dreamed of achieving are scattered everywhere. Yet we have obligations to explore and the diversity of our common good to promote, for the cash value of an educational canon, interpreted in the pragmatic sense I've explicated over the course of this book, is that we are obliged to teach it. Our nation, like any other organized society, has an intellectual canon which our educational institutions should be inculcating through a curriculum of study based on a suitable educational canon. This canon is constantly needing reform but it is constantly needed. Our cultural heritage can only be transmitted by being learned. Minimally, this means constructing a version of E. D. Hirsch's "extensive curriculum" and passing it on to each new generation of students, accomplishing what Richard Rorty calls the "acculturation phase" of education.

This work cannot be left to primary and secondary education. The problem is not that K-12 schooling is inadequate, even though sometimes it is, but that students learn in spirals of increasing sophistication. Acculturation is a recurrent phase of learning, not merely an initial phase to be succeeded by other phases, as though having climbed its ladder to a new level we can then discard the ladder. What we are able to appreciate alters as our understanding broadens and deepens. We return to what we once knew with fresh eyes, and depart it for different reasons and novel destinations. Our initial flight leads us to a new perch, to a moment for taking stock of where we are and what we have accomplished, reorienting us so that we will be ready for the next flight. An educational canon construes that perch insofar as it is a cultural and not merely an individual achievement. As the perches change so do the canons, and so the task of acculturation should recur throughout our schooling—and then on throughout the remainder of our lives.

Hence, liberal arts programs have an obligation to the nation to insist that all freshman students enroll in some kind of required general education core curriculum, some course of study that provides an overview of what is currently thought essential for anyone to know in order to become a decent and productive citizen. Yet as I argued in chapter 1, the weight of this canonical knowledge has become unbearable: dramatically expanded, democratized, and globalized. We need a canonical method for constructing our educational canons. Lists such as Hirsch's, the lists of Great Books and Great Ways among them, are piles of possible canonical candidates, fragments perhaps to be shored against our ruin, but unconnected incoherent jumbles of value. No wonder they strike students as arbitrary arrays imposed by equally arbitrary academic authority figures. The proper selection strategy, I contend, is not to organize this jumble by discipline or theme or even by chronology—but instead to fashion a narrative that tells the story of our culture, and to determine the content of the core curriculum by its relevance to that story.

We share a master narrative as citizens of a nation: the account of its history. It recounts the nation's origins, its successes and failures, its virtues and sins, its changing character as it stretches out across the decades and centuries, expanding or contracting its geographic boundaries and its spheres of influence. This master narrative is the most important schema of interpretation we share as a people, and so it is the appropriate criterion by which to select a canon that teaches us the what and how and why and worth of our being one people. Embedded in this narrative are other subnarratives—stories about ethnic groups, geographic or political regions, neighborhoods, religious communities, voluntary societies, extended families—and it is in turn embedded in narratives about the modern West, the rise of civilizations, the story of humankind from its origins on the African savanna to the present day.

Anti-canonists such as Jean-François Lyotard, as we saw in chapter 4, find a master narrative confining, an attempt by others to limit our freedom, to force us to conform to its imperialistic determination of what constitutes right thinking and right action. The problem is not that such a story is overarching, however, but that it is closed: deterministic, progressive, triumphalist. Richard Rorty can talk positively about a narrative of national accomplishment precisely because he is imagining it to be open-ended: revisable, contingent, fallible.

Imagine an American Culture core course in which students attend general lectures by a historian, who offers them a narrative about the clash of peoples and histories out of which the United States once emerged as a nation and because of which it has ever since struggled to endure as a united people. We need not be social Darwinists trumpeting the manifest destiny of our Anglo-Saxon ancestors when we spin this tale. If the story is to be worthy of our admiration, after all, it must be an adequate account. It must therefore encompass the full range of differing contributions to our national character, attending to the ways in which victories and defeats have had unexpected or ironic consequences, including the ways in which the price of someone's achievement has often been another's tragic loss. Our story also needs to affirm the differing perspectives of those caught up in its narrative, not just the viewpoints that define its central tendencies but likewise those that the course of events has marginalized or excluded.

No one anymore would begin American history with the landing of the Pilgrims in Provincetown and proceed with narrowed focus to trace their adventures through the founding of the Republic and on toward global dominance, a tale of Englishmen and those latecomers they have assimilated, the course readings limited to works by the likes of Jonathan Edwards, Thomas Jefferson, Abraham Lincoln, and Josiah Strong. We would insist on a proper attention to other narrative threads and primary sources. We might, for instance, approach the English colonization of the New World from the viewpoint of those whose lands were being encroached upon, reading Daniel Richter's *Facing East from Indian Country*. And we might parallel this account with one about contacts at that same time far to the west between Spanish colonizers and the Pueblo nations, reading Ramón Gutiérrez's *When Jesus Came, the Corn Mothers Went Away*.

The general historical narrative for such a core course needs to be complemented by discussion sections that focus on a close reading of primary sources. The particularity of those readings helps students appreciate the generalizing character of a narrative. They will discover that particulars are not miniatures of the general, that they vary from it in all sorts of interesting ways without undermining the adequacy of the general statement they illustrate. For instance, the eighteenth century in America and Europe was an Age of Reason even though it included the rise of Methodists who favored warm hearts rather than good reasons as the keys to truth. The back and forth between these two perspectives, the narrative overview and the specifics composing its content, scuffs the uniform smoothness of the narrative, complicating it, enriching our appreciation of it.

The natural sciences also have a story to tell. In one form, it is the story of scientists, the history of scientific inquiry from earliest times to the present, a tale concerning changing theories and paradigms of scientific understanding. This is not only a story about theories and theorizers, however, but also a story about how our understanding of nature has changed our understanding of ourselves, and how our technological transformation of nature has transformed how we act and think and feel. What we take to be true about our world influences our politics, art, philosophy, and religious belief—and vice versa. And in reshaping our world, we reshape ourselves who are a part of that world. This story of science, I contend, is therefore best woven with our cultural master narrative, for as Eva Brann puts it, "the *science* of nature is indispensable to self-knowledge" and so "it follows that science is a humanly necessary constituent of education, so long as it is science not professionally but reflectively studied" (1979: 110).

Another science story also crucially needs telling: the account provided by contemporary science concerning the evolution of things—the origin and development of the universe, our planet, organic life, the human species. Just as our culture's master narrative needs to be complemented by small group discussions about specific primary texts, so a scientific narrative needs to be complemented by small group laboratory and field assignments. In designing actual experiments to test a theory, students discover that data points cluster around but rarely mimic the smooth curve the theory generates. Thus, the firsthand observations and activities undertaken in the field vividly complicate and extend the descriptions of theories found in textbooks. Students learn to appreciate the elegance and power of a theory by mucking around in the welter of details to which it brings coherence, and they learn as well that scientific theories just like historical narratives are general interpretations, not pictures, of those details.

An interpretive schema is a principle of selection. If we take these two master narratives as canonical, as providing a basic sketch of the cultural and scientific things we need to know and appreciate above all else, then the specifics that flesh it out can vary. There is more than one way to tell the tale, many events that illustrate the story's nodal points, various ways to highlight its key features. What texts the students read or what experiments they conduct need not include all the very best of these contributing elements, need not even always be selected solely from among those very best. What is important is that the specifics be timely, illustrative, influential, symbolic. If the narrative is learned by their means, then a student can return later to the narrative and find other, maybe even better or more striking, relevant particular elements. A canonical narrative gives flexibility to the content of the core course for which it provides the framework, and it encourages students to outgrow the confines of the course by exploring other ways to fill that frame.

I can imagine a full freshman year composed of required core courses—nested sequences of American, Western, and World history, plus a science core—supplemented by required work on the three basic academic skills: mathematics, a foreign language, and written composition in English. Such an approach will seem draconian in today's academic climate, where individual choice is the supreme good and where students typically exercise it by choosing a major as quickly as possible. But there are no shortcuts to an adequate education, one that actually prepares students to be good citizens in a democracy. A basic understanding of how we in this culture understand ourselves and our world must be the first step in that preparation. Our first obligation as students and professors is to recognize our dependence on what our ancestors have wrought, to know the fundamental contours of their achievement, and to appreciate it.

Truth and love come first. To know who and where we are, and to value that fact and how it came to be, is the beginning of wisdom. Bypassing this phase of learning, failing to recur to it often over the course of each student's educational development, yields citizens who are uncritical of the world as they find it because ignorant of its scope and character, who are uncritical even when they possess the tools of criticism a disciplinary focus provides. The prerequisite for critique, for criticizing something in order to make it better, is coming to love it for what it is. As I argued in the previous chapter, without emancipation there can be no motive for us willingly to accept the difficult obligation of participating in any sustained effort at cultural renovation.

The Critical Turn

The academic major is a late-nineteenth-century invention, a result of the steady pressure to push back more and more professional preparation, and eventually other kinds of job training, into the undergraduate years rather than locating it in apprenticeship arrangements and graduate school. The disciplinary major is now thought to be the major aspect of a liberal arts course of study: students often enter college within a major program, and often the major determines which general education courses they will need to take. Any core program becomes minor league, at best a preparation for the major league study of a discipline. So we say a student has earned a baccalaureate degree in biology when what we should say is that the student earned the degree with a concentration in biology. A major, after all, is a concentrate, narrowing the scope of a student's course of study, focusing it in on some single chapter or paragraph or thematic strand of the master narrative.

There are many good reasons for us to concentrate our study. It is a way to fill out a particular part of the story that interests us, to fill in its details. Doing so is a way to test the narrative generalizations we have learned, to see whether the story is adequate to all the facts, not only the facts to which it explicitly refers but to those it glosses over and to those it implies but does not explicitly acknowledge. Our demand for detailed adequacy leads to refining the generalizations: sharpening their focus, tightening their coherence, strengthening their explanatory reach. As we engage in these activities, we also learn to identify which forms of inquiry are most effective, what procedures are the most trustworthy to utilize.

Our appreciation of the master narrative was uncritical, an enjoyment of its story and of the sense it makes of things. As our disciplined theories test the limits of that narrative, they formulate alternatives thought more adequate to the aspect of the wider generalization on which they have concentrated. These alternatives are then further tested, and yet more adequate alternatives devised. And so on recurrently, for disciplines are inherently critical of the inadequacies of generalization. By their means we are able to probe restlessly for the facts our generalizations do not encompass and hence restlessly to fashion better theories and more effective methods for testing them.

Thus, the most important thing we should learn as a result of disciplined learning is to appreciate the possible, to become familiar with ideals. Such ideals are not soft-focus fantasies but specific probabilities, such as a novel proposal for schematizing some limited subject of inquiry. Disciplinary ideals are hypotheses, the creative alternatives that are invented by investigators who are profoundly acquainted with the body of knowledge and methods of which their discipline is composed, but who are confronted with a problem for which that information does not suffice unless imaginatively reworked. A discipline is a way for getting to know some facts and theories intimately enough to see the fresh possibilities they harbor. It takes a lot of practice doing logic proofs to see the conclusion in the premises, to see how the shapes of the latter imply their transformation into the shape of the former. It takes a trained anthropologist to see the indentations in an erosion field as the fossilized footprints of an early female humanoid and the child whose hand she holds.

Disciplinary precision is a method of critique, a technique for exposing the limits of our understanding and, in doing so, for generating new understandings. It is an engine of recurrent hypothesis formation: whatever precision it has so far achieved is never enough. The essence of a discipline is the inexhaustible perfectability of its aspirations, hence its profound sense of fallibility combined with an equally profound hope that any specific failure can be overcome with a little more imaginative effort.

The point of studying a discipline is to learn how to work its engine of inquiry. An academic major therefore needs to be composed from the very first of interactive courses. It is pointless, although certainly harmless, to offer disciplinary introductory survey courses with their little parochial master narratives. The presence in the curriculum of such surveys gains its apparent plausibility in the absence of core courses that teach the genuine master narratives, but with the core in place the major should not attempt to be its pale shadow. It should offer students something different, not more appreciation but instead access to an instrument for critiquing the old appreciations.

A discipline is a way of thinking and acting, a style. It needs to be practiced to be learned. Most colleges and universities recognize that natural science laboratories need to be small, so that every student has firsthand experience running experiments: gathering samples, preparing slides, using a microscope, setting up an apparatus, recording data points and fitting them to a curve. No one can learn these things sitting in a lecture hall. Some science instructors go a step farther, arguing that all their courses should be taught solely in an interactive mode, that the traditional lecture/lab format should be abandoned for a lab-only format, the body of a discipline's results being introduced along the way, when problems and their possibilities suggest the need.

Similarly in the arts and humanities. No one would imagine that students can learn ceramics by sitting in large lecture halls. They learn to make pots by trying to make a decent one: digging clays, refining and mixing them, getting a potters' wheel going, applying their hands or a shaping knife to the clay. Only after students have gotten somewhere doing these things, but not somewhere they want to be, do they lean back and wonder what others are doing, find it useful to visit galleries, talk to potters, browse in art books, attend a lecture. It is equally obvious that foreign language acquisition and creative writing can only be taught in small interactive classroom situations.

However, we seem quite willing to teach other subjects, philosophy for example, in lecture halls—because it is not so obvious that philosophy students who can explicate Plato's theory of Forms may not have the skill needed to develop justified views of their own about the sense in which different things are also the same. Students who study French just by memorizing vocabulary words can't hold an intelligent conversation in a Parisian cafe, and goalkeepers who learn their position just by reading soccer books are scored upon at will. But there are no standard public ways in which it is explicitly evident that a philosophy student who has memorized a few quotes from Plato nonetheless cannot philosophize.

The problem, in other words, is not that we think students learn best in large classes but rather that we don't think we can afford the low student-teacher ratios required for interactive learning. So it is easy to persuade ourselves that where the failure to learn is not obvious there has been no failure. As a result, far too many students receive their baccalaureate degree without having made any identifiable progress toward mastering the ways of the discipline they have selected as their major. If they have a decent appreciation for the little narrative that constitutes that discipline's body of accomplishments, and if they can demonstrate this knowledge on standardized tests, we are content. They know some disciplinary truths but lack the know-how for transforming what they know into new truths, better theories, and more effective methods of inquiry.

Acquiring the skills a discipline provides is emancipatory in Bill Readings's sense, for by learning its methods we gain the autonomy that comes from mastery of a technique. Mastery entails hope, the confidence that for any given situation there is always the possibility that it could be better, and that we possess the requisite tools for finding a way to make it so. When Rorty talks about a narrative of national hope, he means this can-do sensibility, this confidence that we have the capacity to improve on whatever we have been given.

Yet such hope is always in danger of falling into the hubris that results from forgetting that our mastery is bounded, that it is within a focused region of a wider context, and that this context is what makes our mastery possible and to which it must eventually be responsible. Engaging prematurely in the narrowing focus of a disciplinary program of study means decontextualizing the discipline, treating it as self-contained and hence self-sufficient, a mastery unbeholden to truths and schemata of interpretation greater than those of its own invention and discovery. The obvious result is the disciplinary arrogance that abounds in our colleges and universities. A major program of study is, and should be taught as, a transition phase between established schemata, an adventurous flight away from our familiar perch in the hope of reaching a better but as yet unknown one.

The Culminating Experience

Insofar as there is any progression to an undergraduate course of study, insofar as it is a course of study and not just a pile of studied courses, it needs to involve some sort of culminating experience. The usual form this takes is for seniors to do an independent project in their major or to enroll in a majors-only senior seminar—on the one hand a solo effort, on the other hand a group exploration, but in both cases students complete their undergraduate education by doing something that increases the narrowness of the concentration.

For instance, the English department at my college interestingly combines both the independent and group aspects of this process by requiring all senior majors to take a two-course sequence—Senior Literature Seminar and Workshop—which is described as involving the "demonstration, under close supervision, of a command of the critical reading and writing expected of a student major in English. Each workshop requires students to share discoveries and problems as they produce a lengthy manuscript based on work in the previous seminar and on new research" (*Dickinson College Bulletin:* 64). Approaches of this sort are applications of the graduate school model, in which a focusing method is applied in a problem area where it is already known to work, where the details of the result may be unknown but not the intellectual boundaries of acceptability within which those details are safely embedded. Such inquiries are just as Bill Readings describes them: either monologues or parallel monologues, oblivious of their obligation to all that lies beyond the major but upon which it depends.

We should not be surprised that a standard complaint about contemporary students is that they are not interested in debating the important issues of the day. Michiko Kakutani of *The New York Times,* for instance, in an essay for the *Yale Alumni Magazine* (online edition), quotes Joseph Gordon, dean of undergraduate education at Yale, as saying that "students are interested in hearing another person's point of view, but not interested in engaging it, or being challenged." Kakutani wonders why this is so, and decides it is a byproduct of "philosophical relativism": "Because subjectivity enshrines ideas that are partial and fragmentary by definition, it tends to preclude searches for larger, overarching truths, thereby undermining a strong culture of contestation." The search for "overarching truths" is irrelevant because students think their "partial" ideas suffice. Their ideas are beyond criticism because there is no standpoint beyond the partial one they occupy from which they can legitimately be assessed. Tolerating others' monologues is the only moral response available. We can sneer and smear those who look and sound and smell and think and act differently than we do, but the sole ethical response we can make is to respect their differences—to appreciate them. There is no hope that these differences can be reconciled. Indeed, the very possibility of doing so is rejected as hegemonic, as not reconciliation at all but an arbitrary imposition.

Substitute the academic departments for the individual students, and Kakutani's "philosophical relativism" becomes a disciplinary relativism, either the "bipolar dogmatism" of the culture wars between canonists and anti-canonists, or a "scholarly eclecticism—less concerned with large paradigms, and more focused on narrower issues." Universities, indeed, have lost their unity. They have become un-communities composed of monologic voices, overwhelmingly populated by students and faculty who disbelieve in the legitimacy, much less the viability, of "contestation" as a way to seek out "overarching truths."

This attitude is explicitly illustrated by Stanley Fish, in an essay objecting to those who in the aftermath of the 9/11 terrorist attacks railed against our cathedrals of learning for fostering "radical cultural relativism, nonjudgmentalism, and a postmodern conviction that there are no moral norms or truths worth defending" (33; quoting from a 1 October 2001 syndicated column by John Leo). Fish counters that he just as much as Leo believes there are "universal values" and "truths independent of particular perspectives," but believing in them doesn't mean he is able to prove their truth. "In order to assert something and mean it without qualification, I of course have to believe that it is true, but I don't have to believe that I could demonstrate its truth to all rational persons" (34).

Religious beliefs, for example, those of Osama bin Laden's Islam or those of Martin Luther King Jr.'s Christianity, "are entirely *internal* matters." The adherents to a religion "follow a vision" based on certain "revelations, authorities, and texts," and they are not about to accept criticisms from "non-adherents citing *other* revelations, authorities, and texts." In "matters of religion—and I would say in any matter—there is no *public space*, complete with definitions, standards, norms, criteria, etc., to which one can have recourse in order to separate out the truth from the false, the revolutionary from the criminal" (35). According to Fish, we share no common ground. There is no neutral arena to which we can come in order to contend, no market place of ideas, no forum for disputation, no agora in which to negotiate our disagreements.

The problem is not that there is no universal—the universal, the absolutely true, exists, and I know what it is. The problem is that you know, too, and that we know different things, which puts us right back where we were a few sentences ago, armed with universal judgments that are irreconcilable, all dressed up and nowhere to go for an authoritative adjudication. ... We have to live with the knowledge of two things: that we are absolutely right and that there is no generally accepted measure by which our rightness can be independently validated. (37)

Fish insists that the "university is a place of dialogue" (39), and he complains when all voices are not given a chance to be heard there. Yet he simultaneously insists that the public space this dialogue presumes does not exist, that inclusive perspectives are fatuous, merely providing "safe and empty" generalizations (38) that disturb no one because vacuous. "Can the complex reality of particular situations be captured by the abstract vocabulary of so-called universals?" he asks rhetorically. No, he answers—"No, in thunder" (40). And his students echo him, also answering No—No, in silence.

Fish is forgetting that religious and political perspectives, just like disciplinary perspectives, are foci in a field. There is necessarily always a wider context that the disputants with their clashing visions, policies, and methods share. However, this shared context is not some superfaith or global empire or queen of the sciences, as Fish obviously presumes. It is a narrative of the vague important meanings that provide the landscape and horizon of our lives, from which these particular foci have arisen and to which they and we can recur in the hope of working out a reconciling new focus.

The public sphere in which the academic disciplines can cavort together is not empty, because it is not itself a discipline. It is the soil from which the disciplines have sprung, a loam of neglected alternatives and overlooked possibilities that when newly appreciated and creatively adapted can provide an opportunity for fashioning a needed integrating approach. Because Shiites and Sunni both believe in the importance of the *Quran,* their differing visions are in principle reconcilable. As are also the differences that fragment

Christianity into a thousand sects reconcilable, because of the Scripture they all hold sacred. As are the differences among all religions reconcilable, insofar as their histories overlap and intertwine, insofar as their adherents share a common natural world and are the same species of organism.

The one necessary condition for weaving differences together is that we abandon Fish's belief that beliefs are true only when held "without qualification" and that universals are "absolutely true." Fish's world is composed solely of bipolar dogmatists whose differences are irreconcilable because they exist in a world composed only of emancipated perspectives. His world has been washed clean of the open networks of obligation that both motivate our concern to find a reconciling pathway and that give us hope that our journey might not be in vain.

Kakutani complains about our students' "failure to fully engage with the world," their unwillingness to test their convictions "against the logic and passion of others," and is rightly worried that this attitude "suggests a closing off of the possibilities of growth and transformation and a repudiation of the process of consensus building" that is crucial to the viability of American democracy. There is no need for building a consensus if our common ground is a settled perspective and our task merely to appreciate it, as John Leo and the traditional canonists presume. Nor is there any need for consensus building if, as Fish and the anti-canonists presume, the partisan perspectives that question the existing consensus and each other's relevance are all there is. Unless we learn to be aware of both the limitations of any consensus and the limitations of any critique of that consensus, we will not realize that the importance of our convictions is that they lead us beyond themselves, that they are the instruments of our growth and transformation precisely because they and the convictions with which they are in constant contestation are not irreconcilable. To the truths we love and the hope these truths can be improved by their encounter with other truths, we must add the faith needed to endeavor steadfastly to find a way to construct better, more integrative truths.

The culminating senior experience of an undergraduate education, therefore, needs to involve a return to the general education core. Equipped with the critical skills of a discipline, students should not simply be encouraged to undertake yet one more focusing effort. Instead, they should put their emancipatory tools to work on the master narrative they temporarily forsook in order to acquire those tools. Disciplined now, they should be able to see through the master narrative to its sources, to discern its weaknesses, to point out its problem areas. They should be able to ferret out the incompatible stories that the master narrative has ignored or glossed over, and to shed light on the outer limits of that narrative, its boundary lines and the untold story of the things that lie beyond. In short, students in their senior projects should grapple with problems that engage them with a wider region than the one provided by their discipline.

Practical problems have exactly this character. They never behave themselves, constantly sloshing over and seeping through the constraining dikes of any single discipline. Such problems are inherently transdisciplinary, not only requiring a number of specialities in their solving but also requiring that these specialities collaborate—collaborate not in the desiccated way they do when each plays its role in modular isolation from the others, but rather in the full-bodied way that requires each speciality to adapt its approach to the ways of the others in order to achieve a viable result. Practical problems are also time-sensitive: the issues have to be resolved even if all the relevant facts are not at hand or incompletely analyzed. One of the best cures for the dogmatism fostered by an insistence on absolute certainty is to be forced by a deadline to make the best judgment one can given the circumstances.

Environmental matters are rife with exemplary problems of this sort, of course. For instance, students involved in a local effort to secure a law protecting water purity in a nearby stream need many kinds of expertise: chemistry and biology to determine the current quality of the water, geology to identify the scope and character of the stream's drainage basin, economics and history to pinpoint likely sources of pollution, sociology and political science to discover interest groups that might be agents of support or opposition, philosophy and religious studies to characterize the values shaping those interests and the ethical aspects of proposed strategies for success, the arts for articulating these various factors vividly and for designing informative and persuasive proposals, briefs, or reports. Students involved in such a project need both to meld these various disciplinary skills and to coordinate them with those of the sanitary engineers, business leaders, environmentalists, city managers and county commissioners, sports club representatives, and the like, whose authority or influence make them relevant contributors to formulating, enacting, and implementing the sort of effective law sought.

Another example of a multidisciplinary senior project is a theatrical production. This task should begin with studying playwrights and scripts, undertaking close readings of texts and performances, examining the artistic and cultural traditions influencing them and the historical developments in which they are embedded. A script finally selected, actors need to be chosen, sets and costumes designed, advertising and program artwork and written material devised. All of these efforts should be rooted in the insights resulting from the literary studies with which the project began, and then sustained over the weeks of rehearsal, set construction, sewing and fitting, lighting and sound choices, ticket selling, and informational lectures leading up to opening night, continuing through to the last night's performance, and ending when the set is struck and the costumes mothballed. Similar collaborative efforts are required for performing a musical comedy or an opera, for mounting street theatre, or for developing new approaches to a religious community's liturgical expressions.

In the small liberal arts colleges that dominated American education until the coming of the land grant universities, the president's course on ethics was the required capstone experience for all seniors. It was where students were admonished that they should express their emancipation as an obligation, that they should use the mastery they had acquired in a manner that would serve the common good. They learned from their president to see their undergraduate years as intimating a career of service, to take the baccalaureate as preparing them to be contributing members of their local communities, responsible and upright citizens of their country.

Nowadays there are different and probably more pertinent methods for encouraging this moral attitude among our students, such as the ones I've suggested. What remains the same is the goal: emancipating students from their societal obligations in such a way that they will come to express those obligations all the more effectively. The senior year should be devoted to developing this sense of commitment, preparing students for their lives beyond academe not simply by equipping them with good tools for making a living but also by equipping them with a Benedictine sense of the obligation to the common good mastery of those tools entails.

Contestations

An obvious criticism of what I have been saying is that my curriculum proposals are both obvious and unrealistic, exhibiting not only an old-fashioned sense of the curriculum but also an unaffordable one. My response is that a canonically based curriculum needs to be approached pragmatically, in the sense this book has explicated. It needs constantly to be refashioned, and if that labor is constructive rather than destructive, as it should be if pragmatic, then the curriculum will not be old-fashioned but rather the old refashioned for today. The old truths we should celebrate are, as always, truths still in the making.

Such a curriculum is expensive in that it tolerates no shortcuts, insisting on the low student-faculty ratios required for interactive learning. If we really want to educate our students and not just say we have, we will need to be honest with ourselves and take music production rather than widget production as our paradigm for pedagogical effectiveness. If we want to hear Schubert's String Quintet in C Major (D 956), we can't expect to save money by refusing to hire a second cellist nor to save time by having the musicians play the second movement allegro rather than andante. Our willingness to pay whatever it costs to achieve military preparedness should be matched by a similar willingness in regard to the cost of academic preparedness. The demand that students and teachers measure up to high educational standards should be complemented by the demand that governmental and eleemosynary budgets measure up to the high fiduciary standards upon which the educational standards are dependent.

Another obvious criticism is that I have only made a few general comments about the proper shape of an undergraduate curriculum, which is hardly much start on constructing the concrete syllabi and lesson plans needed if a course of study and the courses composing it are actually to be implemented. What I have done, however, is all a generalist can do. I have lightly sketched a curricular narrative, a framework of stages of learning that begins from initial appreciation, moves to acquiring tools of criticism, and ends in critical appreciation. This framework is a version of Whitehead's stages of romance, precision, and generalization, which I discussed in chapters 7 and 10, and also a version of Dewey's stages of inquiry, as chapters 9 and 12 sought to demonstrate. So this present chapter is yet one more articulation of the pedagogical narrative to which I have recurred throughout this book, the story of how students can learn to think and act pragmatically, and so grow throughout their lives in intellectual maturity. Appreciating this narrative is a beginning point for curriculum reform in higher education.

The next steps, which involve developing actual courses and programs of study, then shepherding them through curriculum committees and securing appropriate staff, facilities, and funding, call for the critical acumen and focused precision that comes from firsthand knowledge of one's own local campus situation, its constraints and its possibilities. We who are the faculty on a particular campus must accept this obligation and not shirk its demands. It is we and only we who can create a particular interpretation of a general narrative about the educational canon, bringing the abstractions alive by making them concrete, by putting them to work on our own campus, in these difficult times, for more than a day or a semester.

These specific constructive efforts are never done; they are always contested. Higher education is always in the making because its canon is always needing to be remade, so that it will be able to provide an effective interpretive foundation for understanding and coping with change, with the novelties that are constantly welling up in the midst of even the most stable situation. The ideals by which these canonical renovations are guided, both with regard to goals and means, are implicit in the canon needing to be reformed. They are intrinsic not external features of that canon, disclosed by our persistent contestations, disclosed in the defenders' attempts to save the old truths from destruction and disclosed by the critics' attempts to establish new truths in their place. A canon is always its own best critic, for those who have ears to hear or eyes to see.

In the remaking of the educational canon taught in our colleges and universities, the persons whose cultural context is thereby transformed are thus themselves remade, for individuals also are always in the making. They are always educating who they are, who they have managed to become, by aspiring to actualize an ideal of the more they could be that is implicit in what they have so far achieved. And educational institutions, since they are among the groups by which people associate for mutual improvement, are remade by those they are at the same time remaking. The old truths sometimes need new words lest they seem uncouth, but these new words often carry unintended new meanings that can make the old truths themselves uncouth and not just the words expressing them. Higher education is always in the making because even the most enduring things—whether pedagogical, cultural, or natural—will endure only if constantly remade.

Our aim is always upward, but always from a base of prior achievement that is its resource. The intrinsic values of the past are the ideals it has realized—but also the ideals it exposes that ought to have been realized but were not, ideals that surpass it. So all achievement is necessarily inadequate, valuable for what it is but at the same time limited, harboring a value it lacks and lacks because of that very value it has achieved. This upward aim is therefore a feature even of our failed efforts, of actions that in attempting to improve on things only make them worse. In this sense, a pragmatist-process perspective is optimistic: not that growth is assured, that progress is inevitable, but that it is always reasonable to hope for the better even in the worst of times. Whatever is open-ended—a liberal arts education, growth in individuality, democracy—must necessarily be filled with risk, any possible success problematic, every actual success temporary. The course of things may be upward or downward, progressing or regressing. But the aim is upward.

In agreeing that higher education must always be in the making, we take a pragmatic approach to life, a constructive postmodern approach that is grounded in a Darwinian understanding that dynamic adaptability in a universe rife with contestation is the secret of individual and communal success and hence of cultural worth. Educational pragmatism, so understood, focuses on hope, on our capacity to see the good in the bad and the better in the good, and on faith, the courage resolutely to make for that ideal. It involves, to recall Whitehead's double metaphor from *The Function of Reason,* combining the vision of Plato with the cleverness of Ulysses, the imaginative dream of something better with the knack for finding a way through to its realization. Love of our selves and others, love of country and of the world, grows from this combined hope and faith and in turns strengthens them.

In conserving our cultural past, we need to conserve not only what has been achieved but also the resources for its transformation. Our liberation will come not by repudiating the past but by constantly renovating it. Learning our culture's intellectual canon, both substantive and procedural, is the only way by which to equip ourselves for the task of improving that culture, for the only nontrivial way to change a society is to contest its canonical foundations, and by doing so to refashion the beliefs that frame its worldview and the practices that its institutional structures and common purposes presuppose.

In order for our intellectual canon to function in this transformative way, the educational context for our learning the canon must be one that conserves our freedom to depart from it even as we are discovering how fundamentally it has made us who we are. We must learn to love our cultural heritage in a manner that emphasizes its ideals, that sets what our ancestors have done in the context of what they aspired to accomplish. If we overlook the failure of our predecessors to live up to their own expectations, or if we criticize them for not living up to ours, the tension between the good achieved and the good that might have been is lost. We are left either with a bright cheery, often vapidly jingoistic, view of our culture as somehow beyond reproach—or we are left with a dark and dour view of our past as irredeemably flawed. Neither extreme shows us a country we can love, much less one that warrants our faith and effort because it warrants hope for its improvement.

The hope located at the core of what a liberal arts education should provide is a pragmatic hope, not an idle dream about an impossible utopian society that we either naively embrace or cynically reject. An undergraduate education that educes hope is one that helps students appreciate and then love their past because they discern the possible in the actual, see the conditions for improvement harbored by both previous triumph and previous defeat. Such an education holds together what was and what could have been, affording students opportunities to imagine alternative pasts and hence to envision alternative futures, among them ones worth their seeking. It helps students come to appreciate the difficulty of even the most minimal achievements, to recognize the limitations of even the best that has been achieved, and consequently to believe there are ways, awaiting their invention, by which to use those beloved achievements, great and small, as resources for getting beyond their limitations. A college or university education in these virtues transforms students into the problem solvers that Dewey said every citizen in a democracy must become. It teaches them the skills they will need when as adults they take up as their civic obligation the task of putting to work in the world the love, hope, and faith they have acquired while living amid the world's ruins.

Bill Readings was right when he said the University was in ruins, but so always is the cultural world for which it would prepare us. And so always the chores of citizenship have to do with rebuilding and refurbishing, raising up our society from the ruin of its ideals, knowing that eventually our best efforts will themselves be ruined—but will also serve as the resources for our successors to use in their own hopeful refashionings of the world. Our education must be always in the making because the culture that it would conserve is always in the making. A pragmatic educational canon is a toolbox we can use to rebuild a world that now calls for somewhat different tools than those with which it had previously been built. It is a toolbox for constructing better toolboxes from old ones, a better world from the old. Ever so, worlds without end.

Works Cited

Allan, George. 1990. *The Realizations of the Future: An Inquiry into the Authority of Praxis*. Albany: State University of New York Press.
——. 1997. *Rethinking College Education*. Lawrence: University Press of Kansas.
——. 2001. *The Patterns of the Present: Interpreting the Authority of Form*. Albany: State University of New York Press.
Altieri, Charles. 1984. "An Idea and Ideal of a Literary Canon." *Canons*. Ed. Robert von Hallberg. Chicago: University of Chicago Press.
Anderson, Charles. 1993. *Prescribing the Life of the Mind*. Madison: University of Wisconsin Press.
Anzaldúa, Gloria. 1987. *Borderlands: La Frontera: The New Mestiza*. San Francisco: Spinsters/Aunt Lute Press.
Arendt, Hannah. 1961. *Between Past and Future*. New York: Penguin Books.
Aristotle. 1941. *The Basic Works of* Aristotle. Ed. Richard McKeon. New York: Random House.
Banks, James A. 1993. "Multicultural Education: Development, Dimensions, and Challenges." *Phi Delta Kappan* (September): 22–28.
Bellah, Robert, et al. 1985. *Habits of the Heart: Individualism and Commitment in American Life*. Berkeley: University of California Press.
Bennett, William J. 1984. *To Reclaim a Legacy: A Report on the Humanities in Higher Education*. Washington, D.C.: National Endowment for the Humanities.
Bloom, Allan. 1987. *The Closing of the American Mind*. New York: Simon and Schuster.
Bloom, Harold. 1998. *Shakespeare: The Invention of the Human*. New York: Penguin Putnam.
Bonaventure. 1273. "Conferences on the Hexaemeron." *Philosophy in the Middle Ages: The Christian, Islamic, and Jewish Traditions*. Ed. Arthur Hyman and James J. Walsh. Indianapolis: Hackett, 1974.
Botstein, Leon. 1996. "Some Thoughts on Curriculum and Change." *Rethinking Liberal Education*. Ed. Nicholas H. Farnham and Adam Yarmolinsky. Oxford: Oxford University Press. 51–61.
Brann, Eva T. H. 1979. *Paradoxes of Education in a Republic*. Chicago: University of Chicago Press.
——. 1999. "The American College as *the* Place for Liberal Learning." *Daedelus* 128: 151–171.
Calvino, Italo. 1986. "Why Read the Classics." *The Uses of Literature*. Trans. Patrick Creagh. New York: Harcourt Brace Jovanovich.
Carnochan, W. B. 1993. *The Battleground of the Curriculum: Liberal Education and American Experience*. Stanford: Stanford University Press.

Carr, Jean Ferguson. 1990. "Cultural Studies and Curricular Change." *Academe* (Nov.–Dec.).
Casement, William. 1996. *The Great Canon Controversy: The Battle of the Books in Higher Education*. New Brunswick/London: Transaction.
Caserio, Robert. 1990. Quoted in *The Chronicle for Higher Education* (21 November): 1.
Cheney, Lynne V. 1989. *50 Hours: A Core Curriculum for College Students*. Washington, D.C.: National Endowment for the Humanities.
———. 1990. *Tyrannical Machines: A Report on Educational Practices Gone Wrong and Our Best Hopes for Setting Them Right*. Washington, D.C.: National Endowment for the Humanities.
Chomsky, Noam. 1966. *Cartesian Linguistics: A Chapter in the History of Rational Thought*. New York: Harper and Row.
Descartes, René. 1637. *Discourse on the Method of rightly directing one's Reason and of seeking Truth in the Sciences. Descartes: Philosophical Writings*. Ed. and Trans. Elizabeth Anscombe and Peter Thomas Geach. Indianapolis: Bobbs-Merrill. 5–57.
Dewey, John. 1908. "Religion and Our Schools." *Essays on Pragmatism and Truth 1907–1909: The Middle Works of John Dewey 1899–1914, Volume 4*. Ed. Jo Ann Boydston. Carbondale and Edwardsville: Southern Illinois University Press, 1977. 165–77. Originally published *Hibbert Journal* 6: 796–809.
———. 1920. *Reconstruction in Philosophy*. Boston: Beacon Press, 1957.
———. 1929. *The Quest for Certainty: A Study of the Relation of Knowledge and Action. The Later Works of John Dewey 1925–1953, Volume 4: 1929*. Ed. Jo Ann Boydston. Carbondale and Edwardsville: Southern Illinois University Press, 1984. Originally published New York: Minton, Balch and Co.
———. 1934. *A Common Faith*. New Haven: Yale University Press.
———. 1937. "Whitehead's Philosophy." *The Later Works of John Dewey 1925–1953, Volume 11: 1935–1937*. Ed. Jo Ann Boydston. Cardondale and Edwardsville: Southern Illinois University Press, 1987. 146–54. Originally published *Philosophical Review* 46:170–77.
———. 1938. *Logic: The Theory of Inquiry. The Later Works of John Dewey 1925–1953, Volume 12: 1938*. Ed. Jo Ann Boydston. Carbondale and Edwardsville: Southern Illinois University Press, 1986. Originally published New York: Henry Holt and Co.
———. 1939. *Freedom and Culture*. Buffalo: Prometheus Books, 1989.
———. 1946. *Philosophy of Education*. Paterson, N.J.: Littlefield, Adams, 1958. Originally published as *Problems of Men*. New York: The Philosophical Library. Its chapters are scattered across Boydston, ed., *The Later Works of John Dewey 1925–1953*, volumes 11, 13–15.
Dickinson College. 2000. *2000–2002 Bulletin*. Carlisle: Dickinson College.
Emerson, Ralph Waldo. 1836. "Nature." *Nature, Addresses, and Lectures*. Boston: Houghton Mifflin, 1885.
———. 1837. "The American Scholar." *Selected Essays*. Ed. Larzer Ziff. New York: Viking Penguin, 1982.
Fish, Stanley. 2002. "Postmodern Warfare: The Ignorance of our Warrior Intellectuals." *Harper's Magazine* (July).
Frankel, Charles. 1956. *The Case for Modern Man*. New York: Harper and Brothers.

Freire, Paulo. 1971. *Pedagogy of the Oppressed*. Trans. Myra Bergman Ramos. New York: Herder and Herder.

Foucault, Michel. 1961. *Madness and Civilization: A History of Insanity in the Age of Reason*. Trans. Richard Howard. New York: Pantheon, 1965.

———. 1975. *Discipline and Punish: The Birth of the Prison*. Trans. Alan Sheridan. New York: Pantheon, 1977.

Gardner, Howard. 1996. "The Years Before College." *Rethinking Liberal Education*. Ed. Nicholas H. Farnham and Adam Yarmolinsky. Oxford: Oxford University Press. 91–107.

Gates, Henry Louis, Jr. 1990. "The Master's Pieces: On Canon Formation and the African American Tradition." *The Politics of Liberal Education*. Ed. Darryl J. Gless and Barbara Herrnstein Smith. Durham: Duke University Press 95–117.

———, and Nellie Y. McKay, gen. eds. 1996. *The Norton Anthology of African American Literature (with Audio Companion CD)*. New York: W. W. Norton and Co.

Geertz, Clifford. 1973. *The Interpretation of Cultures: Selected Essays*. New York: Basic.

Goffman, Erving. 1974. *Frame Analysis*. Boston: Northeastern University Press, 1986.

Griffin, David Ray. 2003. "Introduction to SUNY Series in Constructive Postmodern Thought." Albany: State University of New York Press. (Preface to every volume in the CPT Series, including this one).

Gunter, Pete A. Y. 1995. "Coherence Lost." *The Humanist* 55: 25–30.

Gutiérrez, Ramón A. 1991. *When Jesus Came, the Corn Mothers Went Away: Marriage, Sexuality, and Power in New Mexico, 1500–1846*. Stanford: Stanford University Press.

Gutmann, Amy. 1992. "Introduction." *Multiculturalism and "The Politics of Recognition."* Ed. Amy Gutmann. Princeton: Princeton University Press. 3–24.

Graff, Gerald. 1992a. *Beyond the Culture Wars: How Teaching the Conflicts Can Revitalize American Education*. New York: W.W. Norton.

———. 1992b. "Teach the Conflicts." *The Politics of Liberal Education*. Ed. Darryl J. Gless and Barbara Herrnstein Smith. Durham: Duke University Press.

Habermas, Jürgen. 1981. *The Theory of Communicative Action*. Trans. Thomas McCarthy. 2 vols. Boston: Beacon, 1984–1985.

Harvard College Core Curriculum. 2003. <http://www.registrar.fas.harvard.edu/Courses/Core>

Himmelfarb, Gertrude. 1997. "Revolution in the Library." *The Key Reporter* 62: 1–5.

Hirsch, E. D., Jr. 1987. *Cultural Literacy: What Every American Needs to Know*. Boston: Houghton Mifflin.

Hutchins, Robert Maynard. 1936. *The Higher Learning in America*. New Haven: Yale University Press.

James, William. 1907. *Pragmatism*. Indianapolis: Hackett, 1981.

Kant, Immanuel. 1785. *Grounding for the Metaphysics of Morals*. Trans. James W. Ellington. Indianapolis: Hackett, 1985.

———. 1798. *The Conflict of the Faculties*. Trans. Mary J. Gregor. Lincoln: University of Nebraska Press, 1992.

Kakutani, Michiko. 2002. "Debate? Dissent? Discussion? Oh, don't go there!" *Yale Alumni Magazine* (Summer). <http://www.yalealumnimagazine.com issues/02_07/kakutani.html>; no pagination.

Kennedy, George A. 1992. "Classics and Canons." *The Politics of Liberal Education.* Ed. Darryl J. Gless and Barbara Hernnstein Smith. Durham: Duke University Press.

Kierkegaard, Søren. 1843. *Either/Or: A Fragment of Life.* Trans. Walter Lowrie. 2 vols. Princeton: Princeton University Press, 1971.

Kimball, Bruce A. 1986. *Orators and Philosophers: A History of the Idea of Liberal Education.* New York: Columbia University Teachers College Press.

———. 1995. "Toward Pragmatic Liberal Education." *The Condition of American Liberal Education: Pragmatism and a Changing Tradition.* Ed. Robert Orrill. New York: College Entrance Examination Board. 3–122.

———. 1996. "A Historical Perspective." *Rethinking Liberal Education.* Ed. Nicholas H. Farnham and Adam Yarmolinsky. Oxford: Oxford University Press, 11-35.

Kuhn, Thomas. 1970. *The Structure of Scientific Revolutions.* Second Edition. Chicago: University of Chicago Press.

Langer, Susanne K. 1957. *Philosophy in a New Key: A Study in the Symbolism of Reason, Rite, and Art.* Third Edition. Cambridge: Harvard University Press.

Levine, Lawrence W. 1996. *The Opening of the American Mind: Canons, Culture, and History.* Boston: Beacon.

Lovejoy, Arthur O. 1936. *The Great Chain of Being: A Study of the History of an Idea.* New York: Harper and Row, 1960.

Lyotard, Jean-François. 1979. *The Postmodern Condition: A Report on Knowledge.* Trans. Geoff Bennington and Brian Massumi. Minneapolis: University of Minnesota Press, 1984.

McInerny, Ralph. 1983. "Beyond the Liberal Arts." *The Seven Liberal Arts in the Middle Ages.* Ed. David L. Wagner. Bloomington: Indiana University Press. 248–272.

Molière. 1993. *The School for Husbands.* Trans. Richard Wilbur. San Diego: Harcourt Brace and Co.

Nancy, Jean-Luc. 1991. *The Inoperative Community.* Trans. Peter Connor et al. Minneapolis: University of Minnesota Press.

Newman, John Henry. 1873. *The Idea of a University.* Ninth Edition. Ed. I. T. Ker. Oxford: Clarendon Press, 1976.

Nussbaum, Martha C. 1997. *Cultivating Humanity: A Classical Defense of Reform in Liberal Education.* Cambridge: Harvard University Press.

Oakley, Francis. 1992a. *Community of Learning: The American College and the Liberal Arts Tradition.* New York: Oxford University Press.

———. 1992b. "Against Nostalgia: Reflections on Our Present Discontents in American Higher Education." *The Politics of Liberal Education.* Ed. Darryl J. Gless and Barbara Herrnstein Smith. Durham: Duke University Press.

O'Brien, Dennis. 1997. "The Disappearing Moral Curriculum." *The Key Reporter* 62.4: 1–5.

Peirce, Charles Sanders. 1960. *Collected Papers.* 6 vols. Cambridge: Belknap Press.

Pepper, Stephen C. 1961. *World Hypotheses: A Study in Evidence.* Berkeley: University of California Press.

Pinker, Steven. 2002. *The Blank Slate: The Modern Denial of Human Nature.* New York: Viking Penguin.

Plato. 1997. *Complete Works*. Ed. John M. Cooper. *Meno, Republic*: Trans. G. M. A. Grube. Indianapolis: Hackett.
Pratt, Mary Louise. 1990. "Humanities for the Future: Reflections on the Western Culture Debate at Stanford." *The Politics of Liberal Education*. Ed. Darryl J. Gless and Barbara Herrnstein Smith. Durham: Duke University Press. 13–31.
Readings, Bill. 1996. *The University in Ruins*. Cambridge: Harvard University Press.
Richter, Daniel. 2002. *Facing East from Indian Country: A Native History of Early America*. Cambridge: Harvard University Press.
Rockefeller, Steven C. 1992. "Comment." *Multiculturalism and "The Politics of Recognition."* Ed. Amy Gutmann. Princeton: Princeton University Press 87–98.
Rorty, Richard. 1979. *Philosophy and the Mirror of Nature*. Princeton: Princeton University Press.
———. 1992. "Two Cheers for the Cultural Left." *The Politics of Liberal Education*. Ed. Darryl J. Gless and Barbara Herrnstein Smith. Durham: Duke University Press.
———. 1998. *Achieving Our Country*. Cambridge: Harvard University Press.
———. 1999. *Philosophy and Social Hope*. New York: Penguin.
Rothenberg, Paula. 1994. "Rural U: A Cautionary Tale." *NWSA Journal* 6: 291–98.
Rousseau, Jean-Jacques. 1762. *Of the Social Contract or Principles of Political Right*. Trans. Charles M. Sherover. New York: Harper and Row, 1984.
Rudolph, Frederick, ed. 1985. *Integrity in the College Curriculum: A Report to the Academic Community*. The Project on Redefining the Meaning and Purpose of Baccalaureate Degrees; Washington, D.C.: Association of American Colleges (and Universities).
Ryle, Gilbert. 1954. *Dilemmas*. Cambridge: Cambridge University Press.
Salisbury, John of. 1159. *The Metalogicon of John of Salisbury*. Trans. Daniel D. McGarry. Berkeley: University of California Press, 1962.
Santayana, George. 1911. "The Genteel Tradition in American Philosophy." *Winds of Doctrine*. New York: Charles Scribner's Sons.
Sartre, Jean-Paul. 1945. "Existentialism." *Existentialism and Human Emotions*. Trans. Bernard Frechtman. Ed. Hazel Barnes. New York: Citadel, 1985. 9–51.
Shakespeare, William. 1986. *Romeo and Juliet. The Complete Works*. Ed. Stanley Wells and Gary Taylor. New York: Oxford University Press.
Shweder, Richard A. 1994. "Fundamentalism for Highbrows." *Academe* (Nov./Dec.): 13–21.
Searle John. 1990. "The Storm Over the University." *New York Review of Books*. 6 December.
Smith, Barbara Herrnstein. 1984. "Contingencies of Value." *Canons*. Ed. Robert von Hallberg. Chicago: University of Chicago Press. 5–39.
Spengler, Oswald. 1918. *The Decline of the West*. Trans. Charles Francis Atkinson. New York: The Modern Library, 1965: Abridged Edition.
Spinoza, Benedict. 2000. *Ethics*. Trans. G. H. R. Parkinson. New York: Oxford University Press.
Stout Jeffrey. 1981. *The Flight from Authority: Religion, Morality, and the Quest for Autonomy*. South Bend: University of Notre Dame Press.
Strauss, Leo. 1968. "What is Liberal Education?" *Liberalism Ancient and Modern*. New York: Basic Books.

Taylor, Charles. 1992. "The Politics of Recognition." *Multiculturalism and "The Politics of Recognition."* Ed. Amy Gutmann. Princeton: Princeton University Press. 25–73.

Thomas Aquinas. 1273. *On There Being Only One Intellect*. Ralph McInerny, *Aquinas Against the Averroists*. West Lafayette: Purdue University Press, 1993.

———. 1990. *Summa Theologica*. Trans. Lawrence Shapecote. Chicago: Enclyclopaedia Britannica.

Toynbee, Arnold. 1934–1961. *A Study of History*. 12 vols. London: Oxford University Press.

Vreeland, Susan. 1999. *Girl in Hyacinth Blue*. New York: Penguin Books, 2000.

West, Cornel. 1989. *The American Evasion of Philosophy: A Genealogy of Pragmatism*. Madison: University of Wisconsin Press.

Whitehead, Alfred North. 1916. "The Aims of Education: A Plea for Reform." *The Aims of Education and Other Essays*. New York: The Free Press, 1967. Chapter 1: 1–14. Originally published *Mathematical Gazette* 8: 191–203.

———. 1917. "Technical Education and Its Relation to Science and Literature." *The Aims of Education and Other Essays*. New York: The Free Press, 1967. Chapter 4: 43–59. Originally published in *The Organisation of Thought*. London: Williams and Norgate.

———. 1922. "The Rhythm of Education." *The Aims of Education and Other Essays*. New York: The Free Press, 1967. Chapter 2: 15–28. Originally published as a pamphlet, "The Rhythm of Education." London: Christophers.

———. 1929a. *The Function of Reason*. Boston: Beacon, 1958.

———. 1929b. *Process and Reality*. Corrected Edition, edited by David Ray Griffin and Donald W. Sherburne. New York: The Free Press, 1978.

———. 1933. *Adventures of Ideas*. New York: The Free Press, 1967.

Wilson, Edward O. 1998. *Consilience: The Unity of Knowledge*. New York: Alfred A. Knopf.

Wolf, Christa. 1993. "Reading and Writing." *The Author's Dimension: Selected Essays*. Trans. Jan van Heurck. New York: Farrar, Straus and Giroux. 20–48.

Woolf, Virginia. 1930. *A Room of One's Own*. New York: Harcourt Brace Jovanovich, 1967.

Wong, Frank F. 1996. "The Search for American Liberal Education." *Rethinking Liberal Education*. Ed. Nicholas H. Farnham and Adam Yarmolinsky. Oxford: Oxford University Press 64–76.

Note on Supporting Center

This series is published under the auspices of the Center for Process Studies, a research organization affiliated with the Claremont School of Theology and Claremont Graduate University. It was founded in 1973 by John B. Cobb Jr., Founding Director, and David Ray Griffin, Executive Director; Marjorie Suchocki is now also a Co-Director. It encourages research and reflection on the process philosophy of Alfred North Whitehead, Charles Hartshorne, and related thinkers, and on the application and testing of this viewpoint in all areas of thought and practice. The center sponsors conferences, welcomes visiting scholars to use its library, and publishes a scholarly journal, *Process Studies,* and a newsletter, *Process Perspectives.* Located at 1325 North College, Claremont, CA 91711, it gratefully accepts (tax-deductible) contributions to support its work.

Index

AAC&U. *See* Rudolph, Frederick
aesthetic esotericism, 159–60
agonized conscience, 31–32, 47–48, 50, 64
Altieri, Charles, 60, 87, 108, 109
Anderson, Charles, 40–41, 118–19
anti-canonists, 53–69, 86–87, 89–91, 111–14, 123, 130–31, 133, 200, 216, 225
anti-foundationalism, 10–13
Anzaldúa, Gloria, 143
apprentices. *See* masters and apprentices
Aquinas. *See* Thomas Aquinas
Arendt, Hannah, 206–10
Aristotle, 9–10, 28, 32, 44, 121–22, 140–41, 172–75, 200
Arnold, Matthew, 22, 185
autonomy. *See* education, emancipatory
Averoes, 121–22

Banks, James A., 115, 143
Bellah, Robert, 98
Bellow, Saul, 91, 124–25
Benedictine ideal, 183, 186, 196–98, 227
Bennett, William, 22, 24–25, 26, 82, 83, 85, 91
Bentham, Jeremy, 162, 195
Bernard of Chartres, 40
Bloom, Allan, 22, 32, 82–83, 85, 91
Bonaventure, 121–22
borderlands, 143
Botstein, Leon, 78–79
Brann, Eva, 20, 24, 26, 27, 38, 58, 82, 110, 119, 185, 218

Calvino, Italo, 23–24, 110
canon
    definition, 21–22
    educational, 22, 26, 31, 39, 59, 61, 103–4, 107, 108, 136, 138–40, 142, 215–27, 229–31
    intellectual, 22, 31, 39, 44, 94–96, 102, 104–5, 108–9, 112, 114, 116, 177–78, 195, 215, 230
    canonless (*see* anti-canonists)
    contemporary (*see* relative canonists)
    ethnic (*see* relative canonists)
    great ways (*see* procedural canonists)
    great books (*see* content canonists)
    progressive (*see* relative canonists)
    self-transcending (*see* pragmatic canonists)
Carnochan, W. B., 24, 83–84, 86
Carr, Jean Ferguson, 60–61
Caserio, Robert, 137
Cassirer, Ernst, 57
Cheney, Lynne, 23, 25, 26
Chomsky, Noam, 190
Columbia University, 81
common good, 168, 177–78, 187, 192–96, 227
content canonists, 17–33, 44, 61–62, 83, 133, 156, 157, 184–85
    great books, 21–26, 86, 95, 110, 119, 184–85, 191, 200, 216
contestation, 223, 227–31
contextualism, 71–76
conversation, 135–36, 142, 178, 201, 224
creativity, 118–19, 152, 161, 163, 174–75, 179–80
cultural Left/Right, 203–4
cultural perspectives, 153–55, 159, 162–63
cultural literacy, 205–6
curriculum
    back-to-basics, 26–29, 32–33
    compaction of, 61–63
    core, 215–19
    disciplinary major, 45–47, 219–22
    culminating experience, 222–27
    extensive/intensive, 205–6, 215

deans, academic, 22, 137–40
democracy, 96, 123, 125, 145–48,
    153–58, 162–66, 177–78,
    181–82, 186, 196, 204, 205, 208,
    210, 212, 213, 219, 225, 229–30
Descartes, René, 36–39, 48, 132
Dewey, John, 2, 32, 49, 145–48,
    158–82, 185, 190, 205, 206, 208,
    210–13, 228, 230
Dickinson College, 46, 136–37, 222

education
    pragmatic theory of, 3
    modes (liberal, scientific, technical),
        184–96
    phases (romance, precision,
        generalization), 116–20,
        180–81, 186–96, 216–27, 228
    emancipatory (autonomy), 199–204,
        210–11, 221, 227
    ethical (obligation), 201–4, 211,
        213, 225, 227, 230
egalitarianism, 53–59, 88, 134–35,
    145–46, 211–12
Einstein, Alfred, 151
emancipation. See education,
    emancipatory
Emerson, Ralph Waldo, 64, 77, 83, 84

faith, 225, 229, 230
Fish, Stanley, 223–25
Foucault, Michel, 54–55, 68–69
foundationalism, 9–10, 17–21, 71–73,
    140, 182
frameworks. See schemata of
    interpretation
Frankel, Charles, 160
Freire, Paulo, 94

Gadamer, Hans-Georg, 125
Gardner, Howard, 79
Garfield, James, 24
Gates, Henry Louis, Jr., 85–86
Geertz, Clifford, 75–76
God, 178–79
Goffman, Erving, 102, 149, 170
Gordon, Joseph, 223

Graff, Gerald, 91, 123–24
Greeley, Horace, 27
Griffin, David Ray, xi–xv, 3
Gunter, Pete A. Y., 130
Gutiérrez, Ramón, 217
Gutmann, Amy, 77, 91

Habermas, Jürgen, 200
Harvard University, 42–44
Hegel, G. W. F., 14, 73, 74, 81, 180
hierarchy
    natural, 18–19, 32, 37, 54–55,
        71–73, 84
    social, 3, 19, 37, 53–55, 75, 115,
        135
    educational, 20–22, 24, 38, 44, 54,
        60, 88, 89, 145
Himmelfarb, Gertrude, 23, 59
Hiram College, 24
Hirsch, E. D., Jr., 205–6, 215, 216
historicism, 57–58, 73, 131
holism, 131, 132
hope, 208, 209, 220, 222, 225, 229,
    230. See also meliorism; ideals
Hume, David, 57
Hutchins, Robert Maynard, 23
hypothesizing, 152, 173, 220

ideals, 136, 208–9. See also meliorism;
    hope
inert ideas, 166
inquiry. See thinking, experimental
intelligence. See thinking, experimental

James, William, 2, 26, 72–73, 92, 97,
    101–2, 104–5, 107, 113–14, 115,
    127, 134, 138–40, 154
Jefferson, Thomas, 56
John of Salisbury, 40
Juvenal, 91

Kakutani, Michiko, 223, 225
Kant, Immanuel, 49–51, 53–54, 57,
    64, 134, 162, 195, 200, 201
Kennedy, George A., 39, 91
Kimball, Bruce, 90, 121, 123, 128–29,
    145

Index

knowledge
  expansion of, 4–6
  globalization of, 7–8, 28
  democratization of, 6–7, 27–28
  assumed, 8–9
Kuhn, Thomas, 57, 120

Leo, John, 223, 225
Leverrier, Urbain, 150–52
Levine, Lawrence W., 40, 95
love, 219, 225, 229, 230
Lovejoy, Arthur, 18–19, 32, 71–72
Lyotard, Jean-François, 56–57, 73–74, 84, 112, 114, 216

Machiavelli, Niccolo, 137–38, 139
Marx, Karl, 133–34
masters and apprentices, 107–10, 177, 187, 202
McInerny, Ralph, 122
meliorism, 113, 176, 177, 178, 181, 182, 190, 195, 197, 211, 222, 229–31. *See also* ideals; hope
metaphor, root, 171
methodism, 35–39, 48–49, 73
  scientific, 146–53, 156, 162–64, 166, 171, 176–77, 180
models. *See* schemata of interpretation

Nancy, Jean-Luc, 213
narratives
  grand (master), 56–57, 73, 216–18, 225
  little, 74, 84, 210, 221
  of hope, 208, 209
  core, 215–19
  curricular, 228
Newman, John Henry, 30, 32, 124
Newton, Isaac, 150–52
Nussbaum, Martha, 79–81, 114

O'Brien, Dennis, 142–43
Oakley, Francis, 90–91, 95, 96, 140–41
obligation. *See* education, ethical

patterns. *See* schemata of interpretation

Pepper, Stephen, 171
Petrarch, 119
Pinker, Steven, 38, 155
Plato, 19, 32, 95, 103–4, 111, 160, 190, 203, 221
  Meno, 20, 115, 157, 202
play, 158–59, 164, 197, 207
Polybius, 208
Pope, Alexander, 18, 72
Port Royal logicians, 132
postmodernism, constructive, 3, 181–82, 229
pragmatic canonists, 93–96, 105, 120, 125, 127–40, 133–37, 143, 146, 164, 168, 178, 185, 228, 231
pragmatism, 1–3, 96–97, 127–33, 140, 202
Pratt, Mary Louise, 60, 91
procedural canonists, 35–52, 61–63, 83, 146, 156–57, 185
  great ways, 39–44, 110, 191, 200, 216
process philosophy, 1–3, 97–100, 140
Protagoras, 54

Quintillian, 39

Readings, Bill, x, 13–14, 29–32, 50–51, 65–69, 199–203, 210, 213, 221–23, 230
reason, speculative/practical, 99–100, 190, 229
relative canonists, 71–88
  contemporary, 76–81, 89
  progressive, 81–84, 89, 182
  ethnic, 84–89, 155
religion, 176–77, 224
religious education, 165–69
Richter, Daniel, 217
Rockefeller, Steven, 96, 125
Rorty, Richard, 17, 57–58, 76–77, 83, 87, 90, 203–10, 215, 216, 222
Rosovsky, Henry, 42, 83
Rothenberg, Paula, 114–15, 161
Rousseau, Jean-Jacques, 53–54, 64
Rudolph, Frederick, 23, 42, 43

Santayana, George, 31–32, 48, 64–65, 127–28
schemata of interpretation, 98–99, 102, 116–20, 130–32, 134, 138–39, 148–58, 159, 161, 162, 174, 176, 186, 189–90, 193, 205, 216, 218, 222
  metaphysical, 170–71, 178
  root models, 171–75, 176
Schiller, F. C. S., 101–2
Schiller, Friedrich, 30
Schleiermacher, Friedrich, 30
scientific method. *See* methodism, scientific
scripts, 174, 190, 204, 205
  scientific, 148–53
  democratic, 153–58
Searle, John, 90
Shweder, Richard, 67–68, 91
Smith, Barbara Herrnstein, 55, 60, 77–78
social Darwinism, 83–84
Spengler, Oswald, 74, 81, 84
Spinoza, Benedict, 24
St. Johns College, 24, 25–26, 82
Stout, Jeffery, 130–33
Strauss, Leo, 119, 123
style, 167

Taylor, Charles, 54, 86–87, 124, 125
thinking, experimental, 146–47, 152, 164, 169, 172–75, 178, 228

Thomas Aquinas, 121–22, 125
Tocqueville, Alex de, 98
traditional canonists, 60, 90, 110, 123, 130–31, 225. *See also* content canonists; procedural canonists
trivium, 39–40
understanding, 166–67

University
  of Culture (Faithful Community), x, 29–31
  of Reason (Guild of Inquirers), x, 50–51
  of Excellence (Resource Center), x, 66–67
University of Chicago, 67–68

versions, 153–54, 159, 162–63, 164, 171, 190, 195, 198, 204
Vonnegut, Kurt, 67–68
Vreeland, Susan, 112

West, Cornel, 84
Whitehead, Alfred North, 2, 83, 97–100, 117–18, 130, 159, 166–82, 183–98, 228, 229
Whitman, Walt, 65
Wilson, E. O., 21, 185
Wolf, Christa, 108–9
Wong, Frank, 83, 96
Woolf, Virginia, 112

SUNY series in Constructive Postmodern Thought
David Ray Griffin, series editor

David Ray Griffin, editor, *The Reenchantment of Science: Postmodern Proposals*

David Ray Griffin, editor, *Spirituality and Society: Postmodern Visions*

David Ray Griffin, *God and Religion in the Postmodern World: Essays in Postmodern Theology*

David Ray Griffin, William A. Beardslee, and Joe Holland, *Varieties of Postmodern Theology*

David Ray Griffin and Huston Smith, *Primordial Truth and Postmodern Theology*

David Ray Griffin, editor, *Sacred Interconnections: Postmodern Spirituality, Political Economy, and Art*

Robert Inchausti, *The Ignorant Perfection of Ordinary People*

David W. Orr, *Ecological Literacy: Education and the Transition to a Postmodern World*

David Ray Griffin, John B. Cobb Jr., Marcus P. Ford, Pete A. Y. Gunter, and Peter Ochs, *Founders of Constructive Postmodern Philosophy: Peirce, James, Bergson, Whitehead, and Hartshorne*

David Ray Griffin and Richard A. Falk, editors, *Postmodern Politics for a Planet in Crisis: Policy, Process, and Presidential Vision*

Steve Odin, *The Social Self in Zen and American Pragmatism*

Frederick Ferré, *Being and Value: Toward a Constructive Postmodern Metaphysics*

Sandra B. Lubarsky and David Ray Griffin, editors, *Jewish Theology and Process Thought*

J. Baird Callicott and Fernando J. R. da Rocha, editors, *Earth Summit Ethics: Toward a Reconstructive Postmodern Philosophy of Environmental Education*

David Ray Griffin, *Parapsychology, Philosophy, and Spirituality: A Postmodern Exploration*

Jay Earley, *Transforming Human Culture: Social Evolution and the Planetary Crisis*

Daniel A. Dombrowski, *Kazantzakis and God*

E. M. Adams, *A Society Fit for Human Beings*

Frederick Ferré, *Knowing and Value: Toward a Constructive Postmodern Epistemology*

Jerry H. Gill, *The Tacit Mode: Michael Polanyi's Postmodern Philosophy*

Nicholas F. Gier, *Spiritual Titanism: Indian, Chinese, and Western Perspectives*

David Ray Griffin, *Religion and Scientific Naturalism: Overcoming the Conflicts*

John A. Jungerman, *World in Process: Creativity and Interconnection in the New Physics*

Frederick Ferré, *Living and Value: Toward a Constructive Postmodern Ethics*

Laurence Foss, *The End of Modern Medicine: Biomedical Science Under a Microscope*

John B. Cobb Jr., *Postmodernism and Public Policy: Reframing Religion, Culture, Education, Sexuality, Class, Race, Politics, and the Economy*

Catherine Keller and Anne Daniell, editors, *Process and Difference: Between Cosmological and Poststructuralist Postmodernisms*

Timothy E. Eastman and Hank Keeton, editors, *Physics and Whitehead: Quantum, Process, and Experience*

Nicholas F. Gier, *The Virtue of Nonviolence: From Gautama to Gandhi*

George Allan, *Higher Education in the Making: Pragmatism, Whitehead, and the Canon*

www.ingramcontent.com/pod-product-compliance
Lightning Source LLC
Chambersburg PA
CBHW030536230426
43665CB00010B/910